A Cool Drink
of Water

A Cool Drink

of Water
INSPIRING TRUE STORIES
to REFRESH
your SPIRIT

Introduction by Edward Grinnan
Editor-in-Chief, *Guideposts* Magazine

Guideposts
New York, New York

A Cool Drink of Water: Inspiring True Stories to Refresh Your Spirit

Published by Guideposts
16 East 34th Street
New York, New York 10016
Guideposts.org

Acknowledgments

Every attempt has been made to credit the sources of copyrighted material used in this book. If any such acknowledgment has been inadvertently omitted or miscredited, receipt of such information would be appreciated.

All material that originally appeared in *Guideposts* is reprinted with permission.

Library of Congress Cataloging-in-Publication Data

A cool drink of water : inspiring true stories to refresh your spirit / edited by the editors of Guideposts.
    p. cm.
ISBN 978-0-8249-4756-9
1. Christian life—Anecdotes. 2. Inspiration—Anecdotes. I. Guideposts Associates.
BV4517.T56 2008
242—dc22

                                    2008020842

Cover design by James Iacobelli
Cover photograph by Getty Images
Interior design by Smartt Guys Design
Typeset by Nancy Tardi

Printed and bound in the United States of America
10 9 8 7 6 5 4 3

CONTENTS

INTRODUCTION

Is there anyone these days who doesn't need to be refreshed and rejuvenated, to experience a cool drink of water for their spirit? Yet being refreshed doesn't necessarily mean retreating or escaping, as the book you are holding in your hands will prove. For you are about to meet some amazing people with equally amazing and inspiring stories: stories of faith, courage and love . . . stories to refresh your spirit.

I am blessed to be editor-in-chief of *Guideposts*, the monthly magazine that has featured true stories of hope and inspiration for sixty-five years. Many of the personal accounts that you are about to read came from its pages, and more than a few are among my favorite stories of all time, which is saying a lot. I arrived at Guideposts more than twenty years ago, thinking it was a good place to catch my breath for a year and work on my résumé. But I ended up finding more than a career at Guideposts; I found a home.

It was the power of stories like these that kept me here, stories that showed how people used their faith-based values in everyday living, people who deepened their love for family, friends and community, who found meaning in their work and grew in their relationship with God. The range of human experience in this collection is breathtaking, from the very famous to the very humble. Yet these stories have one durable thread: a belief that a power greater than ourselves is at work in the world and touches us at every moment of our lives.

Take a cool drink of water from the depth of these stories, and let their comfort and peace refresh you.

Edward Grinnan
Editor-in-Chief, *Guideposts*

CHAPTER

1

Renewal *of the* Spirit

The Maple
by Chuck West

I knelt beside the Japanese maple and grasped a slender, brittle branch. It felt dry in my hand. I twisted it gently, and it snapped. I tested another, larger branch. It, too, broke off with a sharp crack. I hung my head. Only a few months old, and the tree was already dead. All around it, plants were thriving. Delicate-leafed azaleas. Hydrangeas with their moplike blooms. But the Japanese maple was supposed to be the centerpiece of this backyard garden. A memorial to my son Danny, who had been killed a few months earlier in a robbery. I had nurtured the sapling so carefully.

I stood and surveyed the rest of the garden. I had planted it myself in the weeks after Danny's death. Literally carved it out of our back lawn. Most everything else had taken during the hot, humid Georgia summer. Everything but this maple, which sprouted from the soil just a few feet from a bench at the garden's heart. I had done all I could to keep it going. Watered it carefully. Added fertilizer. Put mulch around the base. Nothing worked. *It's like Danny's life*, I thought bitterly. *Nothing we did worked there either. Maybe I just need to accept that what's gone is gone—and that's it.*

Danny had been a wonderful child: bright, good grades, well-behaved. Then, in high school, he had struggled to fit in—until he found the wrong crowd. He had begun hanging out with kids who did drugs. He tried marijuana and then moved on to LSD and, later, cocaine. Before we quite knew what had hit us, he was addicted.

We battled those drugs for eight long years, starting when Danny was just fifteen. We tried counselors, hospitals, tough love, kicking him out, moving him back in. And prayer. Lots of prayer. I prayed every day that Danny would find healing. That we all would. That somehow he, with our help, could kick this terrible addiction. But those prayers never seemed to get answered.

The day Danny was murdered, he was hanging out in a motel room. A few fellow drug users had come to the room to do some cocaine with him. Thinking that he had some money, they decided to hit him over the head and rob him. But they hit him too hard and he died. Police caught the killers a short time later.

That afternoon two plainclothes officers showed up at our door, I was sitting at my desk, getting started on our taxes. It was April, when the sun shines and the air is fresh in Atlanta. Just the day before, my wife Sharon and I had gone to a nursery to buy spring plants—including a fifteen-dollar Japanese maple sapling, all of eighteen inches high. The officers walked into the living room, asked if Sharon could come downstairs and told us in matter-of-fact voices what had happened. Numb, I went to find our daughter Laura, who was living at home at the time while attending Emory University. Then came the phone calls to our families.

The following weeks were chaotic, with the funeral arrangements to be made, calls from the police about the murder case, friends and family visiting. Sharon and I were overwhelmed. Every task reminded me of the years of ache and helplessness.

One day I wandered out into the garage, where I had been putting all of the condolence gifts. There, scattered on the floor, was yet another chore: bunches of plants, sent with cards in pretty pots. They were thoughtful, but even contemplating disposing of them depressed me. I walked back inside to the family room, which looks onto our backyard. It was a clear day, and the lawn shone green in the sunshine. I stared at it for a while, until a thought began forming: *What if, instead of throwing those plants away, I put them in the ground?* I like gardening, and I could picture a neatly bordered oval alive with blooms and deep green leaves. Maybe a path and a bench. A memory garden. A place to remember. But also a place where we might find peace. Peace we hadn't felt in eight long years.

That evening, I discussed my gardening idea with Laura and Sharon.

"That's a great idea, Dad," said Laura. "I think it will help you too."

Sharon, who had grown withdrawn since Danny's death, said only, "I guess. But it seems like a lot of work. If it were up to me, I'd just throw them away."

But I needed that garden. The very next day I walked out to the backyard with a shovel and a twenty-pound post-hole digger. Over the next week—time off I had after the funeral—I dug up a twenty-by-thirty-foot section of lawn, setting aside any rocks I found to use as a border. Sweating in the warm sun, I chiseled the ground and prepared it for planting. After much agonizing over the right balance of sun and shade, I took the plants out of their pots, spread soil and fertilizer and began putting roots into the ground. Those first days, hacking into Georgia's hard clay dirt, I found myself cursing and railing with nearly every swing of the shovel. I cursed the drugs, the murderers. And I called out to Danny. *Why?* Pound. *Why?* Pound. *Why?*

As the garden progressed, though, my anger started to subside. I went back to my job at work and began doing most of the planting in the evenings. Working by twilight, I arranged azaleas into eye-catching patterns of white, coral and red. I grouped the hydrangeas to set off the other plants. I bought a bench and situated it beneath a canopy of dogwood branches. The stones I had dug up earlier worked perfectly as a border, and I used others to make a path from an arched trellis to the bench. Sometimes, bent to the ground, my hands in the soil, I looked back and saw Sharon watching me through the kitchen window. *Maybe when I'm done, we can sit on this bench together and enjoy these flowers*, I thought.

When the last azalea had been placed in the ground and the last stone laid, I stood back and examined my handiwork. It looked pretty good. But it still lacked one thing. A focal point. I looked around the patio and saw the Japanese maple sapling, still sitting in its pot. *Perfect!* I thought. *I'll plant it next to the bench.* Sharon and I had bought the little tree the day before Danny died. It would be as if a part of him were still alive, still with us.

Now, five months later, holding the maple's dead branches in my hand, that earlier glimmer of hope seemed mocking. Yes, just like Danny. *Another hope shattered*, I thought. Twisting the branches in my fingers, I thought long and hard. I knew what I should do with the tree. Dig it up and throw it away. After all, hadn't counselors sometimes advised us to give up on Danny? Kick him out and dust off our hands? We hadn't—and what had our persistence accomplished?

Still, looking at that small maple, I thought about everything that it signified, and felt something stir inside me: a flicker of determination, a tiny spark of hope. I wouldn't quit—not yet.

I'll give it one last chance, I decided. So I dug the maple out of its spot by the bench and dragged it to a walled ledge that got morning sunlight. I scooped out a new hole, put the tree in, shoveled dirt on top, and went inside the house.

The following spring, the azaleas bloomed again. Sharon, who had begun taking walks in the garden, occasionally hurried into the house to tell me about the appearance of a new, particularly beautiful flower. And in those moments I could see her beginning to heal.

One day I was standing in the family room surveying the yard myself. Everything was bright with new spring growth. I glanced toward the maple, about fifty feet away, and saw a patch of red in it. *Is there a cardinal in that tree?* I wondered. I grabbed a pair of binoculars and looked. The red patch wasn't moving. What on earth could it be? I set down the binoculars and went outside. I walked around the garden, past the trellis laced with Carolina jasmine, and stood before the maple. A small batch of red leaves was growing from a branch. They shivered in the afternoon breeze. I reached out and touched one. It was soft and delicate. *Impossible*, I thought. *This tree was dead. But these leaves are alive.*

I stood, uncertain whether I should even tell Sharon. It didn't seem quite real—the maple, come back to life. And yet, looking around that vibrant, peaceful garden, I knew it was true. I smiled. An image came to mind, an image of Danny, an image that filled me with peace and reassurance. I stood by the maple a moment longer. Then I went inside to tell Sharon.

Thy Proper Summer Home

by Bruce Coates

It all came very clearly to me one Sunday morning during our adult class at the United Methodist church in East Naples, Florida. Our teacher had handed each of us a blank sheet of paper and said, "Imagine you could do anything you wanted; then write down your dream."

I found myself scribbling straight out: "My dream is to own a country inn with a beautiful view in a community good for raising a child."

Later, when I showed the paper to my wife Michele, she said, "I love it, especially the part about a child!"

Since 1977 and our first days together as waitress and dishwasher, Michele and I had been partners. From our marriage in 1983 and my years in school for hotel administration, to our involvement in a string of restaurants in Florida, we had worked as a team.

The dream of owning a country inn had always been in the back of my mind. But I never gave it any serious thought until my mother died of cancer in 1997. She'd always approached the future with a deep sense of faith that remained undimmed by her illness and the weeks of constant pain. While taking care of her, I had plenty of time to think. Mom had believed in facing life directly and making the best of your opportunities. If I really wanted to achieve my dreams, I had to act now, not someday or when I retired.

Michele and I tacked the dream I had written in Sunday school to the kitchen wall as a kind of mission statement, a star to guide our many steps along the way. Our first move would be to write a letter to our restaurant partners, asking for a buyout that could become the down payment for an inn of our own. Michele and I told friends about our idea, took seminars on innkeeping and put our house in Florida on the market. All the while, we were met with disbelief. "You're throwing away your future," one friend said, shaking his head.

"Do you think they're right?" I asked Michele one night.

"No," she said, "I think we're right—let's follow our dreams."

As the weeks passed, we refined our wish list for the perfect inn: It should be large enough to be profitable, but not too large; it should have separate owners' quarters; it must be somewhere in New England, close to our family. And when we found we were expecting a child, we added good schools and parks to the list.

Thankfully my partners in Florida came through with a fair price for our share of the restaurants. And that December 1997, with our down payment, wish list and mission statement in hand, Michele and I set out to find the inn of our dreams. We drove north, combing realty listings and guidebooks, writing ahead to ask inn owners if they'd be interested in selling. We visited bed-and-breakfasts along the way and stood enthralled before an idyllic old farmhouse in Vermont, which proved too small for us. We inspected a rambling lodge on the coast of Maine, which was way too large. In New Hampshire we bid on a beautiful mountainside roadhouse, but another couple bought it out from under us. Then, just north of

Boston on Cape Ann, we drove into the seaside town of Rockport, Massachusetts. "What a cozy little town," Michele sighed as we drove the oak-shaded streets, past the neighborhoods of clapboard colonials and stone walls, invigorated by the crisp air of the sea.

Then we turned a corner and saw it: the Emerson Inn.

Thirty-six rooms in all, the Emerson stood atop a rocky sweep of cove known as Cathedral Rocks. Built in 1856 and enlarged in 1913, the inn exuded an old-world ambiance; its woodwork and detailing and perfectly proportioned rooms sang out to us as both stately and welcoming. It was as one of its early guests and subsequent namesake Ralph Waldo Emerson had described it, "Thy proper summer home." If we had closed our eyes to envision the ideal place, it would not have outmatched the Emerson.

But as we surveyed the faded grandeur of the old inn's heavily draped interior with more practical eyes, it became obvious an awful lot of work would have to be done.

When we stepped out of the dining room doors onto the pillared veranda, smelled the lilac bushes in sweet bloom and saw the wide diamond-lit ocean before us, Michele and I both gasped. I leaned against her and whispered, "What do you think?"

Michele looked back at the inn. "I don't know, Bruce," she said. "The place needs a lot of work, which means a lot of time and money. Besides," she added, "it has no owners' quarters."

Then we heard the price. It was more than we could afford. We left, driving slowly along the piers, watching the fishing boats of Rockport. "It costs more than we can ever hope to come up with," I said, "especially with a baby on the way and all the renovation we'd have to do."

"Yes," Michele agreed, "I'm sure it's all for the best. We'll find something more affordable and practical." But during the next months of searching, we found ourselves measuring everything else we saw against the Emerson—its breathtaking views, its unique character, its gentle charm. As Emerson wrote, "The things that are really for thee, gravitate to thee."

One afternoon, while visiting a Maine inn, we happened to mention the Emerson to a friend. "You ought to try again," he said. "I heard they've just dropped their price." That next morning we drove to the Emerson, and a few days later, after securing financing, made an offer. By the end of that summer, 1998, Michele and I were proud innkeepers—and even prouder parents to a beautiful new daughter, Bailey.

We moved in, rolled up our sleeves and started renovations for the following spring. Anything that could break or go wrong seemed to break and go expensively and time-consumingly wrong. When rain fell through the attic and pooled over the ceiling of our rooms upstairs, a handyman explained what had been going on for years. "They'd poke a broomstick through the plaster, let the water drain, and patch and paint the hole," he explained. Michele and I looked at each other, shook our heads, and replaced the roof. When lightning struck and shattered the chimney, we felt shattered as well. Despite it all, we forged ahead, installed an accounting system and new spa equipment and relandscaped the oceanside lawn. And then there were the floor refinishers, painters, decorators, plumbers, bricklayers, electricians, swimming pool repairmen. . . .

Friends back in Florida would send oranges or phone to joke about our latest blizzard. "Very funny," I'd tell them, sometimes admitting things weren't going so well. But that was a gross understatement.

Our reopening that April for the 1999 season should have been a red-letter day, but by that time the Emerson Inn By The Sea had nearly ruined us. We were broke, exhausted and emotionally drained. The next day, I sat on the veranda, the inn to my back, and stared over the cold, gloomy sea, my stomach in knots. Gulls swooped over the lobster boats, and I felt ashamed—ashamed at my total failure. I leaned against one of the pillars, fully expecting it to topple over.

Anything this miserable, I thought as I gritted my teeth, *anything this failed and hopeless could never be our calling.* The truth was I somehow felt betrayed—not just by our inn but by our dreams as well.

The drizzle had turned to rain before Michele came out back to find me. "There you are," she said. "I've been looking everywhere. We just got our first reservation!"

I looked up at her. "Do you realize how overbudgeted, overextended, overdebted, over our heads we are?" I asked. "I'm afraid we're really in trouble here, Michele."

"Sure, I realize," she said, putting her hand on my shoulder, "but all I see is that we're open for business! Our dream has come true, Bruce. We're innkeepers!"

"I've forgotten why we ever wanted to do this in the first place," I said.

"Well, I haven't," she said. "And no matter what you say, I wish your mother were here to see this, because she'd be proud of us and the baby and all we've done, and you know it."

I stared at the horizon of clouds and sea and just sat there.

"Listen for the phone," said Michele. "I've got to run into town for a minute—to buy a new guest book!" I heard her drive away and felt ashamed all over again, but at a different kind of failure: I had failed our dreams, I realized, our dreams hadn't failed us. I sat for a long time, going through all the things that had inspired our vision of owning an inn.

As I watched the billowing ocean, I thought of something else Emerson wrote: "All I have seen teaches me to trust the Creator for all I have not seen." I breathed in the rich sea air. I couldn't let my fears take over now.

We didn't have many guests to sign the book those first weeks, but the weather brightened with spring. It was a pleasure to see that where bulbs had been planted, daffodils and tulips appeared, and I smiled as Bailey took her first steps. I don't know what changed, but I often walked the Cathedral Rocks and heard my mother's voice in the crashing waves, her faith and humor returning to me like a gift from the sea. Gradually, all the discouraging toil of the inn began to seem worth it. It was our home to share: Michele, Bailey and me. Now if only some guests would come to share it too.

That June a family booked their reunion with us. I looked up from my work whenever a new member of the clan arrived, in from the airport or hours of highway driving. I could see the smiles and long embraces, the way they breathed in the sea and the inn and fell into the happy circles of family. I felt the weight of the past year's work and struggle lift off my shoulders as I saw our dream had come true. We had always dreamed of giving this gift to people, yet I had been so busy I hadn't lifted my eyes to see it.

As the moon rose, huge and golden above the sea, I brought Michele and little Bailey out back to watch that sparkling bridge of light lying from the Cathedral Rocks, over the water, to the moon. As our guests, the reunited family, gathered on the back lawn for the evening's clambake, there was the clink of silverware and chatter of people over the sounds of waves. I slipped my arm around Michele and Bailey.

"A country inn," Michele recited my first note back to me, "with a beautiful view in a community good for raising a child."

I pulled her closer to me as I recited another quote, from Emerson himself, "Happy is the house that shelters a friend."

A Priest, A Rabbi and Me

by Rhoda Blecker

One summer day several years ago I headed north to a Benedictine monastery near the Canadian border. Although my husband Keith and I are Jewish, for years I'd been visiting this rustic retreat where my old friend Mother Miriam had once lived.

Usually I went up in the fall, but that year our summer vacation plans had fallen through. Knowing how much I needed to get away from the city, Keith suggested I spend a week at the monastery instead. The atmosphere of work and prayer there never failed to renew my spirit.

As I drove through deep woods, I found myself wondering about the nature of my relationship with the nuns. I had never felt called upon to be a Christian, only to love Christians. Indeed, Mother Miriam had encouraged me not to convert but to explore my own faith, to become a better Jew. Still, I worried. The nuns had given so much to me. What could I give back to them?

At the monastery, the sisters greeted me warmly. Then they told me their predicament. "We must find a new priest," Mother Prioress said. The priest who had been with the monastery since its founding fifteen years earlier had left for another assignment. The nuns had no one to say daily Mass. Since the monastery was in a remote location, the nuns were losing several hours each morning traveling to the nearest church. Yet they still had to squeeze in all their work before nightfall.

"It's very hard to choose between going to Mass and doing our daily chores," Mother Prioress said sadly. They'd written to every Benedictine house in the country, but there were no priests to spare for an area that had so few Catholics.

"Even retired priests say it's too isolated here," she went on. Then she brightened. "Several of them did agree, however, to visit and say Mass for us. One of them will be here this weekend."

During the next few days, as I weeded and planted in the monastery garden, I kept thinking about what I could do to help my friends. But it wasn't as if I knew a lot of priests.

On Saturday the priest who had volunteered his time for the weekend arrived. Father William was a white-haired man with a ready smile and a mellifluous Irish accent. His celebration of the Mass was fairly routine until he reached the homily. "Now," he said, "I'd like to tell you an old rabbinic story."

He proceeded to tell a midrash, a Jewish parable, one I'd heard my rabbi tell just a few months earlier. Later in his sermon, he said, "There's another rabbinic story that fits here," and told another midrash in his delightful brogue.

I nudged the person next to me and whispered, "I don't know about you, but this is going to be a great priest for me." After Mass was over, I asked one of the nuns to give Father William some of my writings about my experiences as a Jew in relationship with a Catholic monastery.

Sunday Mass was less rabbinic, but afterward the priest took me aside and said, "Take a walk with me."

Strolling the paths of the monastery grounds, Father William told me that as a young priest fresh from Ireland many years earlier, he'd been assigned by his archbishop to appear on a new interfaith television show. His co-host was a prominent, much older rabbi. They worked together for twenty years, and Father William came to regard the rabbi as his spiritual mentor.

"My life's mission has been interfaith work between Christians and Jews," he said with a smile. "So when the nuns wrote asking me to be their priest, I refused because this place is so isolated. I was convinced if I came here I would never meet Jewish people anymore."

He took my hands in his. The sunlight slanted through the pine trees onto his white hair. "Then I came and found you," he said. "I believe this is God's way of telling me this is where he wants me. I'm going to talk to Mother Prioress about becoming their priest."

As we walked back to the main house hand in hand, I felt such overwhelming joy that I knew I must have been touched by the Shekhinah, the Hebrew word for the indwelling presence of God. Although I'd understood the concept intellectually, I had never truly experienced it until then—when my being a Jew filled my Christian friends' most pressing need.

"My Toughest Day"

by Meredith Vieira

S even months after coming to the *TODAY* show, I had one of my toughest assignments ever: the terrible shootings at Virginia Tech. Cohost Matt Lauer and I, along with the rest of the *TODAY* team, were on campus within twenty-four hours. Twenty-four hours is not enough time to comprehend such an overwhelming event: thirty-two people dead, most of them kids, slain by a fellow student. As a reporter I had some hard questions to ponder: Where was the shooter and when? Who were the victims? Did any of them know him? Viewers wanted to know the facts so they could make sense of this tragedy. But I also couldn't escape being a mom and thinking of my own kids, especially my oldest son, who would soon head off to college himself.

Ever since I started this job I've worn a charm bracelet with my husband's and children's names engraved on it. I can see it dangle from my wrist no matter what I'm doing, and that day in Blacksburg, Virginia, as I was about to go on the air, just a glance at it made me wish I could wrap my arms around them and hold them tight.

My husband Richard and I have three teens: Ben, Gabe and Lily. As careful as I am about not talking about their personal lives on air (teenagers do not appreciate having their privacy invaded on national television, to say the least), I think about them all the time. Most reporters are also parents, and it is hard sometimes for us not to see the news at least partly from that perspective—especially something as shocking as the Virginia Tech slayings.

Of course, it's a balancing act, one faced by working moms everywhere. I mean, what mom hasn't missed an important announcement buried in the slew of papers that's come home in the backpack? For me it was Colonial Day at Gabe's second-grade class when he showed up sans costume. I took it a lot harder than he did and vowed never to let my kids down, no matter how busy I got.

Maybe I take it a little far sometimes. Recently I was heading to one of Ben's soccer games, after which I had a commitment to host the MS Dinner of Champions—a benefit for multiple sclerosis, which means a lot to me because Richard has the disease. Still, nothing was going to stop me from seeing Ben's game, even if it meant being a little overdressed. I pulled off the highway and jumped out of the car in my three-inch heels, only to discover that there was a three-foot-high fence standing between me and Ben's team out on the field.

No problem, I thought. I hiked up my skirt, balanced on a rock, and threw one leg over the fence and then the other, telling myself, *Please don't let my stocking tear.* I barely made it over. I headed toward the game, wobbling, my heels sinking in the dirt. Finally I reached Ben's coach on the sidelines. I beamed a smile at seventeen-year-old Ben out on the field and turned to the coach, feeling heroic. "Excuse me," he said, "but you're not allowed to stand on this side of the field. You've got to go around to where the other parents are."

It's not that I'm trying to be an alpha mom. I just want my kids to know that I'm there for them. I want to meet their friends, know their teachers and watch them play. There's a lot of support a parent can give a child just by standing on the sidelines—even in three-inch heels.

Then there are the times when your kids show up for you. Last year, after being on *The View* for nearly a decade, I was offered the cohosting job on the *TODAY* show. I had to be sure that my family was behind me. This would be a big change for all of us.

To Richard it was a no-brainer. "What a great challenge for you," he said. "Take it."

But how would Lily and Gabe and Ben feel about it? I would have to leave the house early in the morning, long before they got up. And the hours could be brutal. "Mom, what would you be missing?" fifteen-year-old Gabe said. "All of us fighting over the breakfast cereal?"

I spoke privately to fourteen-year-old Lily, who is the quietest of the three. She is thoughtful and a very good writer, like her father. "Mom, you have to do what's going to make you happy," she said. Then that night, going through my e-mail, I found one message from Lily. *Maybe something I'm supposed to do for school*, I thought. I opened it up and read, "Mom, I love you on *The View* and I will love you on the *TODAY* show. Love, Lily." Tears flooded my eyes. Her encouragement was incredibly touching. It meant everything to me.

Ben is the oldest of the three, and I felt I could be pretty frank with him about all my insecurities. *Would I be good enough for the job? Would I be able to keep it up week after week?*

"Mom," he said, "remember when I had to change schools going into fifth grade and I was scared about leaving my old friends behind and making new friends? Remember what you said to me then? You promised me that after the first few days I'd really love it, and I did. So will you."

That should have been enough. But I still had my doubts. The job would be huge and all-consuming. The night before my first day, I had a terrible case of cold feet. Before dinner I went out for a walk—ever since my days in a Quaker school, solitude has been my way to find peace. I walked and walked, but I didn't feel any better. Finally I came home and sat at my place at the kitchen table. There in front of me was a jewelry box.

"Open it," said Richard and the kids. Inside was the bracelet with the gold charm: "We are with you. Love, Richard, Ben, Gabe, Lily." My doubts vanished. It was as though everyone were hugging me and supporting me at once. Now, looking at that charm bracelet and the pain and confusion at Virginia Tech, I knew my family's love would support me. All day long I thought of them, ached for them.

The last segment we filmed that day was at the sprawling drill field where some students had erected a spontaneous memorial of flowers and signs. It was dusk. Students took turns writing their messages on poster boards, things like, "We love you.... We miss you.... We won't forget you.... We will survive." *But how?* I wondered. *How will they survive?*

When the interviews were all finished, I had the urge to step out of my role as a *TODAY* show host. If I couldn't be with my own kids, I just wanted to be a mom hanging out with these kids. I stood there, part of the crowd. One girl looked up at me, an empty poster board and a marker in her hand. "What should I say?" she asked.

"Anything that comes to you," I told her. "Anything your heart tells you will be right."

Then a girl came up to me and handed me a candle. I tried to give it back to her. "You'll probably need this for some of the others," I said.

"Take it," she insisted. I did. My candle was lit by another candle until all of us standing there—there must have been hundreds of us—were illuminated as if by one single light. A silence—a wonderful, peaceable, healing silence—came over the crowd. We could all feel a presence.

That's when one girl came over to me and asked, "Can you give me a hug?" I wrapped my arms around her and she broke down. For the first time since coming to Blacksburg, Virginia, I was able to cry too, feeling her pain and the pain of all the other students around me, but so grateful that I could somehow offer them comfort. After the first girl walked away, another student came up to me for a hug and then another. I couldn't be at home, hugging my own children, but I could certainly hug these kids. And it felt so right. I looked down at the charm bracelet on my wrist. I read the names again in the flickering candlelight.

Yes, it had been a long day, both as a reporter and a mom. But in the end I had found comfort in the simple act of connecting with these students. It is in these small moments that healing begins.

A New Me

by Jay Earle

Your tests show you have rheumatoid arthritis, Jay," my doctor said. Arthritis? Wasn't that what everyone my age had a touch of? Besides, I felt so great that day, it never dawned on me that I might have a serious problem.

Two weeks earlier I'd been to him when my knee stiffened up—the result of a sixty-seven-year-old guy taking one too many runs on the slalom course waterskiing, I assumed. I headed to the doctor so he could "fix it." And fix it he did. The cortisone shot worked its magic and my knee felt as good as new. Sure, I suffered the usual aches and pains of getting older, but it wasn't anything I couldn't handle.

I drove home and spent the afternoon spreading mulch and spiffing up my boat. I didn't give my diagnosis another thought. And yet, as the shot wore off over the following weeks, it became impossible to ignore the symptoms. At first it was just hard to get up off the ground after playing with my grandkids. Then I started having trouble standing at my workbench using a saw or drill. What was happening to my body?

I'd always thought of physical pain as a temporary condition, something I could tough out or work through. Only if it got really bad would I see a doctor. But this rheumatoid arthritis was unlike anything I'd ever experienced. The pain was constant and everywhere, and instead of getting better, it got worse. I couldn't sleep, I couldn't read, I could barely even watch TV. Waterskiing? Hiking? Forget about it. Overnight I'd become an old man.

My doctor sent me to a rheumatologist, who tried me on a variety of medications. "It may take some trial and error to find the right combination," he warned. I'm not the most patient guy. While I waited in vain for relief, I wanted to scream, Don't you people understand? I'm Jay Earle. I'm not some cranky old man who hobbles around complaining about how he feels. Everything I'd ever done came through determination and hard work—swabbing decks in the Navy, putting myself through college playing saxophone in a dance band, working harder than the next guy in my banking career. I had always counted on my own strength, so now when friends said that they were praying for me, I said thanks but didn't put much stock in it. Never had, really. All I wanted was the old me back.

One morning I snapped at my wife over nothing, an all too common occurrence since my diagnosis. I retreated to my workshop and picked up my power drill. I made a few holes in a nice piece of hardwood. All at once my hands failed me. The drill slipped, gouging the wood. In a blind rage I slammed the drill to the ground. For about a minute I felt better. Then the adrenaline subsided. There I was with a useless aching body and a broken drill.

That night, I couldn't sleep. I couldn't even get out of bed and go downstairs and try to watch some TV. I was alone in the dark with my pain, a pain that had become the largest presence in my life. My mind jumped from thought to thought, trying to outrun it. Yet the pain invaded everything. I found myself thinking about the prayer list my wife had put me on at her church. Prayer had always struck me as a pretty passive approach to solving problems. But now my mind flashed back to other people I'd known with chronic conditions, friends who got hurt in terrible car accidents, family members who'd fought cancer. So much suffering, yet people survived, even prevailed over pain. All of them had faith. Was it the hand of God that supported them? Was it the power of prayer and the thankfulness that people felt for His blessings?

Yes, I'd been lucky. Great jobs. A wonderful family. My patient, loving wife. My house by the lake. I had always assumed that most of it came by way of brains and some tough decision-making. Hard work. But maybe . . . maybe it was because God was looking out for me. Maybe he would look out for me now. "Lord," I whispered in the dark, "I turn to you. If I must have this pain, help me to bear it." Soon I fell back to sleep.

The doctor kept juggling my meds until gradually there was improvement. "I think we've hit on the right combination," he said. I couldn't ski anymore but I could spend the day boating with hardly any pain. The joints in my hands improved so much I picked up the saxophone again. I'd forgotten what a pleasure it was to play music. The doctor might have found the right combination of drugs, but I had found another powerful combination—faith and gratitude.

Arthritis is part of my life these days, but it doesn't control it. For that I am boundlessly grateful. I did something I should have done years ago: I joined my wife's church. Now I not only have a congregation of people praying for me, but I also have a list of people I'm saying prayers for. I work just as hard on it as any of the jobs I've ever done. And I visit the sick in the hospital. It helps me to help them.

Physically I'd say I'm back to 90 percent of where I was before the arthritis hit. But spiritually I'm a different person. And you know what? At my age that's pretty exciting. I don't have the old me back. I've got something new, something I've needed for a long time.

One Perfect Rose

by Ellen Ingersoll Plum

My mother had just passed away after a long illness. Though I was accustomed to seeing death, having helped my husband run a funeral home in New Jersey for many years, all the comfort I usually offered to mourners seemed inadequate in the face of my own sorrow. I styled women's hair for their viewings, and now, three days before Christmas, it was time to do this one last thing for my own mother.

I went downstairs from the apartment where my husband and I lived and had raised our two daughters and began doing Mother's hair, her swirling curls reminding me of the roses she'd loved to grow. I'd left myself plenty of time to finish before the Snyders—my husband's three o'clock appointment—showed up, so I worked slowly, wanting everything to be perfect. I had just completed the finishing touches when the office doorbell rang. It was the Snyders—half an hour early. My first impulse was to tell them to come back later, but looking at their grief-stricken expressions was like looking in a mirror. I ushered them inside to wait for my husband. Mr. Snyder leaned so heavily on his cane I wondered if it would support him.

"I don't want anyone to see her," he declared, dropping onto a chair.

"Please, Dad," his daughter pleaded. "I couldn't live with myself for not getting home in time to say good-bye if I can't ever see Mom again."

"She wouldn't want you to see her like that," Mr. Snyder snapped. "Her hair was all matted, and she looked awful. There will be no viewing."

The daughter turned to me. We tried to stay out of our clients' family matters, but I couldn't help but respond to the desperation in her eyes. "Mr. Snyder, we style women's hair whether or not there is a viewing," I explained. "At least your daughter can see her mother if you come early for the funeral."

Just then my husband arrived, and as he showed Mr. Snyder and his daughter into his office, I stepped outside. I knelt beside our rosebush to take another look at the only thing that had comforted me since my mother's death: a tiny bud on the tip of an almost leafless branch. "If roses could only last till Christmas," Mother used to say, "winter wouldn't seem so long." I had heard people talk about the signs that helped them after the death of a loved one. *When this rose blooms*, I decided, *it will be God's sign that Mother is at peace.*

My daughters arrived with their families that evening, and I showed them the rosebud. "There's never been a bud later than Thanksgiving," one said. "It's got to be for Grandma." The next day was Mother's funeral. What better time for it to bloom? But by morning the bud had not opened. Standing at Mother's grave after the funeral service, I longed to feel her close to me again. I had been to so many funerals for strangers, surrounded by grief yet apart from it. Now I was in its midst, and I wondered how I would get through.

As soon as we got home, I hurried out back with my daughters, searching for velvety red petals in the gray gloom. But we found the bud withered from frost. "It's dead," I said.

"But it was there," one of my daughters assured me. "We all saw it."

"And we all know it was meant to comfort us," said the other.

I nodded, though I had the crushing feeling there would never be any relief from my sorrow, that I would never feel hopeful again, that winter would never end. All I wanted was to go to bed and stay there, but then I remembered I had to do Mrs. Snyder's hair. Her funeral was the next day. I knew I could not let her daughter down.

The next morning, Christmas Eve, I reminded my husband how much Mrs. Snyder's daughter wanted to see her mother.

At breakfast, we sat around the table in silence. *Is this what Christmas will be like now?* I wondered. "Mother would want us to celebrate," I said. "Let's start with the tree." So we set up the tree in the living room, decorating it with lights and ornaments—all except the star, lying broken in its box. The empty spot atop the tree made me feel Mother's absence more than ever.

That evening, as my daughters and I prepared dinner, a car pulled up outside. From the kitchen window I saw Mr. Snyder struggle out of the front seat with his cane. "No!" he boomed at his daughter, who had rushed to his side. "I want to tell Mrs. Plum myself."

Now you've done it, I thought. *This is what you get for sticking your nose into other people's affairs.*

I opened the door and invited them into the living room. "I want to thank you," Mr. Snyder said. "My wife looked beautiful. I will carry that last image of her with me for the rest of my life." The twinkling Christmas-tree lights played across his face as he continued, "We want to share something of hers with you." The daughter held out a small box.

"Oh," I said, "I couldn't—"

"Please," the daughter insisted. "It's nothing valuable, but it meant a lot to Mom."

As she gave me the gift, her hand touched mine. I opened the box. There, on a bed of red velvet, lay a pin, a silver rose. A legend was printed on the inside of the lid: "A little shepherd girl in Bethlehem was weeping because she had no gift to give the newborn baby Jesus, when suddenly a rose appeared where her tears had fallen." This pin was, unmistakably, God's sign, a Christmas rose.

My husband clipped the silver rose to the top of the tree. Standing before it with my family all around me, I knew spring would come again.

Boat Out of Water

by Kathie Kania

When we first laid eyes on the *Belle Isle* in a vacant lot of a small town in Idaho, hundreds of miles from the ocean, my husband Michael nearly flew out of our pickup. "Honey, look at her!" he exclaimed. I did. What I saw was a mastless sailboat carcass on a rusty trailer, morning glories entwined around the ribs of the hull, hornets buzzing out of a nest in the stern. Michael, however, saw a sleek, beautiful boat skimming across the water—his lifelong dream. "Somebody built the frame and then didn't finish it," he marveled as he walked around the boat, knocking on her sides as though inspecting a car. "It's good mahogany and a nice design. Let's find the owner. See how much he wants for it."

Right then I should have said no. We had a four-year-old daughter and I was several months pregnant with our second child. We didn't have time to work on a boat. We lived more than five thousand feet above sea level in the high desert. Michael worked for the USDA Forest Service. True, he had put in for a transfer, but even in the unlikely event it came through, chances were we'd still be living inland, in some other dry, mountainous region. What on earth would we do with a boat?

And yet, for a brief instant, I caught a glimpse of my husband's vision. The two of us working side by side, sanding, varnishing, painting. The kids sound asleep while we pursued a project together, a husband and wife with a shared goal. Besides, Michael was getting frustrated at his job. He needed the outlet, and he was a gifted woodworker. "It wouldn't hurt to ask," I admitted.

And so we became the proud owners of the *Belle Isle*. At first, fixing it up was a lot of fun. I rushed to the garage with hot, steaming towels that we wrapped around wooden boards, warping them to fit the frame. Michael clamped a vise at one end and I gently maneuvered the plank. I loved being with Michael that way, moving closer to each other, fitting together like wood to the frame.

"What's that?" friends asked when they saw the hull in our garage.

"That's the *Belle Isle*," we'd say. "We're going to sail it someday."

"Yeah, sure, in the desert? Are the animals lining up outside two by two?"

I smiled at the good-natured teasing. We would build this boat, plank by plank. And when it was done, we'd find somewhere to sail. Michael and I had faith in our dream.

But then our second baby arrived. I clocked the contractions inside the house while Michael worked up to the last minute in the garage. Finally he emerged, Bogart-like, from a fog of sanding sealer and rushed me to the hospital. After we brought our baby home, I launched into all the activities a newborn demands, not to mention reassuring her older sister that Mommy had enough love for two girls. Michael did his part, too, doing the wash, cooking, cleaning up. But invariably he'd end up drifting out to the garage.

I sometimes ventured there to show the baby what Daddy was doing. "Don't bring her too close," he warned. "This epoxy has really strong fumes." Or, with his goggles on and the electric sander in one hand, he waved us away. "The baby shouldn't be near all this sawdust," he said. Gradually, the boat turned into Michael's project.

That's all right, I told myself. *It'll have to be this way until we get used to two kids. Then I can get back into it.* For Michael, the boat had become his escape from the mounting pressures at work. Nothing was happening with his request for a transfer, and he was growing increasingly frustrated and disheartened. The boat consumed all his spare time, and the details were endless. I found myself wondering, *Is the boat an excuse to get away from me too?*

One day Michael came in from the garage, his hair full of sawdust, his face freckled with paint. "Did you notice the varnish on the hull?" he asked. "Doesn't it look great? It's so shiny you can see your reflection in it!"

I tried to summon up enthusiasm to match his, but I was beginning to resent the *Belle Isle. Am I actually jealous of a boat?* I wondered. Yet he did seem to spend more time with her than with me.

One afternoon a neighborhood busybody, spying the monstrous hulk under a tarp like a body in a morgue, exclaimed, "Now there's a project that'll never get done!"

Too bad Michael can't understand that, I thought. Then Michael's energies flagged. He had built a beautiful cabin lined with cedar and cherry cabinetry, all the corners carefully beveled and fitted. It was the sort of workmanship I wished we had in our kitchen.

"I don't know if I can keep going," he said one evening.

"Give it a rest for a while," I replied. In my mind I added, *And spend a little more time with your family.*

Michael hesitated. "I'm afraid if I stop, I'll never get back to it."

"Sure you will," I said, my sympathy getting the better of me. I hated to see Michael so down! "You'll finish the *Belle Isle.* I won't let you give up." I couldn't believe what I was saying. Hadn't I wished the *Belle Isle* would die a peaceful death? Hadn't I resented

Michael's dream for all the time it took him away from me? And yet I realized that the dream was still alive in me too. Even overwhelmed with caring for our two children, I had never given up the vision of our beautiful sailboat. I still wanted to see it skimming across a crystal-blue sea. "You have to finish her," I said again.

"But how? I just don't have the energy."

"Is there anything I can do to help?"

"Maybe you can take a look at the interior of the cabin. . . ."

The next thing I knew, I was lying on my back, sawdust sprinkling on my face as I sanded the cabin ceiling. With each square foot, my neck and forearms ached more. This was a lot harder than planking the hull. *Michael is probably lounging on the sofa, watching TV with the baby asleep on his chest.* I told myself that it would be a brisk day in a bad place before I worked on the *Belle Isle* again. . . . Yet, slowly, I came to look forward to it, even to love it. When Michael returned from work, I handed him the baby and put on my dirtiest overalls and grungiest T-shirt. Working in the cabin was peaceful, even serene. No crying, no endless loads of wash, no blaring TV. With the soft swish-swish of the sandpaper, I daydreamed about sailing with our girls when they got a little older. One of them would be at the tiller, the other roping in the jib, and their father would show them how to tack against the wind.

God, is this what You've been trying to tell me? That raising children and building a boat take a lot of hard work, detail work, but as long as we keep the faith, we'll make it? When I was with the children all day long I'd forget this, losing myself in juice spills and soiled diapers. But when I was away for several hours in the garage, I could put everything in perspective. Now I knew what drew Michael to the *Belle Isle*. Although the stench of varnish filled my nose and dirt caked under my nails, I had the perfect opportunity for reflection.

That was how the *Belle Isle* finally got done. Michael and I took turns. Sometimes I worked with my paintbrushes and sandpaper blocks. Other evenings it was Michael with his screwdriver and hammer and nails. No, it wasn't how I'd envisioned it, but there was an amazing intimacy in the process. Time and again I'd see something he'd done and appreciate Michael even more. His craftsmanship, his delicate care. It thrilled me to see such good work.

"You know," Michael said, "I used to tell myself that I should have tackled a project like this before I had a wife and family. Now I know I couldn't have done it without you."

I laughed. "Without you, I wouldn't even have known I wanted to do it!"

As a finishing touch, I carved a wreath of roses in the walnut molding at the top of the cabin and touched it up with red paint. "It's the prettiest boat you'll ever see," Michael said.

"Sure is," I agreed.

"Now we just have to find a place to sail it. . . ."

That summer we took the girls on vacation, leaving the *Belle Isle* under her tarp in the garage. *Too bad we can't put her in the water*, I thought. But we weren't close enough to any good sailing spots. Instead, we camped in the woods. One day we stopped at a filling station so Michael could call his office, just to be sure things were okay. He came back from the phone booth with the strangest expression on his face, as though he'd just won the lottery.

"You know that transfer we've been waiting for?"

"Yes?"

"Well, it finally came through! We're going to the Hood River in Oregon. The office is right on the water."

The *Belle Isle* filled slip number one at the marina near Michael's new office in Oregon. And just as I had dreamed and prayed, on summer weekends when the girls grew older, we went sailing. Father, mother and two daughters. One girl took the tiller and one the jib, and I trailed my hand through the water.

"Just what you dreamed it would be?" Michael asked, squinting into the sun.

"No," I replied. "Better."

Compassion *for* Others

Annie's Soldier

by Elizabeth Hassee

Mom!" my ten-year-old daughter Annie shouted as she burst through the front door after school that fall afternoon nearly three years ago. "I just got a letter from a soldier!"

Annie's teacher had given them a project: Write a letter to a US serviceman or woman in Iraq. Annie had worked hard on a big picture of a red, white and blue cat. On the bottom of the page she'd written, "Be safe, and thank you."

I'd cautioned Annie not to get her hopes up too much. "There are a lot of soldiers over there," I told her. "And they're very busy. I'm sure they'll appreciate hearing from you, but you might not get an answer from them."

"That's okay, Mom," Annie had said. "It was fun making the picture." Now Annie pulled the letter from her schoolbag and read it to me.

Hi, my name is Scott Montgomery. I am a sergeant in the South Carolina Army National Guard currently stationed in Kuwait. Two weeks ago in Iraq, on a mission just north of Baghdad, my truck was hit by a bomb. A piece of shrapnel struck me in the arm and I had to be rushed to the hospital. I had two operations and was feeling pretty sad. While I was recuperating, someone gave me an envelope addressed to a US soldier. I found a beautiful handmade card from you. It brought a big smile to my face to know that a young girl in Indiana took the time to wish good luck to someone she doesn't even know. Thank you, Annie. You really brightened this soldier's day. I hope you get a chance to write back. Take care, Scott.

"That is so cool!" Annie said. She raced upstairs to show the letter to her sisters while the words she'd just read echoed in my head. *Kuwait. Baghdad. Trucks. Bombs. Shrapnel.* The kinds of words I read every day in the paper, along with another one: *casualties.* I instantly liked the young man who had been thoughtful enough to write back to Annie—to make her feel so special. But to be honest, I was worried. My daughter was a sweet little fourth grader. Her world was small and, I hoped, protected. Scott was a man in the middle of a war where people were getting maimed and killed. A conflict that adults argued about every day . . . on TV, the radio, even in our own church parking lot. The ugly realities of war were nearly everywhere. Did I really need to expose my ten-year-old to them? Wouldn't the world find her soon enough?

"She's going to grow up fast enough as it is," I said to my husband Jim that night. "War is the most horrible thing in the world. Does she have to learn about it now, when she doesn't even know that Santa's not real?"

"Look," said Jim. "We're the ones who taught the girls that we need to support the troops over there. Annie's just putting that idea into action. She can learn from this. It is scary, true. But you're never too young to do the right thing."

The next day after school, Annie showed me a letter she'd written to Scott. It was short, but I could see the work she'd put into it in every carefully lettered word.

Dear Scott, I'm in fourth grade. I'm in gymnastics twelve hours a week. I like SpongeBob and using my dad's computer to play office. Annie.

"That's nice," I told her, and she sent off the letter.

Starting almost immediately, the first thing Annie did when she got home from school or gymnastics class was to check the mailbox. Three weeks passed. I figured Scott wasn't going to write back. "Don't feel bad," I told Annie one afternoon following another fruitless check of the mailbox. "Scott's a soldier. He's got all kinds of things to think about over there. Writing you a letter right now might not be so easy for him."

"I know, Mom," Annie said, her voice upbeat as usual. "But I can still think he's going to write back. I can hope."

A month flew by, and I hoped Annie had moved on. Then one day a package with a military return address showed up. Inside was a bracelet made of rope, a small stuffed camel and another handwritten note from Scott. "Every guy in my unit wears a bracelet like the one enclosed," it read. Annie immediately wrapped it around her tiny wrist; it was a perfect fit. She went to bed that night with it on and the camel tucked in beside her. I peeked in on her later. Her face, bathed in the soft pink glow of her half-moon nightlight, was peaceful almost beyond imagining, so opposite of the way our world was now. How would she react if Scott or someone in his unit got hurt or worse? I went to bed more worried than ever.

"Christmas is only a month away," Annie said the next morning at breakfast. "Let's send Scott a holiday goodie package. We can put cookies in it. The frosted cutout kind. And Chex mix. You can't have Christmas without Chex mix." Christmas in Iraq. I closed my eyes and tried to imagine it. Broiling heat. Constant danger. And homesickness.

I opened my eyes and saw Annie staring at me, a big, eager grin on her face. I looked at that innocent, completely trusting face and decided I had to say something more than I had so far. "War isn't nice, Honey. This isn't just another fun school project. It's real. And dangerous. I want you to know that."

Annie fixed me with one of those looks she gives me from time to time. A look that basically says: *Mom, how can you be so dumb?* "I know, Mom," she said. "And that's why I wanted to write the letter! That's why I put Scott and the soldiers in my prayers every night."

Now I was the one being naive. I should have known Annie had thought this through and that there was no hiding the world from her. Certainly there was no holding back her prayers. And how could she pray if she didn't know what she was praying for? "Christmas in Kuwait!" I said to Annie. "We should put some practical things in the package too. Things he can use every day, like gum and lip balm. He can't drive down to Target like we can." Annie nodded vigorously, as if this fact had already occurred to her. By the time we'd gotten everything packed into Scott's holiday package and sent it off, I was as excited for Scott to get it as Annie was.

The holidays came and went. No word from Scott. I kept my eye on the mailbox. I was as bad as Annie. Worse, probably. Finally a box arrived—a big box. Inside was an American flag. With a mix of awe and excitement, Annie and I spread it across the dining room table. It was covered with written messages from everyone in Scott's unit, like a page from a high school yearbook.

Dear Annie, Scott's letter read, We flew this American flag in Iraq and Kuwait. As you can see, all the soldiers on my team have signed it for you. They know all about you, and it is our way of saying thank you for your support. You aren't really supposed to write on the flag, but we made an exception. I hope you like it. Take care. God bless. Scott.

I turned my head away. Wars make us cry for the right reasons too.

That spring, Annie developed an injury to her back due to gymnastics class. Her flexibility caused her to develop a hairline crack on one of her vertebra. This meant limited activities for her, and she needed to wear a back brace for several months. She told Scott all about it in a letter. *Dear Scott, I had to quit gymnastics. I hurt my back. I have a brace that I wear, and I have to do therapy. Ugh!* Scott wrote back—in an envelope covered with some of the SpongeBob stickers Annie had sent him.

Dear Annie, How are you doing? Is your back still bothering you? I hope by now it is all better. Take it easy and be patient. I know you're upset about not being able to do gymnastics right now. Try not to get too upset. When I got wounded back in October, I was pretty upset about it. I wondered why that happened to me. I now know that it happened so I could get your letter and we could become friends. Your friend, Scott.

"See, Mom?" Annie whispered after we read the letter. I couldn't say anything. I pulled her close to me, kissed the top of her head and breathed in her little girl smell. Sometimes moms forget that there are even bigger plans than their own, and how fast children grow up.

In the fall of 2005, Annie's friend Sergeant Scott Montgomery came home to Myrtle Beach, South Carolina, to resume duty as a police patrolman—the job he had held before shipping out to Iraq. He invited our family down in February 2006 to meet him face-to-face. We decided to meet Scott and his fiancée down at the beach. Annie hesitated at first, feeling a little shy; then she threw her arms around Scott like she'd known him her whole life. So did I. It was so good to see him and see that all his wounds were healed. We had dinner with Scott and his fiancée. Scott had arranged for us to attend a tribute to our Armed Forces at the Alabama Theatre the next day. He greeted us at the auditorium and showed us to our seats.

"Just to let you know," he whispered in my ear, "I have a little surprise to give to Annie." When the announcer called Scott up, he walked nervously to the stage. After the applause, Scott called to Annie, "Annie, get up here. I'm not doing this by myself.

"This young lady was always there for me when I was in Iraq," he told the audience. "She deserves to share this award." The room broke into applause as Scott handed a plaque and a bronze eagle to Annie. Someone snapped a picture. "Annie, while we're up here," Scott continued, "there's one more thing I'd like to give you." Scott reached into his pocket and pulled something out: his Purple Heart, the award wounded soldiers are given by their country. Annie's eyes widened as Scott pinned his Purple Heart on her jacket. The whole house erupted in applause. Scott's fiancée gave me a hug.

Annie made her way back to her seat, the plaque and eagle in her hands, the medal pinned proudly to her, and an impossibly huge grin on her face. "Mom, can you believe how cool this is?" she said.

"It's pretty cool, all right," I said, putting my arms around my daughter. "And so are you."

Along Came Santa

by Cimeri Miller

I was traveling home for the holidays, from Sacramento to Fort Smith, Arkansas, by bus, taking my two young boys to see their beloved granddad. Sounds like the makings of a Hallmark story, right? It was anything but. Truth is, I was broke. Flat broke. Dad had wired me seven hundred dollars—enough for three bus fares and food for my kids and me for the four-day trip to his house. I was afraid to tell him just how bad off I really was, that I wanted to move back in with him for a few months until I could save some money and get back on my feet.

I hadn't seen Dad in more than a year, we lived so far apart. But he had always been my rock. When I was a little girl, I would crawl up on his lap and snuggle against his chest and he'd wrap his arms around me. "Don't worry, baby girl, God will be with you," he'd always say. Dad was a man of faith. A minister, in fact. Riding through the pitch-dark along lonely Interstate 70 on day four, somewhere in Kansas, I gazed at my sleeping children: Zachary, four, and Blake, two. *I could use some of Dad's faith right about now,* I thought.

I checked my watch. Four o'clock in the morning. Two more

hours till we reached Kansas City. A short layover and then we would be on our way to Fort Smith, to Dad. *We're going to make it home*, I thought with relief. *Home to Dad for Christmas Eve.* My eyes closed. I began to relax.

Suddenly, the bus lurched to a stop. I jolted awake. *Where are we?* I wondered. *What's wrong?*

The bus driver threw open the door, tramped down the steps and popped the hood. A few minutes later, he climbed back aboard. "This bus ain't goin' nowhere," he announced.

By the time we finally arrived in Kansas City, we'd missed our connection to Fort Smith. I checked the bus schedule. Twelve hours till the next bus. I called Dad in tears. "We're not going to make it in time for Christmas Eve," I sobbed. I hung up the phone and herded the kids to the waiting room. I checked my purse. Ten dollars. Not even enough for a real meal. I slumped in a seat.

There was a commotion in the bus station. I craned my neck. A tall, plump man dressed in white overalls and a Santa cap was walking around the waiting room, handing things out to people. "Look, kids," I said, "it's Santa Claus." The man stopped directly in front of me. He smiled and looked into my eyes. It was a kind look, incredibly kind.

"Merry Christmas," he said. He reached into his pocket and pulled out a one-hundred-dollar bill, handing it to me.

"I can't accept this," I gasped, waving his hand away.

He held out the bill again. "Are these your boys?" he asked.

"Yes," I answered. He reached into his pocket and pulled out two more hundred-dollar bills, holding them out to me.

My eyes welled up. "Mister, you don't know how bad I need that money," I said, my voice quavering. "But there's no way I can accept it." I looked around. There was a policeman standing nearby with a fire chief. They both seemed to know him. The man bent down close to me.

"I came here in 1971 on a Greyhound bus with everything I owned in one suitcase," he said. "I know exactly how you feel." He reached into his pocket once more and pulled out another two hundred dollars. "Take it," he said gently, placing all of the bills in my hand.

I broke down and told that Santa everything—how I had no money, how the bus had had engine trouble, how we had missed our connection to Fort Smith, how we couldn't make it home to Dad. The man turned solemn. "I'm going to get you to Arkansas tonight," he said, beckoning to the policeman and the fire chief, "but I think you need something to eat first. Can we take you and the boys out to lunch?"

"Yes, thank you," I said. We were whisked away to a restaurant where Zachary and Blake were given all they could eat, and Santa— he never told me his real name—arranged for a limousine. That's right. A limo. It was the first time I had ever ridden in one, but I think I would have taken a ride in the back of a pickup truck if it would have gotten me home to my dad.

The limo and the money—they weren't what was important. What restored my faith that night was kindness . . . simple, powerful kindness, kindness that gets you home for Christmas.

Just for Joshua

by Susie Vaccaro Hardeman

August 3, 2001, the day after my husband's funeral. Tyler had inoperable cancer. We'd moved to Little Rock and rented an apartment in a quiet complex so he could spend his last days in the town where he had grown up. We'd been here only three weeks before he died. Now I was on my own. I looked around the living room. Stacks of unopened boxes. *Get busy,* I told myself. Maybe it would take my mind off missing Tyler. I shifted my legs, trying to muster the strength to get up out of my armchair. The answering ache in my hip—still mending from a recent fall and fracture—was a rude reminder of the state I was in. How much could I hope to accomplish, really?

There was a rustle at my feet. The boys—that's what Tyler and I called Albert and Mouche, our two miniature poodles—stared at me expectantly. "I know, I know. It's time," I said. I reached for my walker, thinking, *You won't be able to give the boys near the exercise they need.* Tyler's hospice volunteers had been taking the dogs out for me, and I hadn't found anyone to assume the dog-walking chores. Not that I knew anyone in town well enough to ask. I sank back in the armchair, feeling defeated. Alone. More alone than I'd felt in all my sixty-plus years. *If this is what life on my own is going to be like, how am I going to deal with it?*

The doorbell rang. Who could that be? "Just a minute," I called, bracing myself on the walker and struggling to my feet. I shuffled between the boxes, the boys right at my heels, and opened the door. Standing there was a young man with a backpack, a clipboard and a handful of what looked like magazines.

"Good afternoon, ma'am. My name is Joshua Matthews. I play saxophone in the Forest Heights Junior High School band. Would you like to see our Christmas gift catalog?"

Christmas? I hadn't gotten used to the idea of a single week without Tyler—a week without our laughing at the boys' antics, our debates about current events. Christmas? I couldn't think that far ahead. I was about to say I wasn't interested, when I stopped. *He seems like a nice young man, and it's for a good cause.* "All right, let me take a look."

I rested the catalog on my walker and leafed through it. Joshua stood quietly, his eyes riveted on the dogs. "I could use one of these cheese crocks, I guess," I said. It came out half-heartedly, but I meant it.

"Great!" He took down my name and address and handed me a copy of my order. "Thank you, ma'am." He hadn't gone two steps before he turned around again. "Those are some good-looking poodles. What're their names?"

"This is Mouche. And that's Albert."

"I love dogs." He glanced at my walker. "Would you like me to take them out? I have to ask my mom first, but I live right here in the complex and I know she'll say yes."

Albert and Mouche looked up at me pleadingly, almost as if they understood. Normally, I wouldn't have let a stranger take my dogs. But they needed a walk, and it wasn't as if I was up to it. "I'd appreciate that, Joshua. So would the boys. Why don't you check with your mom while I get their leashes?"

"All right!" Joshua grinned and dashed off. He was back before I'd finished clipping on the leashes. I liked the way Joshua knelt to introduce himself to my dogs and let them sniff his hand. The boys liked it too. Dogs appreciate being treated respectfully. They went on a good long walk. I don't know who came back happier, Joshua or the boys. "If you want, I could come by every day and walk them," he offered.

"How much would you charge?"

"Nothing, ma'am." I must have looked surprised, because he went on. "I want to be a veterinarian someday, so helping with your dogs would be good practice. Besides, they're great dogs."

The boys' tails started going a mile a minute. I chuckled. "No need to ask if they like you too. All right, Joshua, you've got the job. And you don't have to call me ma'am. Mrs. Hardeman is fine."

"Thank you, Mrs. Hardeman. See you tomorrow," Joshua said, and then looked at Albert and Mouche. "And you guys too."

Four o'clock the next afternoon, Joshua was at the door. The boys ran right up to him. Once they got their exercise, I got to know Joshua a little more. He was thirteen, about to start ninth grade. He lived with his mom in the next building over. Besides music, he liked math, literature and biology, because it had to do with animals.

I knew how most teenagers were—their interests jumping from one thing to the next—so I figured I would just enjoy Joshua's help while it lasted. A thirteen-year-old was bound to find something more exciting eventually. Don't tell that to my dogs, though. I didn't even need to look at my clock anymore. Right around four, Albert and Mouche would watch the door for their new friend. Joshua never let them down.

I looked forward to his visits too. The boys would head straight for the water dish after their walks. Joshua and I would sit down in the living room with a couple of glasses of lemonade. At first we'd just chat about things like what the dogs had been up to and how I liked the apartment complex.

"Mrs. Hardeman," Joshua asked one afternoon, "what do you think about what's going on in Afghanistan?" We ended up having a big discussion about the chances for democracy in that troubled country. I'd spent my working years as an administrative assistant in brokerage firms. To understand the stock market, you had to know what was going on in the world. That's where my fascination with current events had taken hold. It was a nice surprise to find someone else to share it with now that Tyler was gone. By then I knew Joshua was no ordinary thirteen-year-old.

The blazing summer mellowed into fall. My hip got better, but the boys were way too stuck on Joshua for me to take back that afternoon walk. And I wasn't about to give up our afternoon talks. I had a feeling Tyler would be pleased that I'd found a friend in Little Rock. Joshua still refused to let me pay him, so I was looking forward to the holidays. No young man could turn down a Christmas gift.

"Joshua," I asked one November afternoon, "what are you going to do with the first paycheck you earn as a veterinarian?"

"That's easy, Mrs. Hardeman. I'm going to buy some Coca-Cola stock."

"Do you know much about stocks?"

"Not really. I just heard that Coca-Cola is a good one. Makes sense. Everyone I know drinks it."

"Joshua," I blurted out, "I'm going to buy you some Coca-Cola stock for Christmas and put it into a college fund."

Joshua's eyes lit up. "Really?"

"That's not all. I'm going to get you a book so you can learn about how the stock market works and keep up with your investment."

It took just a few phone calls to my broker to open an account for Joshua and get him some shares of Coca-Cola. But a book? That was another story. The investment guides I came across were dry, technical, intimidating even to me. I was looking for a book that would show Joshua how fascinating the ins and outs of the stock market were. I could just picture it: small enough to fit in his backpack and full of the kind of clever, colorful illustrations kids love.

But there weren't any books like that. Someone would have to write one. *Someone? Why can't that someone be me? After all, I have a built-in critic.* I told Joshua my idea.

"Your own book, huh?" Joshua said. "That's pretty cool. Can I help with it?"

I laughed. "I was counting on it."

Our afternoon visits turned into editorial sessions. Sometimes we would talk for so long the boys would clamor for another walk. Joshua was a tough editor. And he had plenty of suggestions. Like the day I gave him a short but detailed history of Wall Street. Joshua read through what I had written. Finally, he looked up and said, "This is okay, Mrs. Hardeman, but how about doing it like a Q and A?"

Why not do the whole thing Q and A? I thought.

Last fall, *Stock Market Knowledge for All Ages* was published. The entire book is done in simple question-and-answer format, with fun illustrations, the kind that keep kids—and adults—reading. I have to say I'm pleased with every page. My favorite, though, is the dedication: "To Joshua Matthews, my friend," who showed up at my door just when I'd thought I might have been forgotten; but I wasn't. My friend Joshua is proof enough of that.

The Arlington Ladies

by Richard H. Schneider

The widow flew alone from Orlando. The only fare she could afford required two stops before landing in Washington, DC. The trip took nearly a day. She rode in a cab to Arlington National Cemetery, holding her husband's ashes in a wooden box on her lap.

Before her husband died suddenly, she had been looking forward to a long, happy retirement. Her husband had begun building a deck behind their house. They had no children, and their only surviving family lived in Peru. But they had each other.

Now she had no one. She might have attended her husband's funeral by herself. But he had retired after twenty years as a senior Navy technician. And so, when she arrived at Arlington, she was met by a woman named Paula McKinley, whose mission it is to ensure that no one in the United States military's large extended family is left to endure the death of a loved one alone.

Paula is an Arlington Lady, one of about 150 women who volunteer to stand by the freshly dug graves of American soldiers and veterans, comforting survivors and, when there are no survivors, embodying the military's commitment to never abandon its dead.

The women—wives and widows of servicemen or retired from the service themselves—are all busy. Some work full-time. Yet they are drawn to the Arlington cemetery because "everyone who has served in the military is a hero," says Paula. "It is without a doubt the most gratifying volunteer work I've ever done."

When Paula arrived for the Orlando technician's ceremony, she found his widow in a cemetery waiting room, cradling a picture of her husband. The wooden box with the sailor's ashes had been given to an attendant. Paula introduced herself and put her arm around the widow. "She buried her head in my shoulder and she didn't say anything for five minutes. Then she looked at me and said, 'I'm so sorry.' And I said, 'For what? You have every right to cry.'" Paula stood by the widow while her husband's ashes were interred. When a sailor handed the woman a folded flag, she again cried on Paula's shoulder. The next day, Paula drove her to the airport. "I didn't want her to be by herself," she says.

The Arlington Ladies began attending funerals in 1948, when Gladys Vandenberg, wife of the Air Force Chief of Staff, noticed airmen being buried without any mourners, says Linda Willey, chair of the Air Force Arlington Ladies. Troubled, Mrs. Vandenburg enlisted members of the Officers' Wives' Club to attend funerals that were otherwise unaccompanied. Soon after, the women offered to attend all funerals—to give comfort and to present condolence cards from the entire Air Force family. After the service, the women wrote letters to any survivors who couldn't make it to Arlington, reassuring them that their loved one was buried with dignity. Army wives inaugurated their own Arlington Ladies branch in 1973, which is now chaired by Margaret Mensch. Navy wives followed suit in 1985.

"You can't understand what these survivors have gone through in their lives unless you've experienced the same," says Paula, who began serving in 1991, when she and her husband David, a Navy captain, returned from an extended deployment in Japan and the Philippines. As a Navy wife, Paula believes she knows a widow's loneliness. During the years her husband was deployed, she sometimes woke up Christmas morning to find she was the only one in the house. It was "the loneliest feeling I've ever felt in my life," she says. "It gives me empathy with a widow. She wakes up every morning without her husband."

Arlington holds twenty-five to thirty funerals every day. Veterans who have been given an honorable discharge are entitled to have their ashes put in the columbarium. Soldiers retired from extended service are entitled to a ground burial. Although Arlington conjures images of full-dress funerals with a horse-drawn caisson and honor guard, most ceremonies are simple, with a chaplain, survivors and a few casket bearers.

Paula, who chairs the Navy Arlington Ladies, has attended burials for Marines and Navy SEALS killed in Iraq, and a Navy officer killed at the Pentagon on September 11, 2001. "It can be heartbreaking to see the young ones," she says. Sheila Brown, secretary to Arlington's Navy chaplain, Ronald Nordan, has seen many widows comforted by the Arlington Ladies later become members of the group themselves. That's because Arlington Ladies keep in touch, sometimes forming friendships with the men and women they comfort. Once, Paula got a call from a widow in Pennsylvania distraught that she couldn't make it to her husband's grave on their wedding anniversary. The couple had been so in love that, even when the husband was far out to sea, they had arranged times to look at the full moon. He would stand on deck, she in her yard, and both knew what the other was seeing. On anniversaries, the husband always sent a red rose. Paula went to her yard, took three roses from her own garden and went down to the cemetery, where she placed them on the sailor's grave and took pictures to send to the Pennsylvania widow.

Paula says she knows that, one day, either she or her husband will be accompanied by an Arlington Lady. "It's the closeness that we have," she said. "That's why I'm an Arlington Lady. I'm part of a military family."

If I Could Trade Places . . .

by Sam Vargo

J ust about this time last year I started as a staff writer for the *State
Journal* in Charleston, West Virginia. It was a new city to me, and
I found it to be a nice place, clean and pretty free of crime. My
co-workers were friendly, honest and sincere. I wasn't really used to
working with folks like that. I was starting fresh and assumed I'd be
happy. But just a week later I got a call from my thirty-seven-year-old
brother Tom.

"Sam, he said, "I've got some bad news." Doctors had discovered
a tumor in his stomach. "It's about the size of a football," he said.
The doctors estimated the mass at about nineteen pounds. "They're
going to do some more tests, and probably surgery."

Why my little brother? I wondered after hanging up. We'd been
best pals ever since he was a toddler and he climbed up on my back
so he could ride me around like I was a horse. We'd lived together in
college, and after Dad died in 1982 we grew even closer. Tom went
on to become a coach and a schoolteacher, a clean-living, church-
going guy with a wife, two daughters and a new baby on the way. He
believed in the goodness of life and had a serenity about him it
seemed I'd never have. *He doesn't deserve this. Why couldn't it be*

me? Unlike Tom, I hadn't always stayed on the straight and narrow. When I was younger, I used to smoke and drink a lot. I was still single with no family depending on me. As for my faith, I was more of a worrier than a believer.

I'd been taking Tom for granted lately, I felt. He lived several hundred miles away in Columbus, Ohio, and with my new job I couldn't easily get away to see him. It seemed I'd never visited or called him as often as I should, never thought about him enough. After the phone call I started thinking about him all the time, about the likelihood of his death.

Especially in the parking deck near my office, where I'd race at 5:00 PM and break down crying behind the wheel of my car after a long day of keeping my emotions in check. The parking deck fit my mood, all right. It was cold and full of dark shadows, a nothing sort of place. I was beginning to think life was a lot like that too, especially with the raw deal it was giving my brother.

Terry, who sits in the cubicle next to me, overheard me talking grimly about my brother's condition one day and called me over. "He hasn't even had the surgery. Don't bury him yet," he counseled.

Shame flashed through me. How could I have been so negative about my own brother? That day after leaving work I didn't notice the bleakness of the parking deck so much.

Then, while flipping through TV channels one night, I saw part of a fishing show. Some guy caught a very large fish. It was green, long, fat, scaly and weighed in at sixteen pounds.

Look at the size of that thing! And still it's three pounds lighter than my brother's tumor! How could anyone survive having such a large thing inside of them? Worse, how could they survive the surgery needed to get it out? All over again I was consumed by doom and gloom. I couldn't escape it, not even watching TV.

A few weeks later Tom went in for the operation, right around the time I went to work. It was nearly 5:00 PM when my sister Barbara called from the hospital to let me know everything had gone smoothly.

"I told you not to bury him yet," my co-worker Terry gently reminded me.

Before bed that night, I got on my knees and thanked God my brother was still alive. I thanked him that Tom had survived a tough surgery. I even tried to apologize for having been such a bummer. And then I slept like a baby.

Tom did so well that he was released from the hospital two days earlier than expected. We waited for the biopsy. Things were good overall, the doctors said. The tumor had been removed and the malignancy had been contained. Tom would need follow-up tests every so often. *How do they know they got it all? What if the tests show something?* I started in again and then caught myself. *Wait. He's got faith in God, and maybe it's God's will for Tom to live. Who am I to say otherwise?*

My fears wouldn't go away, though. I woke up worrying and went to sleep the same way. I even started to break down in the parking deck after work again. I'd look through my tears at the cold, drab walls around me, as if searching for some meaning in the mass of gray rock.

I called my mom one night and she told me, "Tom's fine. It's you we're beginning to wonder about. Why don't you go visit?"

So I drove to Columbus the weekend of my birthday. My sister-in-law Tressa baked me a cake and my nieces helped me blow out the candles. "I hope Tom gets better" was my wish, but really it was more of a prayer.

The next day Tom asked if I wanted to go for a walk with him. "I've been walking a lot lately," he said. "To church, mostly, twice a day." That was a pretty long trip by car, let alone on foot. I was impressed. We headed out, and while we walked I told him how worried I'd been. He got upset with me. "You know what, Sam?" he said. "I believe God is going to see me through this. It'll be okay either way. I'm not so sure about you. Your worries aren't helping anyone; they're dragging us down, and you most of all."

I thought about what he'd said the whole drive back to Charleston. *Tom's the one who's facing this, not me. This worry is self-centered. It's taken over my thoughts, my life.* When I should have been thinking about my brother, all I could do was imagine how sad my own life would be without him. For once, I really thought about Tom and what this meant for him. If I could trade places with Tom, I'd do it in a heartbeat. Not only so he wouldn't have to suffer, but also because I wanted the kind of faith he had, really wanted it. Why couldn't I be more like Tom?

I visited again over Christmas. Tom, Tressa and I walked to midnight Mass in subzero temperatures. On the way home, we stopped at a diner. Inside it was warm, and the coffee brought the color back to our cheeks. I looked at Tom sitting across the table, laughing with Tressa, when it struck me: My brother had survived and was doing a much better job than I ever could have dreamed. Or than I ever could have done had I really been able to trade places with him. And he was doing it bravely, with a faith that wouldn't allow worries to drag him down. *Thank you, God,* I prayed. *Help me to be more like Tom.*

All at once I felt a sense of peace—everything was right in God's world, and there was no reason I shouldn't be able to say the same thing in the days ahead. I didn't have to worry about it. I don't know why it happened then and there. Maybe God just got sick of hearing me complain. But starting in my neck and going all the way down my body, I felt myself relax muscles I hadn't even known I'd tensed.

I felt the worry being physically released from my body, like the steam rising up from the coffee.

Today, Tom is doing great. He still goes in for tests, but so far the news has all been good, and he's been able to go back to teaching. Plus, at the beginning of this year he and Tressa had a bouncing baby boy.

As for me, I don't worry so much anymore. I used to sit in the parking deck thinking life was dark, bleak and unyielding, just like the mass of cold gray stone around me. Things looked that way because that's the way I was looking at them. We all go through changes, good and bad, but that's just life. How we face those rough patches is what living is all about.

Mr. Thanksgiving

by Ashley Johnson

Thanksgiving eve, Bob Vogelbaugh, owner of a small grocery store in Moline, Illinois, was bagging Rose Hanson's purchases. "Hey, there's no turkey here," Bob said.

"My family's all grown," Rose said. "Why bother with dinner? It's just me now."

That got Bob wondering. Were there other folks in the same boat as Rose? He asked other customers that day about their holiday plans. "My kids have moved away." "It's too far to travel just for dinner." "Why go to all the trouble?"

Closing up, Bob took note of an old table and some folding chairs in his storeroom. *I bet that table would seat eight*, he thought. He scratched his plans to go to a family reunion (his mom was disappointed, but she understood) and called his customers. First, Rose. "I'm inviting you to Thanksgiving dinner," he said.

"Does this mean I have to buy all my groceries from you?" she teased.

Bob laughed. "It's just dinner! Come by the shop at six and bring your favorite dish. I'll supply the bird." The next night, Rose and a half-dozen others gathered for green beans, mashed potatoes, turkey and pumpkin pie. "It was like the first Thanksgiving: people from different backgrounds getting together to share their blessings," Bob said. "And a great meal."

Thirty-four years later, Bob's annual Thanksgiving potluck has grown into a buffet extravaganza that overflows the food court at a local mall. Dinner is served free of charge to anyone who shows up. Weeks ahead of time Bob collects donations, rounds up volunteers and books buses (provided free by the transit authority) for the diners unable to drive. On the big day, he wakes up at five and heads to the mall to put up decorations. He checks in with the four hundred volunteers preparing the salad, rolls and side dishes and arranges for the delivery of the two thousand pounds of turkey he's ordered. At 2:30 PM, buses pull up to the mall, carrying hungry folks from four counties in Illinois and even a few from as far as Iowa.

Vicki Baker, Bob's right hand for the day, directs volunteers, who pass out plates piled with food. "As for dessert," Bob says, "it's every man for himself. People show up with a half-dozen pumpkin pies, stacks of angel food cakes. We always have enough for everyone." "Everyone" was more than two thousand people last year. Bob makes his way from table to table, saying hi to newcomers and regulars alike. "I know the ladies who bring the best pies," he says. "And one family still comes back to do all the dishes!"

The dinner costs about nine thousand dollars in turkey, stuffing and fixin's. "We have a couple of large donors," Bob says. The third-grade class at nearby C. R. Hanna Elementary School raised more than eighteen hundred dollars last year. "Mostly, we get letters with a few crumpled bills in them. The people always say they wish they could give more—those are the ones that really get me!"

After the last turkey is carved, Bob sits down with a slice of pumpkin pie and surveys the contented diners. What is Bob most grateful for, you might ask? "I don't believe the man upstairs meant for us to be alone at Thanksgiving," Bob says. "He gave me the chance to help bring all these people together for the day. That's what I'm most grateful for."

A Healing Net

by Sona Mehring

Darrin and JoAnn are two of my closest friends. So when JoAnn suffered a difficult pregnancy, I wanted to help them somehow. Their baby Brighid was born extremely premature and was in the Newborn Intensive Care Unit. JoAnn was also in critical condition. Darrin spent nearly twenty-four hours a day at the hospital. "What can I do?" I asked him.

"Just let everyone know what's going on," Darrin said. They had a lot of friends and relatives spread out all across the world, wanting to know what was happening, wanting to send their love and support. But Darrin was so occupied with everything, he couldn't keep retelling the story. There had to be an easy way to keep everyone informed and show support for Darrin and JoAnn without overwhelming them and the hospital staff.

I ran a consulting company that produced Web sites for small businesses and organizations. What if there were a Web site where Darrin and JoAnn's friends and relatives could go to share their messages and find out how JoAnn and Brighid were doing? It could save a bunch of phone calls, to be sure. And Darrin and JoAnn could check it when they were able to. I set up the site that night, with Darrin's blessing. At the bottom of the page I inserted a guest-book so people could type messages and prayers.

JoAnn needed her rest, so the doctors unplugged her phone and limited her visiting hours. But the Web site allowed everyone to stay in touch and updated, without intruding. Every day I updated it with news about JoAnn and Brighid's conditions. And the messages started pouring in. One of JoAnn's uncles, living in Switzerland, was happy he could feel connected to what was going on. "Finally a good use for the Internet," he wrote. I printed out the prayers and messages from the Web site for Darrin and JoAnn to read. "It helps so much to know there are people out there praying for Brighid and me," JoAnn said. "People I can picture in my mind."

JoAnn steadily improved, but Brighid's condition was a roller coaster. After nine days of fighting, she died. As much as the Web site had been great for keeping people updated, I worried it might seem like a terrible place to tell about something so tragic. But having to call everyone—all the extended family, far-off friends and others who had reached out through the Web site—seemed just as heartbreaking. I posted the sad announcement. JoAnn and Darrin left a message on the site, thanking everyone for their support: "Brighid left us after a nine-day struggle against tremendous odds. Even though she was with us a very short time, she has touched us all and brought us together in a huge circle of love."

I was surprised at how true that was. At Brighid's funeral service, everyone was already acquainted. We had read each other's words, learned the trials and tribulations Brighid had gone through in her short life and the miracle of JoAnn's recovery. We had all experienced a bit of what JoAnn and Darrin had experienced, and it had brought us closer together. *This could really help others*, I thought. JoAnn and Darrin thought the same thing. "We want to start a memorial fund in Brighid's honor," JoAnn told me. "We want to dedicate a computer and Internet access for families at the children's hospital, so they can create a Web page for their friends and relatives too."

JoAnn and Darrin's gift helped families at Children's Hospitals and Clinics of Minnesota in St. Paul set up Web sites to update friends and relatives about their situations. Word spread, and soon other hospitals were interested in helping their patients get online too. I dedicated myself to making it simple for anyone to create their own site filled with journal entries and photos, absolutely free. I called the program CaringBridge, in honor of Brighid. Most of the Web sites were initially set up by the close friends or family of patients. But even long-lost friends, co-workers and acquaintances left prayers, Bible verses and positive thoughts, told stories and jokes and talked about similar experiences. I've even seen people use the site to organize feeding schedules for one hospital-stranded couple's dogs and recruit volunteers to do chores around a patient's house.

The service is free, so we rely on donations to keep things running. Thankfully, many CaringBridge users give back. There are nearly sixty thousand CaringBridge sites today, with nine million guestbook messages of love and hope. I never could have imagined it when I first got the call that my friend JoAnn and her baby Brighid were in crisis. All I wanted to do was support them. And in ways I never could have foreseen, I was able to do that—for my dear friends and, amazingly, for millions of others.

Never Far from Family

by Pat Egan Dexter

My dog Balaam put her chin on my knee and eyed me expectantly. "Want to go for a walk, girl?" I asked. Immediately she circled and pranced. I held her still long enough to snap on her leash and then stepped out into the fresh air. It was a clear, hot August morning. Neighborhood sprinklers already chugged away, irrigating the southwestern desert lawns. Sunlight glinted off the leaves of the lemon and orange trees. I opened the wrought-iron gate in the wall that surrounded my front yard, and out we trotted. Early morning walks always invigorated me. Or at least they used to. Lately I'd been fighting a nagging sense of loneliness and fear that I always seemed to wake up with. I knew it was because my youngest son, David—the last of my children to still live in the area—had recently moved away.

I was thrilled about my son's new job and the exciting prospects it held for him, his wife and their three children. But on this particular day the reality of their departure—and the feeling of being all alone—hit me full force. My husband Ralph had died two years earlier. My closest family at the moment was Balaam, a black Labrador mix I'd found in a shelter and named after an Old Testament prophet. Balaam bounded off with her usual energy and I had to move fast to keep up. I nodded to two young men cutting hedges and trimming grass on a neighbor's lawn and then moved on past my friend Dorothy's house. *She's lucky*, I thought. *She's got family close by.* It occurred to me I could stop in and chat with her about how I was feeling, but I dismissed the urge. *I don't want to burden her with my problems.*

Balaam trotted off toward a fig tree, wrapped her leash around the trunk and gave a yip. "Don't worry, girl. I'll take care of you," I said, but as I fumbled to free her, the thought came loud and clear: *Who will take care of me if I get tangled up?* My mind raced with woeful scenarios—a bad case of the flu, a flat tire in the middle of nowhere, a gas leak, emergency surgery. Step by step, scare by scare, my apprehension intensified. By then Balaam and I had spent forty minutes circling the neighborhood. Once we got back to our street, I didn't even glance at Dorothy's house to see if her door was open or acknowledge the two young gardeners who were now hoisting their lawn equipment into a blue pickup truck. I just wanted to go back inside and brood. I was several feet from my front gate when I stumbled on a raised area in the walk. I fell down and landed hard on the cement. Balaam's leash flew out of my hand. My right arm had smashed into the pavement and my head had grazed the wall. As I lay there stunned, the young men left their pickup and raced toward me.

"Señora," one of them called, "are you all right?" As they approached, Balaam growled, her neck fur standing on end. She jumped up to protect me.

"Girl, it's okay," I murmured, putting out my hand.

The young men stopped, afraid of the dog. One spoke Spanish to the other, who quickly translated. "He wants to know if we should call 911."

I wriggled my legs to see if there was any real damage. None. "I'm okay. I live here." I gestured toward my house. "If I can get inside, I'll be fine."

Now that she was sure the men meant me no harm, Balaam stopped growling and backed away. They eased me to my feet and watched with concern as I gingerly moved about. "Can we call your family?" one asked.

"I don't have family," I said. "*Nada.*"

"No *familia*?"

I shook my head again. "Not here, anyway." They looked puzzled and then saddened. One on each side, the men guided me into the house, where they eased me onto a chair beside the telephone. They offered to drive me to the hospital.

"Thank you, no," I said. Then as an afterthought I reached for my purse nearby. "Let me give you something for helping me," I told them.

"No, no." They both were emphatic. "You could have been our mother," one said. "We were glad to help. We are all familia." They asked once again if I was sure I'd be okay and if there was anyone they could contact. I assured them I was fine and sent them on their way.

After a few minutes, I checked myself in the mirror. I had blue-purple bruises on my arm and knees and a scrape on my forehead, but other than that I wasn't seriously injured. The pain was almost gone, but what lingered just as forcefully were the young men's words: "We are all familia." I thought about it and realized family isn't just spouses and children and cousins and aunts. It's my neighbors, my community, the people I pass on the street. The mailman, who makes sure my mail is taken care of and welcomes me home when I get back from a trip. And Rosie, the cashier at the grocery store who asks how I'm doing and points out items on sale. There's the Bemis family, who live next door and whose daughter Makenzie has watched Balaam on occasion. And then there was the kindness of strangers, sometimes unexpected but welcome nonetheless, people ready to rush to help you up when you took a tumble, like the two young gardeners.

I picked up the phone and called my neighbor. "Hi, Dorothy," I said. "I tripped on the pavement and had a spill. No serious damage done but I'm a little shaken up. Would you mind coming over and having tea with me later?" Dorothy showed up as soon as she could. I greeted her as familia.

The Love
of a Child

Then Came Annie

by Dee Abrams

*G*randma. Oh, how I'd hoped I'd be one. All my life I'd wanted children—and grandchildren. My beloved husband Arthur and I hadn't been able to have kids, and when he died I felt so alone. Sure, I had friends. But it wasn't the same. There was no daughter to call to fuss with over an old family recipe. No son to be proud of. Arthur's children from his previous marriage dropped out of my life after his death. All I had left of my stepgrandchildren was an old photo album. I'd buried it in a closet after not seeing or hearing from them for years. But I couldn't bury my broken heart.

Then one day the phone rang. "I'm from the foster grandparents program at Ruth Rales Jewish Family Service," the caller said. Several weeks earlier, as much out of loneliness as charity, I'd volunteered to be paired with a child needing a grandparent. I'd done it somewhat hesitantly. Now my heart raced. "We have a match for you," the woman said. "Her name is Annie and she's three."

"That's wonderful!" I said. Still, a part of me hesitated.

"Just meet her," the woman urged. "Her mother's divorced and it's just the two of them. No other family. Annie could really use someone else in her life."

No other family. I knew how that felt. "Okay," I said. "I'll try." I spent the rest of the day preparing for our meeting. *I don't know if I can do this. How do you entertain a three-year-old?* Stories! I drove to the local bookstore, where I saw *Miss Spider's Tea Party.* I snatched it up. That was one of my stepgrandchildren's favorites!

I went to the community center to meet Annie. She wasn't anything like I'd imagined. She had beautiful ebony skin and black, tightly curled hair. The woman hadn't told me that Annie's mother was Jewish and her father African American. But that didn't faze me. What got me was her smile. So innocent, so trusting, it put me completely at ease. "Hi, Annie," I said. "My name is Dee. Would you like me to read to you?" Her eyes lit up. She led me to two chairs across the room. I opened the book and began to read. I felt her cheek brush against my arm.

"That's Miss Spider!" she said, pointing.

By the last page, I thought, *Maybe this can work.*

I closed the book when another woman entered the room. "I'm Barbara, Annie's mother," she told me. "You two seem to have hit it off." She pulled me aside and said, "Annie is turning four next week. Would you like to come to her party?"

Memories of my stepgrandchildren came rushing back. That photo album in the closet was stuffed full of pictures of birthday parties over the years. I thought we'd been so happy. But after Arthur died, my birthday cards and letters to them came back marked, "Moved. No forwarding address." Did I really want to get attached to another child who'd walk out of my life? I glanced over at Annie. That smile of hers . . . "I'd love to come," I said.

The party was at a park. A dozen kids ate cake, played on the swings and sang. Annie had such fun with her friends. So much so that it felt as if I were invisible. *What are you doing?* I wondered.

Annie doesn't need you. Not like you thought. But I couldn't keep away from her. I asked Barb if I could take Annie to a local arts festival.

"She'd love that," Barb said.

The festival was packed. "Hold my hand," I said. "I don't want to lose you." Annie slipped her tiny hand into mine. A tingle went through me.

At one of the booths a woman was painting children's faces. "Can I get a butterfly?" Annie asked.

"Of course you can." I reached into my purse and pulled out the camera I had brought along. "As long as I can take your picture. I want to make a scrapbook." Annie agreed. While the woman painted the butterfly on Annie's face, I snapped picture after picture until the whole roll of film was gone.

I hated having to drop her off at home. Until . . . right before Annie ran inside, she gave me a big hug and a kiss. "Can I call you Grandma?" she asked.

I took at least one picture of Annie every time we met after that day. I'd get double sets—one for me and one for Annie.

"Why don't you come for dinner on Friday?" Barb asked one afternoon. She made roast chicken and vegetables. It was excellent. After we ate, Barb lit some candles and said a prayer in Hebrew. I closed my eyes and silently said a prayer of my own.

I adopted Annie and Barb as fully as they adopted me. Many a Friday I had dinner with them. I was there when Barb remarried, to a wonderful man named Gordie. I was at the hospital when she gave birth to Leah and then to Noa. Yet after eight and a half years, there are still days I fear Annie's leaving me behind. She's thirteen now. How long will she want to hang around with me? It's at times like these that I remember one day when I visited Annie and Barb. Annie grabbed my hand and said, "Grandma, Mommy and I have a big surprise for you." From behind her back she pulled a thick book. The cover read, *A Book about Grandma Dee and Me.* I took it in both hands and sat down. Page after page was filled with photos of Annie, or Annie and me. She'd made a photo album too! At the end of the book she'd pasted a crayon drawing of a child and a woman holding hands. "From your loving granddaughter," it read. "Forever."

Saving Diyar

by Lee Hill Kavanaugh

I covered the conflict in Iraq for my newspaper, and the horror of war got overwhelming at times. But every once in a while, even in war, you come across something that reminds you of the goodness in people. For me, it was the story of US Air Force Tech Sergeant Roxanne Dowell and a four-year-old Iraqi girl named Diyar Fiaz.

Diyar was badly injured in a barrage of gunfire at a Nasiriyah checkpoint. Her parents were killed. Coalition soldiers carried the girl's bullet-riddled body to the trauma clinic at Tallil Air Base in Iraq. Doctors worked through the night to save Diyar, removing the bullets. Except one. It was too close to her spinal cord. Taking it out would require an expert neurosurgeon, and there wasn't one at Tallil. Among the volunteers at the hospital was Tech Sergeant Dowell, the information manager for the Army's 22nd Communications Squadron. Dowell, forty-one, from Wichita, Kansas, worked with children during her off-hours, in part because she missed her own three kids. She fell in love with Diyar, who was quick to giggle and dole out kisses as thank-yous.

Dowell was hopeful the little girl would heal. Then the doctors gave their grave diagnosis: Unless the bullet was removed, Diyar would never walk again. Her life would be severely limited, because in Iraq specialized medical care is scarce. Diyar's grandparents were overcome by the news. Her grandmother turned to Dowell and begged in Arabic: "Please, please help her. Isn't there something you can do?" Tech Sergeant Dowell flooded doctors and clinics around the world with e-mail requests on Diyar's behalf.

One person who read Dowell's e-mail was Baghdad-based Dr. Eaman Algobory, the director for the Medical Evacuation and Health Rehabilitation Program in Iraq. Part of Dr. Algobory's job was to link Iraqi children with the specialists they needed, anywhere in the world. Never before had she received a message from an American service member asking help for an Iraqi child. Moved, she requested Diyar's medical records. Dowell sent the file. Dr. Algobory reviewed it and immediately contacted neurosurgeon Jeff Poffenbarger, a lieutenant colonel with the Army's 31st Combat Support Hospital, based in Baghdad. Poffenbarger agreed to see Diyar if she could be transported the 250 miles from Tallil to Baghdad.

Dowell was overjoyed. So were Diyar's grandparents. Dowell offered to accompany them and arranged transportation. But the day they were set to leave, Dowell received orders sending her home to Kansas. How would Diyar get to Baghdad now? Dowell found an Iraqi man who agreed to drive them. She hugged Diyar and her grandparents and then boarded a transport to reunite with her own family. Dowell prayed for Diyar, knowing the highway to Baghdad was littered with wrecked cars of other civilians who had tried, unsuccessfully, to elude insurgents and their homemade bombs.

Diyar's car reached Baghdad safely. When her grandparents met Dr. Poffenbarger, they held up a photograph of Dowell and kissed it. He thought, *At least one American has won an Iraqi's love.*

Diyar's surgery took many hours. The damage from the bullet was severe, even to hands used to treating the wounds of war. Two days later, though, Diyar was standing. Five months after that, she was walking, exceeding Dr. Poffenbarger's greatest hopes. When Dowell heard, she mailed Diyar a pair of shoes. As Dr. Algobory says, "Many prayers went out. Diyar had many angels helping her." Yes, many angels. Even in the ugliness of war.

America's Weatherman

by Al Roker

Y ou've probably noticed—if you start your morning watching me, Matt Lauer and Meredith Vieira on the *TODAY* show—I don't take up as much of the screen as I used to. Not since I had my stomach stapled. It's a very risky operation that I don't recommend for everyone. But I was willing to take my chances, as much for my family as myself. I want to be around for them as long as I can.

My wife Deborah—who's a correspondent on 20/20—and I had been married for about a year when we decided to have a child. We already had an adopted daughter, ten-year-old Courtney, from my previous marriage. To me, there is no difference between "natural" and "adopted." My own childhood showed me that when it comes to loving your kids, concepts like that don't apply. I was the oldest of six; three of my siblings were adopted. Mom and Dad even took in foster children. "There are no limits to how much you can love," Dad always said.

Dad would do anything for us. He'd get up early and leave our house in Queens to go to work as a New York City bus driver. He put in back-to-back shifts and took odd jobs to provide for us. But to him, it wasn't work; it was an expression of his love. And the more kids, the more love. That's why I wanted to have a child with

Deborah. But try as we might—for more than a year—she didn't conceive. "This is taking longer than it should," Deborah's ob-gyn, Dr. Janice Marks, told us. "Let's get you both tested."

The problem was me. I was more relieved than anything else. Now we knew for sure what the trouble was. Besides, as a weatherman I'm used to a certain amount of failure. Dr. Marks recommended we pay a visit to the New York Fertility Institute for a consultation. Deborah hesitated. "Let's try it on our own just one more time," she said. "If it's meant to be, God will make it happen."

Dr. Marks pinpointed Deborah's window of ovulation. "Knowing when should help," she told us. But it didn't. Every time I saw one of those commercials showing a happy couple with a positive on their home pregnancy test, I wanted to throw something at the TV.

Three weeks later, Deborah surprised me. "Al, I'm late," she said. I scrambled off to the drugstore for a home pregnancy test. Deborah went into the bathroom the next morning while I paced in the hall outside. Finally she opened the door, a smile on her face and test strip in hand. Two pink lines.

"Positive?" I asked. She nodded. Was this really happening?

I wouldn't let myself get excited. Not yet. We tried another test. That one came back positive too. *Oh man. We're pregnant!* We stayed up almost all night talking. *What do we do now? Who do we tell and when? What about Courtney, who had ruled the roost for so long?* We decided to wait to give her the news, just in case. I didn't sleep much that night. I got out of bed around 3:00 AM—a little earlier than usual—gave Deborah a peck on the cheek while she slept, and then left for Studio 1A at Rockefeller Center.

"You're looking mighty chipper, Al," my then co-worker Katie Couric said.

"Really?" I answered nonchalantly. Inside, I was ready to burst. I wanted to tell Katie, Matt, everyone. But I kept quiet and gave the weather report as usual. "Nine months from now," I felt like telling the whole country, "it looks like we're due for a nice, warm baby. And a high probability of an overly sunny dad."

It was good I didn't. A sonogram at two months showed the baby wasn't growing. Its heart rate was way too slow. "I'm sorry," Dr. Marks told us. "I know this is going to hurt, but it doesn't look like the baby will reach term." Deborah miscarried on Labor Day weekend.

"I'd just started to think of myself as a mother," Deborah told me. "And now it's all changed." I squeezed her hand. I knew just what she meant. It wasn't that we weren't parents already. But ever since the day Deborah showed me that test strip, we'd both felt something new at work in our lives. The incredible mystery of God working through us to create a new life. I think we both knew then and there that there was no turning back.

A few weeks before our second anniversary, Deborah got a checkup with Dr. Marks. She asked about the possibility of trying to get pregnant again. "I see no reason why you couldn't," Dr. Marks told her. "You've healed well, and you're in good health. But you're going to need medical and scientific help." We went to see Drs. Majid Fateh and Khalid Sultan at the New York Fertility Institute. Dr. Sultan told us about artificial insemination and in vitro fertilization. Then he said, "I'm not going to lie to you. If you choose this road, it is a long one. And difficult. For both of you, but especially for Deborah. There will be a lot of work involved, a lot of discomfort and no guarantees. Are you willing to go through it?"

That night Deborah and I talked it over. "It's your decision," I finally said. "Like the doc told us, you're the one who has to do the real work. But . . ." Deborah took my hand and I knew I didn't have to finish my sentence. We wanted a baby. Come what may, we were going to try.

We opted for in vitro fertilization. It was a success; Deborah got pregnant again. This time I was afraid to be too happy. The doctors told us how critical the first trimester was. I prayed every day, asking God to keep my wife and our unborn child in His hands. Twelve weeks later we went into the sonogram room together. I had years of live TV under my belt and thought I was well past the butterflies-in-the-stomach phase. But I'd never felt so unsettled before. The doctor turned on the monitor and the screen flickered to life. He ran the wand over Deborah's belly. "There," he said. Deborah and I squinted at the black, white and gray image on the screen, trying to figure out what the doctor was pointing out. "Those are the arms," the doctor said. Then he ran his finger along two thin shapes near the bottom of the screen. "Those are the legs right there." He flipped a switch and the room filled with sound. A steady, thumping beat. "Good, strong heartbeat. Congratulations!" In that moment, all my doubts and worries, all my questions about whether or not Deborah and I had done the right thing, completely vanished. Science may have helped us on our path to pregnancy, but it couldn't get us all the way to the end. The only thing that could do that was the power and grace of God. He'd been with us on this journey every step of the way. This was His miracle; the beautiful, glorious, humbling mystery of life.

At 9:17 AM on Tuesday, November 17, 1998, I heard the most wonderful sound: the cries of our newborn daughter, Leila Ruth Roker. A nurse held her up for Deborah to see. My wife started to cry, and so did I. I held my new daughter and looked into her eyes. *Is this how Mom and Dad felt when they held me?* I wondered. I thought back to growing up with my five siblings. They were my brothers and sisters, but to my parents they were much more. Each of us was a miracle. My little girl wriggled in my arms and all at once I felt warmth surge through me. Love. For Courtney, for Leila and for Deborah. This was the answer to the mystery that had driven Deborah and me to want a child so much. Love without limits, just like God's love for all His children.

Zeke the Geek

by Susan McMichael

A paper Santa smiled up at me from the top of my desk, one hand waving, the other holding a bag of toys. I'd followed Teacher's instructions to a tee and cut out the mimeograph with my mother's snub-nosed safety scissors, trimming carefully around the lines. Then I used every crayon in the box to color Santa's suit, hat and the gifts in his sack. My final touch was cotton, which I glued to his face as a beard. "Very good, Suzie," Teacher said when she collected my Santa. She pinned him at the top of the bulletin board, along with some others. But the drawing at the bottom of the board caught my eye. That Santa seemed to have survived some terrible accident— barely. His beard dangled from his left ear. His hat was chopped off. Streaks of crayon shot off in every direction. His hand, missing a thumb, was raised in a defiant fist. Only one kid in my class would have turned in a Santa like that: Zeke.

Zeke was, without a doubt, the most unpopular boy in school. Zeke the Geek, we called him. He wasn't like the rest of us. His clothes were tattered and clearly secondhand, his hair stood up in clumps as if he'd just tumbled out of bed, and his hands were always grimy. He was in a special reading group for kids who couldn't get past Dick and Jane. Zeke couldn't do anything right.

Zeke got onto our school bus at a farm camp, which was a cluster of ramshackle huts off the side of a rural route. That morning he had stumbled down the aisle and plopped down on the seat beside me—not waiting for an invitation.

"Hey, Suzie," he said. "D'you want to see my slingshot?" *Ugh.* I concentrated on my book, fighting the urge to crawl under the seat. I was so embarrassed. Martha and Helene—the popular girls—sat right in front of us. Did I detect a giggle? My stony silence didn't deter Zeke. He reached in his back pocket and pulled out his home-made slingshot and a funny-colored rock he'd found.

"Did I show you my Lone Ranger Atom Bomb Ring?" he said, a lopsided grin lighting his face. He uncurled his fingers to reveal a small, tarnished brass ring with a silver bullet on top. "I got it from a box of Kix," he said. "If you take off the bottom, you can see flashing lights like an atom bomb blast." Back then, in 1947, this was a big deal. I knew all about the ring already because Zeke never got tired of showing it off. He wore it so much, it turned his finger green. To make sure the ring wouldn't fall off, he'd wrapped it with adhesive tape. The tape quickly became dirty and frayed, like everything else he owned. Zeke held out his prized possession for me to examine, demonstrating the flashing light effect.

I rolled my eyes. "I don't care about your dumb ring," I said and turned back to my book. I didn't want anything to do with Zeke the Geek.

At school that day, we decorated the classroom with paper snowflakes and streamers and planned a secret Santa party. Teacher wrote all our names on scraps of paper and put them in a shoe box. We'd buy a present for whomever we drew. I squirmed in my seat as Teacher moved up and down the rows of desks with the box. I'd never bought a present for anyone before, but I was full of ideas. There was a tiny tea set at Woolworth's that would be perfect for Martha and a book of Shirley Temple paper dolls that I knew Helene would love. This was going to be fun. Teacher reached my desk. I shut my eyes and plunged my hand into the box. I unfolded my paper and stared at it. My jaw dropped. Zeke! Zeke the Geek! Of all the names in the box.

I trudged home from the bus stop that afternoon in a state. It just wasn't fair. Zeke, with his messy clothes, his broken crayons, his slingshot. What could I possibly give a kid like that? I explained the situation to my mother, but she wasn't sympathetic. "Why don't we go into town?" Mother suggested. "You can find a present for Zeke at Woolworth's."

I wandered reluctantly through the aisles. Why couldn't I buy a nice present for somebody who'd appreciate it? I saw the tea set I had wanted for Martha and the Shirley Temple dolls for Helene. It would be easy to buy presents for them; I just had to think about what I would like myself. But Zeke? I looked at marbles, tin cars, plastic soldiers. I had to get him something. Suddenly, I remembered his sloppy Santa and the crayons he'd brought from home. What he needed, I decided, was a new box of crayons. It wouldn't cost me much, and maybe then he'd do his next art project correctly. I found a box, paid my quarter to the cashier and went home feeling happy about having gotten it over with. The day of the party, I added my present to the pile under the tree in our classroom. Zeke lumbered in, last as usual. I wondered if he'd like his gift. *Probably not. I bet he wouldn't even have the manners to thank me.*

Teacher handed back our Santas so we could show our parents. Mine got a blue star. Zeke jammed his into his desk as soon as he got it, tearing Santa's arm off in the process. The homeroom mothers began passing out the presents. Zeke got his and tore my pretty wrapping paper off without even glancing at it. He emptied the box of crayons and, not even looking at me, pulled out a piece of paper to color. *I knew it,* I thought. *Not so much as a thank-you. He doesn't know anything about presents.*

Pretty soon all the packages had been delivered. Around me, kids showed off new coloring books, cap guns and dolls. I stared at the top of my desk, tears beginning to well up in my eyes. Everyone had a gift but me. Whoever my secret Santa was hadn't bothered to get me anything. I was crushed. Then Teacher put her arm around me. "Susan," she said, "we found this behind the tree. We didn't see it until all the other presents had been given out." Teacher held out a ball of lined notebook paper bound with tape. It looked like a giant spitball. My name—misspelled—was scrawled on the top. "From Zeke." *Zeke the Geek? He was my secret Santa?* I took the package and glanced over at the messy boy bent over his desk, busily coloring. What could Zeke have bought me?

Slowly, I tore open the paper. Only then did it dawn on me what was going to be inside, and it filled me with a mixture of shame and, oddly, joy. Shame at my selfishness, yes, but a kind of joy at Zeke's giving. There was only one thing for Zeke to give, and he would give it rather than give nothing—give it gladly. His slingshot wouldn't do, nor the funny-colored rock. So when his Atom Bomb Ring fell out and clattered noisily onto my desktop, all I could do was look up and see Zeke smiling shyly at me. I wonder if he knew this would be the best present I got that year, a gift that taught me a lesson I never forgot.

"Please! Save My Baby!"

by Tracinda Foxe

I had just drifted off to sleep, curled up on the comforter, when something told me, *Wake up, Tracinda!* I didn't want to wake up. I was exhausted. It was just after eight o'clock on a cold, gray December morning in the Bronx. I had bundled up my two older kids and sent them off to school and then fed my one-month-old Eric and lay down with him in the bedroom for a moment of quiet. I needed time to rest, to think. It hadn't been an easy month. My husband and I had separated. The kids, cooped up in the cold, were rambunctious. If the baby wasn't crying, the older kids were arguing. I never knew if I was making the right decisions. And my family, especially my sister, was a long subway ride away in Manhattan. I felt cut off, alone.

The voice, though, was insistent. *Wake up, Tracinda!* I pulled myself to the edge of the bed and rubbed my eyes. Eric, who had been nuzzled beside me in his white pajamas, stirred. Something wasn't quite right. Usually by this time light was streaming through the third-floor windows of our small two-bedroom apartment. But the air seemed dark, ominous. I hugged myself and padded quickly to the bedroom door. A strange sound came from behind it. I opened the door, and a cloud of choking smoke pushed through. I waved my arm and leaned into the hall. Bright orange flames licked out from the kitchen, singeing the hallway between me and the exit. They were low but too thick to jump over. There was no way out.

Eric! I slammed the door and ran back to the bed. Eric had his head turned to one side, his lips parted slightly. I shuddered to think what the smoke would do to his little lungs. *God, what are we going to do?* I looked at the door. Wisps of smoke were snaking through the cracks.

I picked Eric up and held him. He awoke and began crying. The smoke pumped in more thickly, stinging my eyes. It was getting hard to see. *God, we're trapped!* I had to calm down. *Think, Tracinda.* The window. I ran to the window, which was closed tight against the cold. *Maybe I can at least get some air in.* I jerked it open and held Eric as close to the sill as I dared. *Even if I choke, he might live.* But the warm air in the bedroom only rushed out into the cold, pulling more smoke in from the hallway. Both of us coughed. I could barely keep my eyes open, they stung so much. *Eric can't take much more of this. We have nowhere to go. What now, God?*

I leaned my head out of the window and saw, below, about half-a-dozen people on the apartment-complex lawn, all of them staring up at the fire. A hand pointed and I heard a voice. "There's someone in there!"

Then they saw Eric. "Oh no, she's got a baby!" The group of people bunched together, and more joined them, streaming across the lawn. "A baby! There's a baby up there, trapped!" For a moment, the voices crowded together, and I couldn't understand. Then several people shouted, "Drop him! We'll catch him!"

I heard the words, but—drop Eric? How? He'd die! I looked at him, his soft hair, his face pulled into a scream. He was only one month old. It was hard enough for me sending my two older kids out into the world each day, out of my sight. How could I drop my baby?

"Drop him! It's okay! We'll catch him!"

Eric choked and spluttered in the smoke. *He's not going to make it if he stays up here*, I thought. I looked down. I couldn't even see the ground. But I knew I had no choice. I had to let him go. *God, please take care of my baby.*

I held Eric out the window. The smoke billowed past him. His legs kicked. And in a sudden, agonizing motion, I let him go. He fell into the smoke and disappeared. My heart froze and my body clenched.

Then a voice floated up. "He's fine. He's fine! We caught him! And the firemen are on their way!"

I leaned out of the window into the fresher air and saw someone running across the lawn with a bundle in his arms, toward a building, out of the cold. Eric!

I pulled back and tried holding my breath. When I needed air, I pushed my head out the window as far as it would go, out of the smoke. *Lord, I need to stay alive for my kids.* My eyes burned, my lungs ached. All at once I heard sounds behind me, breaking and splintering wood. Burly men in thick coats crashed into the bedroom, wrapped a jacket around my nightgown and hustled me out into the hall and down to the lobby.

And there was Eric. A man was holding him. He was wrapped in a warm sheet from someone's apartment, his pajamas peeking through. And he was asleep! Peacefully asleep, as though nothing had happened. I took him in my arms and held him as tightly as I could. A few minutes later, the firemen rushed us both to the hospital.

It wasn't until later that day, when Eric and I returned to the apartment complex to face our ruined home that I met the man who had caught my baby. He was a Housing Authority worker, and when he saw me, his eyes widened and he broke into a grin. "You're safe!" he exclaimed. "I was so worried! He wasn't breathing when I caught him. I gave him mouth-to-mouth, but someone took him to wrap him in a sheet, and I lost track of him. I didn't know if he made it."

I barely knew what to say. "You're like a guardian angel for my son," I finally managed.

"Oh, I don't know," the man said. "My name is Felix—Felix Vasquez. I did what anyone else would do. I'm just glad I could be there for him."

Felix was being modest. It turns out he played catcher for a Housing Authority baseball team. So it wasn't just dumb luck that his arms were there for Eric. It was only the first of many good things to come from that fire.

Soon after, I moved to a new apartment—in Manhattan, closer to my sister. And I've decided life is too precious to wait—I'm planning to go back to school to get my G.E.D. so I can find a better job to support my kids. I'm starting over and it feels good.

Eric is getting big now. I know he won't remember what happened that morning when I held him out the window and let him go in the smoke. But I will. I'll remember that moment of agony and my decision to trust. It's still hard being a single parent with three children to care for. But I know now that I'm not alone. Many arms are there for me. Felix's, my sister's—and those arms we never see, the strongest, most loving arms of all.

Homework Cycle

by Georgina Smith

I passed it every night while driving home from Brooklyn College, where I was studying for my master's in education—a Clean Rite launderette in Brooklyn, teeming with children, their parents busy doing the wash. Kids played video games. Some stared at the laundry's TV. A lot of them raced around, playing bumper cars with the laundry carts, until a mother would jump up and yell. Not once did I see a kid reading or doing homework.

Eventually I took a job teaching science at a Brooklyn elementary school. Not many people think of it as a dream job, but it is to me. I left a twenty-year career as a corporate executive to do something more meaningful and fulfilling with my life. Each day I have the opportunity to change children's lives. My biggest challenge—one that every inner-city educator faces—is this: *How can I get the kids interested in reading outside the classroom?*

That's why I started thinking about that Clean Rite I used to drive past. My professors at Brooklyn College had always encouraged me to think outside the box. I could fill the launderette's waiting area with books on every topic under the sun. ABCs, picture books, books on science—books that had everything to do with fun. Kids would pick out whatever they wanted and then sit and read or talk to other kids about their books. They'd run their own book club. I'd be there with other volunteer teachers, though definitely not as an instructor. Kids could come to us for homework help or learning games, but I didn't want them to think they were in school. I wanted this to be fun . . . productive fun.

I got ahold of John Sabino, president of the eighty-one-store laundry chain. "I have a great idea to help your customers," I told him. Within ten minutes, I'd sold him. A few weeks later I pulled up to the Clean Rite a little after 6:00 PM. I lugged fifty books inside and arranged them on tables Mr. Sabino had provided. Some were books my school was discarding, some I'd bought on my own. Then I waited for the kids and their parents. They began arriving after dinner. At first, the kids didn't know what to make of the "library," but soon enough, curiosity got the better of them.

"Hey, this one's about planets and stars," said a boy, maybe nine years old. Another boy plopped down next to him. They read the book together, surprising their parents. Many had never seen their children talk animatedly about a book before. This was as good as any learning miracle I'd seen in a classroom. My instincts had told me that these children—like all children—had learning potential. All we needed was to find a way to tap it.

When I closed the library two hours later, the kids helped me pack up the books—and demanded to know when I was coming back. "Every Monday, Wednesday and Saturday," I promised.

Today we have crates of books at three Clean Rite locations, where we get about ten to fifteen kids at each launderette. I've arranged with Brooklyn College to provide tutors—student education, psychology and literacy majors, both undergrad and grad—at each site. The library has proved as valuable for the student teachers as the students. They get real-life experience and become better teachers for it. You'll still find me there too.

One night, one of my library regulars came running up to me. "Mrs. Smith, I remembered the words you helped me with last time." Abrina, a third grader, read at a first-grade level. With a huge smile, she spelled the four words she'd learned the night before. It was her moment of triumph. Abrina hugged me. That was one of my finest teaching moments. When you get one of those, it means everything.

Our 3,000-Mile Field Trip

by Tanya Walters

I'm a school bus driver. I'm up before the sun, getting kids where they need to go in inner-city Los Angeles—to magnet schools, remedial schools and everything in between. The world boards my bus: college-bound immigrants, strutting football players. Then there are the kids I call the 2 Live Crews—angry troublemakers. Their parents are mostly missing, and they live in a world of gangs, drugs and grown-ups whose only interest in them is the money they might spend on rap music and one-hundred-dollar sneakers. On the bus, though, it's my rules: "No getting up, no acting up. Period." I run a tight ship.

On June 22, I filled a bus with twenty-two teens, some from the projects, and headed out from an intersection two miles from where the 1992 LA riots started. I didn't drive to school. We turned onto the interstate, aiming for a new destination—all the way across the United States. Sound crazy? Stay with me a minute.

I became a bus driver by accident. In high school I was a lot like the kids I drive now, getting by with Cs and Ds. One of my girl-friends invited me to take a test with her to become a school bus driver. "It's a good job," she said. Job? I didn't need a job. I took the test anyway and passed.

When I graduated, I drove a bus. I was nineteen, not much older than my students, and they bullied me. Sometimes I wanted to quit. But my dad always said, "Tanya, get a job with benefits." Working for the Los Angeles Unified School District, I had health insurance and a pension. And money for my real passion—travel. You see, Mom died when I was six. I got passed between my aunt and my dad. Wherever I lived, though, I always went to summer camp and visited relatives on the East Coast. Seeing those faraway places— Pennsylvania, West Virginia, Louisiana—I realized the world was much bigger than south LA.

I spent some of my first paychecks on plane tickets. In the beginning I went by myself. Then with my godchildren, the son and daughter of a girlfriend from high school. I was young and naïve— I even had to look up the word *godparent*. But when I learned my responsibilities, I decided one thing I could do: expose the kids to life beyond LA. I found travel deals and took them to Boston, New York, Phoenix. Soon their friends asked if they could come. Weekends became trips to Magic Mountain, museums, new cities. The trips were educational. I made the kids budget their money and took them to stores to show them how to dress for work.

One day, corralling yet another group of 2 Live Crews, I decided the kids on my bus needed more than discipline. They needed what my godchildren had—a grown-up spending time with them, modeling good behavior, widening their horizons. They needed to travel. So I planned a trip. I knew how to drive a bus. And I knew how to travel with kids. I announced one morning that any student who wrote an essay explaining why he or she wanted to go could join me on the road to San Francisco. Some kids laughed. But others wrote essays, and when they returned from our trip, the stories they told got around. I tried some longer trips, and by summer I had a small nonprofit called Godparents Youth Organization (www.godparentsclub.org), a few local sponsors and a team of six adult chaperones—bus-driver friends and others in the community. Together, we planned our most ambitious trip yet, a month-long drive across the country to visit colleges, civil-rights monuments and historic cities. We left LA on the evening of June 22, the kids slumped in a forty-five-foot-long, black rented motor coach. I asked someone to say a prayer and said a silent one myself. These were not easy kids—some were involved with gangs or drugs, some had been tossed from school to school. One girl's father was in prison. *This is the big time, Lord. We are completely at Your mercy.*

We drove all night and day to a Best Western in Albuquerque— I got the chain to give us a discount, and I always looked for hotels with a pool. The girls sat in back, the boys in front—my rule. In the mornings, the kids wrote in journals and read a chapter from a book I had given them: *The Purpose Driven Life* by Rick Warren. They didn't like it at first—"It's boring, Miss Tanya!"—until one of our mentors, Rhonda Dennis, began reading it aloud like a preacher. "Can I get an amen?" she shouted. And the kids laughed and read along with her.

In Atlanta and Birmingham, we visited Dr. Martin Luther King Jr.'s church and learned about a black church bombed by white supremacists. In Montgomery, the kids boarded a historic bus at the Rosa Parks Library and Museum and felt for themselves the sting of segregation. We visited historically black colleges and a museum in Baltimore that told the story of African Americans, from slavery to modern accomplishments, in wax reenactments. By the time we pulled into Pennsylvania on a rainy night, the kids were making connections. "Back then it was blacks and whites. Now it's Crips and Bloods," said Sam, who's thirteen and lives in Watts. "We're killing ourselves."

We awoke in Philadelphia on July 4 and took a walking tour of America's birthplace. The guide showed us where slaves had been sold, in a park behind Independence Hall, and we ran into a man dressed as Benjamin Franklin, reenacting the days leading up to the Revolution. The guide also showed us a house where MTV filmed one of its *Real World* shows. The kids perked up. "Can we go in? We live on MTV!"

That afternoon, we drove to the spacious suburb of Dresher, where Vernon Walker, an attorney who is friends with one of our Los Angeles sponsors, had invited all the kids for a barbecue. Neighbors stared as our bus pulled up and the kids piled out. Soon we were spread on Vernon's lawn, playing volleyball and badminton, while chicken, burgers and hot dogs were prepared for the grill. A girl named Shamika, who's sixteen, asked Vernon, "Do you get nervous in court?"

"I'm nervous till I say my first words, 'May it please the court?' After that, it's on!" he said, laughing.

Inside, a friend of Vernon's, Huntley, was talking to John Dennis, a sixteen-year-old student. "Stay focused," he said. "Keep at it, reach out. Surround yourself with kids who want to go to college. I know you'll get there."

By the time we left Philadelphia and headed for a tour of Princeton, all the kids were talking about what college they wanted to go to. Some said a Black college. Others were awed by the ivy-drenched halls of Princeton, which we walked through with a student tour guide.

"What percentage of students here are of other ethnicities?" John asked.

"Twenty," she said.

"Maybe I could be at home here," he said quietly.

On the bus, a mentor had all the kids write down subjects they wanted to study in college—a list they could take to high school counselors. Shamika wrote, "Law. Dance. Criminal justice." Someone asked why. "I want to be a public defender," she said. "My dad's in jail, and before we went on this trip, I had to write a letter helping him get parole. I want to be part of the justice system." By that point, I knew the trip had succeeded. We still had many more destinations—over a dozen cities, including New York, plus colleges and museums. And once I almost sent a boy home, until he knocked on my door after midnight and we stayed up talking about his priorities. But when we arrived back in LA on July 18, I knew John and Shamika were aiming toward college. I knew Sam understood the true cost of ghetto violence. And I knew I'd soon be announcing another trip. Because that's what a bus driver does. I get my kids where they need to go. To a new and better path. To all the possibilities life holds. As I told the Lord, *That's the big time*.

In Mrs. Lake's Eyes

by Laurie B.

A soft-spoken woman with a firm touch, Mrs. Lake taught sixth grade. She kept her long auburn hair up in a barrette, showing off the drop earrings she always wore. From my first moment in her class, I loved her. Though I was a good student, I was shy about speaking up in front of my classmates and could easily be overlooked. Not with Mrs. Lake.

That year had been a hard one at home. My father's alcoholism had grown worse. At night as I lay in bed, I listened with dread to the pop of beer cans opening or the clink of ice cubes in a glass as whiskey was poured. Then came the loud slurred voice from the kitchen, my mother's tears, the slamming of doors. Dad was an attorney, and meticulous about polishing his wingtips every morning before work. So for Christmas, I took the babysitting money I had saved and bought the best shoe-shine kit I could find. I was so excited on Christmas Eve when he opened the heavy box. But I watched in stunned silence as Dad—in an incomprehensible rage—threw it across the living room, breaking it into pieces. Somehow I thought I was to blame.

How much safer I felt in Mrs. Lake's class. This was my sanctuary, the place where I felt appreciated, my papers coming back with her distinctive scrawl, my tests decorated with stars and smiley faces. When I gave oral reports, standing in front of the class, my knees shaking, I looked in her encouraging blue eyes and my fears subsided.

At the end of the year came the day for parent-teacher conferences, each student meeting with her parents and Mrs. Lake for a final evaluation and progress report. On the blackboard was an alphabetical schedule with a twenty-minute slot for each family. I was puzzled that I had been put at the end of the list, even though my last name began with *B*. It didn't matter. My parents would not be coming. When I brought home papers with Mrs. Lake's glowing remarks, they ended up in the trash, unnoticed. Letters reminding them about the school conference were ignored.

All day I tried to stay busy with our assigned projects while the room mother escorted my classmates to the doorway at the back of the class. Every twenty minutes, a different name was called, a student walked out, and through the closed door I could hear the muffled voices of parents asking questions while Mrs. Lake offered suggestions. I couldn't even imagine having parents like that. Finally, after everyone's name had been called, Mrs. Lake opened the door and motioned for me to join her. Three folding chairs were set up in the hallway in front of a desk covered with files, class projects and Mrs. Lake's grade book. I watched as she folded up two of the chairs. Then she gestured for me to sit down in the one remaining.

Moving her chair next to mine, Mrs. Lake lifted my chin. "First of all," she said, "I want you to know how much I love you." I saw all the warmth and compassion in those beautiful blue eyes that I had observed all year long. "Secondly," she continued, "you need to know it is not your fault that your parents are not here today."

It was the first time someone had said such a thing to me. For a moment I was scared. *She knows our secret.* But then I realized she had understood all along.

"You deserve a conference whether your parents are here or not," she said. "You deserve to know how well I think you're doing."

She took out a stack of my papers and congratulated me on the good grades, pointing out my strengths. She showed me my diagnostic test scores and explained how high I had ranked nationally. She had even saved some of my watercolors—those things my mother usually consigned to the trash. During that meeting my perception changed. I was allowed to see myself objectively, and because I knew Mrs. Lake cared for me, I believed what she told me. My home situation was the same, but I was a different person. For a long moment Mrs. Lake and I looked at each other in silence. Then she gave me a hug. Afterward she gathered her papers and we returned to class. None of my friends ever asked me what she said, and if they had, I don't know what I would have told them. It was too precious, too private, too wonderful.

The growing-up years that followed were often difficult, but my teacher had given me an extraordinary gift. For the first time I knew I was worthy of being loved. That made all the difference.

CHAPTER 4

Forgiveness

My Perfect Neighbor

by Patricia Butler Dyson

Hi, I'm Jerri," she said. "Jerri with an *i*." My neighbor stood at my front door with her two little boys. Ten years younger and at least ten pounds thinner than me, she had silky blonde hair and a healthy tan.

"Come on in," I said. I'd arranged this meeting so my five-year-old son Brent could get to know some other boys from the neighborhood who were starting kindergarten in the fall. He would be a little more confident on that first day of school if he just had one friend. I'd gotten the class list from school and noticed that Marty Bradford lived a few blocks from us.

"This is Marty," Jerri said. Her son marched up to Brent and stood face-to-face with him in the hall, sizing him up.

"Brent, why don't you take Marty to the backyard and show him your tree house?" I suggested.

"Go ahead," his mother urged. The two boys scrambled off.

"Y'all come sit down for a minute," I said.

Jerri gestured to the child clinging to her leg. "Max is shy." She followed me into the living room and sat on the sofa, Max perched in her lap. Jerri was everything I wished I could be: elegant, composed, sunny-tempered. She talked about the exercise class she and Max took together and the bread she baked from scratch—yeast, dough and all. There wasn't even a hint of conceit in her voice, yet she stirred up in me a vague feeling of inadequacy. But nothing pained me as much as watching her with that sweet-faced, brown-eyed boy in her lap.

"How old is he?" I finally asked.

"Max?" she said. "Four. He and Marty are eighteen months apart."

Brent's younger brother would have been four too. I almost said it out loud, told Jerri what we had been through in the past months since Blake died, but I stopped myself. I couldn't confide in a stranger, especially one whose life seemed so together.

"I'd better run," Jerri said. "I'm baking my bread for the week."

"I'll bring Marty home in an hour," I responded.

"Super." Then she and her younger son were off.

From that point on, Brent had regular play dates with Marty. They built forts in our backyard and held imaginary sword fights in Brent's room. I was grateful my son had a new friend, but seeing Jerri always made me feel worse about myself. She was so cool and confident. She had moved here from up North when her husband transferred, but even our hot, humid East Texas weather hardly had an effect on her.

I convinced myself that once kindergarten started, I wouldn't have to see her so often. But the day before school began, she called and announced, "Marty wants to ride his bike to school tomorrow with Brent. How about us all going together?"

"Okay," I said hesitantly. "I haven't biked in a while—"

"It'll be fun!" she interrupted. "We'll meet you at the corner of Westgate and Elaine at 7:45 sharp."

The next morning after breakfast, I unearthed my bike from a corner of the garage and Brent hopped on his. Marty and Jerri were waiting at the corner, Max in a baby seat on the back of his mother's bike. "Hi, guys!" Jerri said. "Ready for the big day?"

"Yeah!" Brent said, smiling.

"I guess so," I said. Then—on a day that should have only been about the future and the wonders it would hold for our two boys— Jerri sent me plunging into the past, into my sorrow.

She was staring at the empty baby seat on the back of my bike. "Do you have a little one I haven't met yet?" she asked.

"I did," I said, trying hard to keep my voice steady. The same age as your Max. The same blond hair, the same brown eyes, the same smile beneath a bike helmet. "Brent's brother Blake was three when he died of meningitis last year. I just haven't been up to removing the seat yet."

"Oh, Pat, how awful for you," Jerri said. "I'm so sorry."

"Thanks," I said quickly. "Hey, Marty, what a neat bike!" I didn't want to talk about my grief.

For the next few weeks, as summer mellowed into autumn, Jerri and I would meet and ride with our boys to and from school. Little by little, I learned more about her. She said her husband was often away on business, and that as welcoming as people were in Texas, she hadn't made many friends. No matter what she said, her life still sounded perfect, whether she was sewing Halloween costumes for her kids or baking cookies or cakes for the church bazaar or rushing back from an aerobics class. The hardest thing for me each morning was seeing young Max in the seat behind her, dressed in his Peanuts pajamas. But I choked back my feelings.

One morning it pained me so much I came back home and threw down my bike helmet in a rage. I cried out, "Why is everything in her life so perfect when parts of mine are so empty?"

Later that afternoon, our little caravan was making its way home when suddenly Marty let out a howl as we turned the corner at

Westgate. "Mommy!" he cried. "I forgot the popcorn we made at school. Can we go back and get it?"

"Absolutely not," Jerri said, with surprising sharpness. "Marty, you must learn to keep track of your things."

Brent gave me a woeful look and I knew he felt bad for his friend. So when we parted ways with the Bradfords, I gave Brent a wink and we headed back to the school. Marty's bag of popcorn was just where he had left it, in his cubby in their classroom. Pedaling as fast as we could, we rode to Marty's house. Brent ran up and rang the doorbell and I stood behind him. Jerri opened the door, revealing a trail of toys and clothes littering her foyer.

"We got Marty's popcorn," I said. Jerri frowned. She held a broken toy in her hand.

"I wish you hadn't, Pat," she said. "Marty's so irresponsible. I'm trying to teach him a lesson."

A dozen angry retorts sprang to my lips. Instead of the thank-you I deserved, I was being reprimanded. "I'm sorry," I said coldly. "I had no idea."

The next morning I led Brent on a different route to school so we would be sure to avoid the Bradfords. "What about Marty and his mommy?" Brent asked plaintively.

"They'll catch up with us," I said. At school I gave Brent a quick kiss good-bye and biked home. I sailed into the garage and was starting to yank down the door when Jerri careered into my driveway on her bike with Max strapped in his seat.

"Pat, wait!" Jerri hollered. "I have to talk to you." I stood beside my bike, staring down. "Where were you this morning?" she asked. "We missed you."

"We left early," I replied.

"Pat, please forgive me," Jerri said. "I've hurt your feelings and

I'm sorry. I've just been so stressed out lately." I was surprised to hear a quaver in Jerri's voice.

"Forget it." I turned to go inside.

"You wouldn't understand," Jerri said. "You have everything under control. You're such a good mother, you keep a neat house, and Brent is a happy, well-adjusted little boy. With my husband gone so much, I'm like a single parent. I feel like a failure next to you. You're so together."

"Me? Together?" I whirled back toward her. "Do you know how miserable I feel each morning after I leave you? Do you know how it crushes my heart to see Max every day, the same age as Blake and looking so much like him?"

"How would I?" Jerri said quietly. "You've never let me into your life."

Then it dawned on me: Had Jerri also been keeping her feelings to herself, hiding her pain from anyone who might comfort her? She hadn't lost a child, but she was going through a tough time of her own. Maybe Jerri and I had been brought together to share our problems, not hide them.

"I'm just trying to be a good mother," Jerri went on, "to do the right things. The way you do, Pat. I wish I could be like you."

"But I don't sew costumes or bake bread. And lately I've been so depressed I can hardly make it from day to day." The tears started coming. Jerri got off her bike, unbuckled Max and set him down on the grass and put her arms around me.

"I had no idea what you were going through," she said.

"I was keeping a stiff upper lip."

"So was I."

"Maybe we're more alike than we know," I said as I wiped my face. Instead of reaching out, I had withdrawn, and in a way, so had

Jerri. We were both feeling inadequate and had been unable to say it. "We're not good at putting up fronts."

Jerri nodded. "I know now is not the time, but someday, Pat, would you tell me about Blake?" she asked softly.

"I'd like that. Thank you. And this afternoon . . ."

"Meet you at the corner of Westgate and Elaine at 2:45?"

"I'll be there." I scooped up Max, touched his soft cheek and buckled him into his bike seat. "See you later, alligator." He blew me a kiss as he and Jerri rode off into the crisp, bright morning.

A Chance to Forgive

by Frances McGee-Cromartie

Thursday. My turn to pick up doughnuts for the Montgomery County Prosecutor's office, where I work. I was in a rush, as usual, but it wouldn't take long to swing by my favorite bakery. It was good to see so much activity on a gray February morning: kids holding their parents' hands as they walked to school, folks hurrying to work. But one man stood out. He was pacing in front of the parking lot next to the bakery, wearing a rumpled overcoat and a blue knit hat. His body language made me wary. As a prosecutor, I'm trained to notice these things. I drove past the lot and pulled up on the street, as close to the bakery as I could get.

I quickly paid for my doughnuts and fished my keys from my pocket. I was heading back to my car when I spotted him again. *Probably a crackhead, the way he's slouched.* I picked up my pace. Just then he stepped in front of me. "This is a robbery," he snarled. "Don't make it difficult."

Did he say he's going to rob me? I'd heard it described hundreds of times by victims: Time seemed to slow and a feeling of unreality set in. "Hurry up!" he said. He unzipped his coat, revealing an opened switchblade. Yet, I was frozen with shock, a combination of fear, disbelief and anger. Anger that this could happen to me. He reached out and yanked my purse off my arm in a single, violent motion. My keys and the doughnuts tumbled to the pavement.

The mugger pointed the knife, pushing it at me as a warning. Then he sprinted down the alley and through the parking lot, clutching my bag. I let loose a scream that had been building in the few seconds that the mugging occurred. It curdled my own blood. I trembled uncontrollably. Somehow I made it back to the bakery and used their phone to call my husband. "I've been robbed," I managed to gasp. "My purse is gone. Wallet. Everything."

"I'll be right there," he said. "All that matters is that you're okay."

He was right, of course. I was lucky not to get hurt. I've said the same thing to victims. But okay? Certainly not. This time I was the victim. I'd been violated.

The police came and found the robber's coat and hat in a search of the area. There were hairs that could be used for a DNA sample. The next day I skipped work to review hundreds of mug shots at the police station, but I couldn't match my assailant's face to a known felon's. Worse, all those mug shots of all those criminals made me feel vulnerable. I didn't want to be alone. And I felt I could never go back to my favorite little bakery. I lay in bed that night unable to rest. I should have felt secure beside my husband, but my thoughts were trained on the stranger who'd done this terrible thing. Would he come after me? He knew where I lived now that he had my wallet. I closed my eyes and tried to sleep. Impossible. The anger I felt during the attack welled up and I fantasized that I'd fought back. I felt bolder. I visualized myself standing tall in the courtroom at his sentencing, upbraiding this villain for what he'd done to me. I wanted him to pay.

I awoke in the morning still feeling vengeful. I had a right, though, didn't I? I sat down alone at my dining-room table, sipping my coffee. I felt rage overtaking me, and I didn't like it. I needed to pray. *God, I know you protected me from the mugger's knife. Now protect me from my hateful feelings.* In the stillness of the room, an answer came. *Have the church pray for the robber.*

Pray for him? The criminal? That wasn't what I expected. Yet throughout the day the thought kept popping up. Finally I dialed my pastor's number. I was indignant as I told Father Ben what had happened. "Pray for my attacker!" I said. "That's crazy, right?"

"Maybe not," Father Ben said. "Just make sure to come to church tomorrow."

Next morning during the service, Father Ben stood in front of the altar. "Please join me, Frances," he said. The surprise must have been plain on my face. I rose hesitantly and walked down the aisle till I reached his side. "Frances was mugged on Thursday in an act of terrible violence," he announced. There was a collective gasp. "Let us give thanks for her deliverance from harm." Heads bowed and whispered prayers filled the sanctuary. Next, Father Ben asked us all to pray once more. This time, incredibly, for the robber. "Release him from his dependence on drugs, Lord," he said. "Show him your way. The way to you. The way to forgiveness."

"Your way," I repeated. My way was vengeance. I certainly had a right to be upset, even angry. I had a right to demand justice. But I also needed to let it all go, to let God. I closed my eyes and prayed with my whole being. I would not meet evil with evil. *Show him the way to forgiveness*, I repeated, and laid my fears and anger at the foot of the cross.

When I returned to work on Monday, each of my co-workers stopped by to see me. The support felt good, but things weren't right yet. There was one thing I had to conquer. "I'll bring the doughnuts tomorrow," I announced on Wednesday afternoon. "Thursday's my day."

"Where are you gonna get them?" a colleague asked, furrowing her brow.

"Same place," I said.

Thursday morning. I retraced the steps I'd taken a week earlier. I parked in the same spot, went into the bakery and strode back out minutes later with a box of Dayton's best doughnuts. My co-workers cheered as I carried the box into the office like a trophy. Scared? Yeah, a little bit. I'd learned that there are things out there we need to be scared of, and more so that the Lord protects us from harm not only from others but from our own feelings.

More than a year has passed and my robber hasn't been apprehended. I still ask God to direct his life and deliver him from the forces making him cause pain to others. Of course I still hope he'll be caught. When he is, I hope he'll know he's been given a chance to change. When God gives you a chance, you take it. I know. After all, he gave me one: a chance to forgive.

Brian's Roses

by Rachel Muha

One sixty-five McDowell Avenue. It's the address of an old gray house in a middle-class section in Steubenville, Ohio. The neighborhood is a little run down now, but it is still called La Belle because it was once so beautiful.

My eighteen-year-old son Brian told me about the house when he came home from his freshman year of college early in May two years ago. He and his brother Chris, twenty, were students at Franciscan University about a mile away from the La Belle neighborhood. Chris intended to live at home that summer, but Brian decided to go back to Steubenville for five weeks to take some extra courses. This time, though, instead of staying in a dorm, he was excited about living off campus. "Some seniors are moving out, so there's room for me in the house, Mom," Brian told me. "It has a great big front porch with columns—you'd like it."

I had hoped Brian, too, would be home all summer. I kept busy teaching at a nearby homeschool cooperative I'd helped set up, but I loved having my sons around. Brian and Chris were incredibly close, both honor students and athletes, both generous and thoughtful. The three of us had long conversations, ate out and went to church together. Brian wanted to be a doctor; Chris was thinking about the priesthood. I thought to myself that Brian would help heal bodies while Chris would help heal souls.

Brian's excitement about moving off campus turned out to be contagious. In the late afternoon of May 31, 1999, we kidded around as we loaded canned goods and household supplies into his Chevy Blazer. Chris gave Brian a big bear hug; then I, too, hugged my younger son and waved good-bye. The next morning a bouquet of white roses arrived with a card Brian had written before he left town: "Mom—Just wanted to say hello even though I'm away. Love, Bri." I buried my face in the soft blossoms. At that moment I had no idea that my son was no longer alive.

The night before, Brian had arrived at 165 McDowell Avenue, unloaded his groceries, and fallen asleep on the living room couch while watching a movie. His friend, Aaron Land, twenty, was asleep in the next room. At approximately 4:30 AM three intruders broke in, boys about the same age as my son, drunk and high on crack cocaine. They beat Brian and Aaron savagely with a .44-caliber gun, forced them into Brian's Blazer and drove to a hillside about twenty minutes away. There they shot each of the boys in the head and left their bodies in a thicket. When the killers were apprehended several days later, the only reason they gave for their crime was that they "were looking for somebody to kill." One of those "somebodies" was everything to me.

When the police called to tell us Brian and Aaron were missing, Chris and I immediately drove to Steubenville. My sons' father flew in from Texas, and people came from miles around to join in the search. The boys' bodies were found four days later. Chris started sobbing and I held him close. Even when my own tears stopped, the weight in my heart felt like it would never lighten.

On June 5, Chris and I and dozens of relatives, friends and

students climbed the hillside to the spot where the boys' bodies had been found beneath a bush of white wild roses in full bloom. I sensed that a darkened area to my right was where my son had been slain. I went to it and fell to my knees, kissing the ground where he'd taken his final breath. "Brian," I sobbed, "come back, Bri." As I got to my feet again, someone handed me an armful of white blossoms he'd cut from the rosebush, and I took them home and put them in water, vainly hoping they would never fade but knowing that, like Brian, they would be gone far too soon.

Over a thousand people attended Brian's funeral later that week. Many more wrote me letters or called to offer their condolences. One minute I'd think of how much love Brian had brought into the world, and the next I'd think of how his life was snuffed out so quickly, so casually. I struggled with my deepening grief. *Why,* I asked myself, *did I ever let him go to that house?*

I'd been told the trial would not happen for another year. A year? What would I do in the meantime? How would I cope with the emotions that battled within me?

Trying to ease his grief, Chris resumed his summer classes, but I could not bring myself to go back to teaching youngsters as bright and full of promise as my son had been. I spent my time staring out the window, endlessly pacing the house, or visiting the cemetery, wishing I could rip up the grass and bring my son back. I couldn't look at Brian's photograph without crying. Over and over I thought of how scared Brian must have been that terrible night, jolted out of his dreams into a fight for his life.

Several weeks after the funeral, the police told me their investigation was complete. I could go into 165 McDowell and retrieve Brian's belongings. The thought of entering that house made my heart feel raw again. Yet I ached to hold anything Brian had touched that night.

On a hazy afternoon in late June, Chris and I walked up the steps to 165 McDowell Avenue. I stepped into a room with fading wallpaper and overstuffed furniture. Brian's things were still where he'd left them, but the walls, floors and upholstery had been cleaned. No one would ever suspect the unspeakable crime that had happened there. I sat on the cushions where Brian had fallen asleep. At the end of the sofa were his sandals where he'd kicked them off. Next to them sat his duffel bag and backpack. Each item seemed to cry Brian's name.

I went into the kitchen, where the bags of canned goods we'd loaded into the Blazer were still on the counter. Reaching into a sack, I pulled out a "recipe" I'd playfully written about how to make spaghetti sauce:

1. Open the jar of sauce.
2. Put it in a saucepan.
3. Add a little water if you think it is too thick.
4. Heat slowly.
5. Enjoy.

I held the note against my cheek and then tucked it in my purse. If only my son had never stepped inside this place where his first night became his last. From the porch, I watched Chris loading Brian's stuff into the car. Some young people strolled past on the sidewalk. "That's the house where the boys who were killed lived," one of them said. They turned to look, and I quickly drew back inside. Was this how my son and his friend would be remembered? As victims of a horrific crime instead of as the incredibly special young men they were?

Back in my own home, the image of 165 McDowell haunted me. One afternoon, as the last golden rays of sunlight melted into the soft tones of twilight, I pulled one of Brian's favorite sweaters out of his duffel bag and pressed my face into it. As I did, I saw his eyes sparkle, full of life, as he talked about the old house, saw him stopping at the florist, thinking of me, even in the midst of his excitement about his first "real place." I envisioned him sitting on the couch, gazing out the window at the streets of La Belle, looking forward to all the good times he'd have at 165 McDowell Avenue.

Buy the house. The idea rose clear and strong out of those vivid images of Brian. *Buy the house and make it a symbol of life, rather than death.*

When Chris came home that night, we sat down together and I took his hand. "Maybe this sounds strange," I said, "but I want to buy the house at 165 McDowell. I want it to be a safe haven— a place of hope instead of despair."

"Yeah, Mom," Chris said. "Let's do it."

I had no idea where I'd get the money, but the next morning I called a realtor in Steubenville. "I'm interested in the house at 165 McDowell Avenue," I said. Before long the phone rang.

"I'm sorry, Mrs. Muha," the realtor said. "The owner's not selling."

"Please call him back," I said. "Tell him I'm the mother of one of the murdered boys."

Soon the realtor called again. The owner agreed to sell the house to me for less than its appraised value. Within the next two weeks I was able to secure the necessary loans, and the closing was three weeks later. By this time I had more ideas. I would let seminary students live at 165 McDowell; their "rent" would be their daily prayers. I even came up with a name for 165 McDowell. It would be called Divine Mercy House.

In August, two student priests from Africa, Father Leo and Father Godfrey, moved in. Several hundred students filled the front porch, the yard and the streets as Father Leo and Father Godfrey blessed the house and neighborhood. The police opened a new substation in La Belle. And a "Neighbors Who Care" block association was started, whose members walked daily around the neighborhood praying and building a sense of community. I felt the heaviness in my heart begin to ease.

On what would have been Brian's nineteenth birthday, July 23, 1999, Chris and I and about fifty others again climbed the hill to where Brian and Aaron had died. A five-foot-tall wooden cross, painted gold, now stood at the spot in their memory.

The shoots I'd brought home from that white rose bush on the hill rooted, and in the fall I planted them in my backyard by the kitchen window. By the next spring, there was a beautiful profusion of glorious white roses. Brian's roses.

My *Funny Valentines*

by Marilyn Strube

Sweet sixteen wasn't feeling so sweet to me that Saturday after-noon, Valentine's Day, 1966. Home alone with no plans, I was actually cleaning my room when I heard the mail truck rattle by. I bounded down the stairs two at a time and grabbed the envelopes from the carrier's hand. No cards for me. Just one letter addressed to my mom from my brother Dave, fighting in Vietnam. I trudged back upstairs, where I attacked my room without mercy. Usually I was maddeningly indecisive about what to toss out. Not that day. Mementos, keepsakes, old notes and letters, boxes that would have had me sitting cross-legged on the floor for hours, deliberating over every unearthed trinket—out with the trash! It was as if I were trying to get rid of the whole sentimental idea of Valentine's Day. I felt like Scrooge on Christmas Eve.

Yet I kept thinking of Dave. A couple of months earlier when he had been home on leave, we'd had a huge fight. I loved my big brother, but he made me so mad sometimes! He was five years older and was always telling me what to do with my life, always trying to arrange everything for me. Didn't he know I was becoming my own person, almost all grown up? When he returned to Vietnam, we hadn't parted on good terms. I still felt bad, but not bad enough to write him and make up.

As I was stuffing an old bag into the trash, it burst open, contents spilling at my feet. Valentines from first grade. Irresistibly reverting to my old dilatory ways, I scooped them up and piled them on my bed. Cupids, paper doilies, cowboy cards. A bunch of those chalky candy hearts tumbled out of a pink napkin. "True Love!" announced one. What a memorable Valentine's Day that had been.

I had awakened with a splitting headache and Mom had insisted I stay home from school. Normally it would have been joyous news, but not that day. I didn't want to miss our class party. Mom, though, was adamant. No school. I slept through the day, until my three brothers came home, raced upstairs and surrounded my bed. "Look at all the stuff we got," they bragged. "It was better than Halloween!" Each had a bag full of valentines, candy hearts and smashed sugar cookies.

"Did you bring home mine?" I asked hopefully.

Their blank expressions answered my question. "I'll go back to school and see if there's a bag for you," Dave mumbled. I couldn't tell if he minded going, and I didn't care. I felt as crushed as the cookies.

"Now, don't get your hopes up," Mom warned after Dave had left. Dave was gone for a long time. When he returned he handed me a bag full of candy and cards: Superman, cowboys and cowgirls, ballerinas and clowns, puppy dogs. I thought they were the prettiest things I'd ever seen. I lined up the candy hearts in rows by color. I couldn't read well, but there was one I could make out. "True Love!" it read.

"What's that?" I asked Dave.

"It's like what Mom and Dad have for us, the kind where they love you even if you're stupid or ugly."

"Thanks!" I said, snorting.

I'd forgotten all about those cards until ten years later. Sitting cross-legged on my bed, I fingered one, a puppy with a heart in its mouth. The card read "To Mare." *Funny*, I thought, *no one at school ever called me that. Only my family.* In fact, all the salutations were to "Mare." Looking closer, I could see where another name had been clumsily erased and Mare written over it. Eraser shavings still clung to some of the cards like rubber rust. Holding one up to the light, I could see it had originally been written to "Dave." Someone had changed it. In fact, all the cards had been altered, and it was obvious who the culprit was.

My teenage cynicism crumbled. A tear trickled down my cheek and clung to the edge of my chin. Dave's definition of true love should have included a big brother who arranged nice things for his sister even when she acted like a jerk. I pulled out a Superman valentine from the old first-grade stack and scrawled "Dave" over "Mare." Then I added a note. "I was wrong. Forgive me. Love, Mare." I addressed an airmail envelope to PFC David Lee DeLisle and slipped in the valentine. Just for good measure, I added the "True Love!" heart and said a prayer that Dave would come home safe and soon.

It Takes All Kinds

by Jennifer Clarson

Stepping off our boat, I slung my in-line skates over my shoulder and started the long walk down the dock on my way to work. I was halfway along when I heard the all-too-familiar high-pitched roar of a neighbor's motorboat. I glared in his direction as he tore out of the boat basin, sending up a wake that knocked our boat, *A Moveable Feast*, back against the dock. *Can't he read?* I thought, glancing back at the large No Wake sign on the dock. His boat's powerful wake usually came in quick waves, rocking our boat back and forth three times before it stopped. How often I'd had to reach out to catch a toppling knickknack or keep a meal on the stove from jumping out of the pot as those wakes rocked our boat. Whenever my husband David talked to the guy about his speeding, he'd apologize and promise it wouldn't happen again. But soon enough he'd be back to his old tricks.

It was the only bad point about living on A Moveable Feast. We had a stellar view of the Palisades across the Hudson River, and our jobs in Manhattan were only a few blocks away. Blading to work was easy and quick. But after the manager of the marina spotted me zipping along the dock one day, he posted a No Skating sign. The walk to the sidewalk seemed so long and slow, especially on nippy autumn days. Seeing the speeder fly by rubbed it in.

I'll tell David to talk to him again, I thought, watching the white arc of foam behind the motorboat. What a nuisance!

David was more mellow about it than I was. "It takes all kinds to make a world," he'd say when I'd complain about the speeder. "Everyone does things that annoy others. If we lived in an apartment, we might have a neighbor who played loud music at night. All in all, this isn't too bad."

Still, it grated on me. Why couldn't this guy just play by the rules? Fortunately, he'd soon head elsewhere for the winter and we'd get a few months of peace and quiet. *But until then, God, please make that speeder stop driving me crazy!*

That night I brought up the speeder as soon as David came through the door. "Well, I don't think you'll have to worry about him much longer this year. Turns out he zigged when he should have zagged and hit a log in the water."

Instantly I felt remorseful. "Is he okay?"

"Oh yeah, he's fine, and there wasn't too much damage to his boat. But barring a miracle, he's done for the season."

Wow, that was fast, I thought. *Thanks, God.* And that was that. Problem solved—at least for this year.

The weather turned bitterly cold later that week. As I left work I heard a forecast for snow the next morning. *Last day I'll get to blade to work for a while*, I thought as I skated home. Even though I had on several layers of clothing, my teeth were chattering by the time the boat basin was in sight. I couldn't wait to start dinner. I put on a burst of speed, glancing guiltily at the No Skating sign as I whizzed down the dock. *Just this once*, I thought. *It's freezing!* I braked, almost feeling the toasty warmth of our boat's cabin. Next thing I knew I was tumbling down the gangway. I grabbed for the railing but my momentum swept me along. Must have hit a patch of ice. *I'm in for a dunking*, I thought. Being a good swimmer, I wasn't too worried. David will get a kick out of this story when I tell him tonight.

I hit the water headfirst. The cold seemed to soak right into my blood. I was between A Moveable Feast's hull and the dock, upside down in the water. I tried to right myself so I could kick back to the surface, but it felt like someone was pushing me under by my right foot. I bent up from the waist until my head was above water. Then I saw: My bulky skate was tangled in the boat's dock lines.

I couldn't hold myself up. Underwater again, I tried to wrench my leg free. No use. Again I forced my body up, frantically trying to grab hold of the lines. My fingers grazed them before my strength gave out and I fell back underwater. I tried once more. That time I didn't even get close. *I'm going to drown! Please, God, don't let David have to find me like this.* Suddenly, through the water I heard a muffled roar. What's the speeder doing here? I felt a blast of hope. *His wake will push the boat toward the dock and the lines will slacken*, I thought.

The first surge from the boat's wake came in and I tried to pull my foot free. The lines were still too tight. *Two more chances*, I thought, remembering that the wake came in three waves. The second surge came. The boat's hull pushed against me and I reflexively used my last bit of strength to shove it back. Then came the third. The boat hit hard against the dock behind me. That did it. The ropes slackened just enough so that my foot came free. I hauled myself onboard and collapsed on the deck, listening to the speeder's motor growing fainter in the distance.

That evening I told David the whole story. "I can't believe I'm saying this, but I'm so thankful for that speeder."

"Me too," said David, putting his arms around me. "We'll have to make sure to tell him that when we see him again."

I nodded. I actually found myself looking forward to hearing the sound of his motorboat. It would remind me to be more tolerant of people. David was right. It takes all kinds to make a world. And God, who makes all those kinds, has reasons for putting them in our lives.

The Paperweight

by James Winburn

I don't remember what I gave anyone else that Christmas of 1956. But I remember what I gave my dad: a paperweight. I was ten at the time, and Miss Autry, our fourth-grade teacher, assured us that dads loved paperweights. You started out with a smooth, round stone, painted it, covered it with glitter and glued a little piece of felt to the bottom. Presto: the perfect "dad" Christmas gift. Well, maybe for most dads. But my dad didn't fall under the "most dads" category. As far as I could tell, the thing that interested him most was the bottle of gin he'd pick up each Friday when he got off work at the garage-door company. He'd keep company with that bottle and the TV right through till Monday, when he'd sober up and go back to work again.

"Paint it your dad's favorite color," Miss Autry told us, so I chose a deep shade of green that matched Dad's 1953 Hudson Hornet that sat proudly in our driveway. I'd never really given him a present before. I hoped maybe it would change Dad's attitude and bring a smile. I wrapped the paperweight in colored tissue paper and gave it to Dad on Christmas Eve, too excited to wait till morning.

"What's this?" Dad said, shifting his eyes from the TV to the tissue-covered object in my hands.

"I made it myself, Dad." With each layer of tissue he pulled off, I got a little more anxious. Finally, the last layer fell away. Dad held the green rock in his hand, hefting it, feeling its weight, rubbing at the glitter with his thumb. He got a funny look on his face.

"A rock?" he said. "What am I supposed to do with a rock?" Dad put the paperweight on the coffee table next to his drink and went back to his TV. The rock sat right there for months, and every time I saw it, I felt a fresh stab of embarrassment. Finally, one day—inexplicably—it vanished. I didn't know where it went, probably in the trash. The bottom line was I didn't have to look at it anymore.

Sometimes, though, if you caught him at the right place in the bottle, Dad would be downright friendly. He'd served in the Pacific in World War II and could tell some pretty amazing stories. Some pretty harrowing ones too. Stories that made me proud to have him for a dad. But those good moments were fleeting.

I was thirteen when I came home to find Mom and Dad in the middle of an especially ugly fight. I got between them. Dad took a swing, knocking a cup Mom was holding out of her hand. It shattered against the wall. Had Dad been aiming for the cup, or me? It didn't much matter. I ran out of the house and started walking. Mom's car caught up with me a mile down the road. Her things—hastily packed—were in the back.

Mom and Dad divorced soon after, and I never lived with Dad again. But I still came by to visit him—as much out of some vague sense of duty as anything else. It was clear enough he'd never be a father who'd be proud of me, but some part of me simply refused to stop caring about him. He was my dad.

He didn't make it easy, though. Especially in my later teens. "Bring my packages in from the car," he ordered me on one of those visits. It was Friday. Those "packages," I knew, included a fifth of gin.

"Bring your own packages in," I told him, the rebellion that had been building in me for years, spilling out angrily. Dad grabbed my arm.

"I told you to bring that stuff in!" he shouted. My hand shot up—seemingly of its own volition. I backhanded him. The blow wasn't hard at all, more symbolic than real. Yet I regretted it instantly. Dad backed away, tears in his eyes. Tears I'll never forget.

"Why don't you just go," he said, his voice trembling. I turned and left.

I was eighteen in 1966 when I shipped out with the Marines for Vietnam. I caught a bullet in a firefight and came back in a full leg cast, toe to hip. Once I was able to drive, I went over to see Dad. It took me a long time to get out of the car and make my way up to the door. Dad stood in the doorway and watched me approach. Our eyes met. "Hello, Son," he said simply. "I'm glad you're home."

When you're young, you think people are just who they are. You never really think about them changing. Vietnam taught me—painfully—that that wasn't so. The war changed me in more ways than I could count, and more ways than I could talk about. But I did talk about it a little . . . to Dad, of all people. In the weeks and months following my return, we shared stories about war, the things we'd seen. Dad's were long and involved. Mine were short, tentative. But Dad listened to my every word, even when he was drinking. Drinking. That hadn't changed.

In the late seventies, Dad retired and moved back to his home-town in central Mississippi. He indulged his passion for fishing and famously hauled a nine-pound bass around town, showing it off to so many people that it finally spoiled under the sun. Then in his mideighties, he surprised everyone. He quit drinking, just like that.

After another visit a few months later, I got up to leave. Dad got a sad look on his face. "Stay a little longer, Son," he said. So I did. When I finally got in my car, I took one more look back at the porch and saw Dad standing there, tears rolling down his cheeks. I stopped the car and rushed back.

"What's wrong, Dad?" I asked.

"It's okay, Son," he said. "I just had a feeling." A few weeks later I learned the reason for Dad's tears. He had cancer. Nothing could be done. We buried him at Flat Rock Church, near the back fence, under a scrubby old oak that rose obstinately through a growth of poison ivy—a fitting enough image for his life.

Did I wish that Dad had gotten past the poison ivy a little sooner—that he'd been able to love me as a boy in the way that he'd come to when I was a man? You bet. That love would have changed everything. But I was grateful for the love I got, all the same.

I drove over to Dad's house to clean out his belongings. Toward the end of the job, at the very back of his closet, I pulled out a shoebox. It was strangely heavy in my hand. I opened the lid. Inside was a small object, wrapped in tissue. Pulling the tissue away, layer by layer, I found an ungainly green rock, sprinkled with glitter. Holding that rock, the last of my resentment vanished.

People can change. They can grow. I know, because my dad did. So did I. Just like I had hoped all those years ago. I had hoped a little rock paperweight I'd made in fourth grade would change things between Dad and me. And it had. A rock I had made in fourth grade changed everything.

Eight Dozen Roses

by Beatriz Sandoval

My sister Leticia sprang the question on me one Sunday in the car. She, her fiancé Carlos and I were driving to sample brunch at a restaurant that they were considering for their reception. "B!" she exclaimed amid a torrent of wedding talk. (My name is Beatriz, but my friends and siblings call me "B.") "I want you to be my maid of honor!" She turned and flashed a radiant smile at me in the backseat.

"Looty!" I squealed, using my own nickname for her. "I can't believe it, I would love to! I'm so glad you asked me."

I was more than glad. I was honored. Looty and I had been close ever since we shared a room growing up. We were like twins— laughing at the same silly things and embracing life with the same zest. Immediately I began dreaming up ways to make the day really special for her. Part of my job as a marketing executive is to do event planning. I would ensure that my sister's wedding was a gorgeous, fantastic success.

But as the car sped along a Los Angeles freeway, I thought of the guest list and pictured my large Latino family. A familiar worry resurfaced, and I felt my excitement drain away. Of course my mother would be at the wedding. And at Looty's bridal shower.

I hadn't spoken to Mom in five years.

There was no single moment when our relationship soured. Just a lifetime of resentment building from when I was a child, wishing she would defend me against the teasing I got for being chubby and wearing glasses. "Beatriz, you'll never get a boyfriend the way you look," my relatives would say—and my mom would simply nod in agreement. Other times, she would summon me from whatever I was doing to help her translate bills or write checks. She and my father had emigrated from Mexico in the 1960s, and Mom always expected me to be her English-speaking assistant. No matter how hard I worked, I never felt like I earned her approval. Even after I moved out and became successful in my career, Mom and I could never seem to make peace. We would go months without speaking, until finally, after one particularly bad argument, I told her I never wanted to talk to her again. And I didn't.

The day after Looty asked me to be her maid of honor, I sat at work, trying to concentrate on a marketing catalog I was editing. The catalog—of kitchen appliances—had pictures of a loving couple cooking together, and I immediately thought of my family and the looming wedding. At least it was several months away, plenty of time to come up with ways to avoid Mom. Maybe I could hold a separate bridal shower, like the holiday parties I celebrated with my siblings—deliberately Mom-free events. And it wouldn't be hard to avoid her at the reception, would it? There would be a lot of people. But what about family photos? Maybe if we took them at separate times...

Oh, who are you kidding, B? I stood up from my desk. Scheming was useless. I was going to run into Mom at some point. I'd known that since Looty announced her engagement, and it had been eating at me. I tried picturing our encounter. What would I say? Images of her ran through my mind. Her smell, that distinctive Mom smell—part home-cooking, part fresh, clean clothes. I remembered her when I was little, bustling around the kitchen, arranging flowers on the table—she loved roses. Then preparing a massive batch of tamales, my favorite. She was always serving them to family or neighbors—more than anyone could possibly eat. I hadn't had Mom's tamales in a long time.

In fact, I realized, I hadn't seen much of my sister Marisol either, who had recently moved back to Los Angeles from New York with her baby daughter. She and the baby had been over at Mom's a lot. But not me. I couldn't help but see how our feud was dividing our family.

"You should call your mom sometime," my husband Ruben said periodically. But I brushed him off, even when his own mother died of cancer just a few months before. I saw how much he missed her, and I knew he didn't want me to lose my own mom one day without reconciling with her. But I wasn't about to back down. If she could be stubborn, I could too. Mom and I were alike in that sense, at least. *Why should I be the one to give in?* I argued with myself. *She's the one who doesn't know how to treat me.* The self-righteousness felt good. But even as I let it run on, some small part of me knew that it was wrong.

I thought of Mom that last day we had argued. Then Looty. And suddenly I realized what I was actually doing: ruining Looty's wedding for the sake of holding on to a grudge. I walked to the water cooler down the hall, filled a cup and carried it back to my desk. I sat for a while, drinking slowly and pulling my long, dark hair through my fingers. I took a deep breath. I knew what I needed to do.

A few days later I stopped at a florist on my way to work. It was a warm southern California day, but I shivered in my sleeveless blouse as I held the cooler door open, choosing between red bouquets, pink bouquets and white bouquets. I was nervous. "Come on, B, just pick one!" I muttered to myself, wondering what color to get. I agonized until, suddenly, with a sweep of my arm, I grabbed every bouquet from the cooler and struggled to the counter, wrangling bundles of cellophane as they slid over each other. The clerk raised an eyebrow, but I paid quickly and hustled to my car. While driving, I had to hold the huge pile of flowers against the passenger seat with one arm. There were eight dozen roses. *This is crazy*, I thought.

I pulled into my mother's driveway and made the sign of the cross. I looked through the windshield and saw my mom standing in the garage. Were those tears in her eyes? I gathered the flowers, the cellophane quivering in my shaking hands, and stepped out onto the driveway. Mom was crying. I could hardly believe it. My stoic, stubborn mom. Had our separation hurt her too? It didn't fit with my picture of her. And yet here she was—this crying, vulnerable woman. I rushed to the garage, set the flowers on the washing machine and took her in my arms. Her smell! And her body, so soft and small. Hugging her felt exactly right. "You don't have to cry, Mom. I'm here now," I said.

"*Mi hija*," she repeated over and over. "My daughter, my beautiful daughter."

"Let's not talk about it, Mom," I said quickly, forcing back my own tears. I had a meeting to go to soon and I did not want to show up at work with red eyes and smeared mascara.

"What do you think?" I asked, pointing to the flowers in their cellophane wrappers, their colors vivid in the light. "Did I get enough?" We both laughed and went inside to find vases. As Mom reached into a cupboard, I looked at the family photos that she had placed on the living room wall above the fireplace. I realized just how long it had been since I had come to this house, since all of us had been together. Mom began arranging the flowers in her vases, and I realized that it was time for me to go. It was enough for now, just seeing each other. There would be plenty of opportunities later to hash everything out.

"Well, I have to get to a meeting, Mom," I said. "If I get fired, I'll have to move in with you!" It was lame joke, but I always joke when I'm nervous—in fact, Mom does the same thing.

"That would be okay.... I could use a little help around here," she said. She smiled and we walked back to my car, arm in arm.

As I opened the car door, I felt relief, exhaustion, excitement and peace all rush through me. Every part of my being was telling me that I had done something that I had desperately needed to do for a long, long time. Not just these past five silent years, but a lifetime of pent-up resentment.

"Would you like to come to lunch this Sunday?" she asked. I looked at her, and I knew what the question meant—*I forgive you too*.

"Will you make your tamales?" I asked.

"Anything you want, *mi hija*."

Making *a* Difference

Babushka Matrushka

by Linda Neukrug

I slouched in a chair in the back of a room at Chapman University, absolutely fuming. I could probably teach this class. After all, I'd already earned a bachelor's degree as well as a master's. I'd gotten my state certification and had spent three years teaching high school English. But that was back in New York City, before my husband and I had moved to California. In the eyes of my new state I was not qualified until I had completed its two-year process of classes and testing. *This is stupid. What can I learn here that I don't already know?*

I figured I'd breeze through the course, but then the professor announced an important requirement for his class: Each of us would tutor a student for eight weeks. Everyone else was assigned junior high kids, but somehow I got stuck with Fira Menina, an older woman who'd recently emigrated from the former Soviet Union. Tutoring was bad enough, but working with an older immigrant had nothing whatsoever to do with the career path I was on as a teacher. *Lord*, I complained, *what I need is a challenge, not a chore.*

I assumed Mrs. Menina had basic English skills, so the day of our first lesson I went to the library and hurriedly checked out a few books: *Dr. Zhivago*; a romance novel set in Moscow; and *Culture Shock! USA*, which included tips such as "When you eat in a restaurant in America, the waiter may tell you his name. It is not necessary to introduce yourself in return." My lesson plan complete, I headed for the apartment where Mrs. Menina and her husband Villiam lived. I knocked on the door and was greeted by a short, sturdy woman with shiny gray hair in a tight bun, apple cheeks and a wide smile. A typical Russian grandmother, except she was missing her right leg.

"Hello," I said. "I'm Linda, your tutor."

"Hello!" she replied.

"I'm sorry I'm late. Traffic was terrible."

"Hello!" Mrs. Menina said again as I went inside and took off my jacket.

"So, how do you like living in America?"

"Hello!" she said a third time.

Oh dear. This is going to be worse than I feared. As Mrs. Menina motioned me into her cramped kitchen, I sighed. "Do you like to read?" I ventured carefully as I emptied my canvas tote.

She shrugged. "I cannot English," she said, pointing helplessly at the books I'd stacked on the table. But her eyes lit up when she saw the colorful supermarket flyer crumpled at the bottom of my bag. So we spent our lesson saying *meat* and *carrots* and *milk* as we studied the corresponding pictures. When we ran out of foodstuffs, I emptied my pockets and we went over *penny* and *dime* and *quarter*. The hour dragged for me, but Mrs. Menina wore an eager smile the entire time.

"Good-bye, teacher!" she sang as I left.

"I'll see you next week," I said wearily, leaving the books for her to thumb through.

I returned to her apartment with a restaurant menu and two old telephones. We sat in the kitchen again. "Did you look at the books I left?" I asked, pantomiming wildly.

"Good books!" she said, nodding.

"Which one did you look at?" I asked. She stared blankly. Villiam translated for her.

"Ah!" Mrs. Menina said, understanding. "All. I read . . . three . . . books."

I was dumbfounded. "You read all three books?"

"Yes, yes. Good books." She opened an old-fashioned marbled notebook, showing me page after page of cramped handwriting. There were hundreds of English words with their Russian translations alongside. Her conversational English might have been stunted, but her reading ability was remarkable.

"Mrs. Menina," I sputtered, "I must get you a library card."

"Fira," Villiam addressed his wife and rattled off something in Russian.

Mrs. Menina looked at me and shook her head vigorously. "*Nyet.* I no go out," she said, pointing to her missing right leg. She said a word that sounded enough like *diabetes* for me to understand.

I started right in on the lesson. We acted out ordering things from the menu and used the old phones to practice making simple calls. After that I tried a bit of conversation. I was able to piece together that Mrs. Menina had a nine-year-old granddaughter named Elina, who was also in the United States.

"I worry Elina forget Russian," she said. Then she laughed. "It is *babushka*'s job, to worry."

"*Babushka*?" I said.

Villiam looked up from a tattered old book, *The Forty-Eight States*. "That is Russian for *grandmother*," he told me. "Fira is *babushka*. I am *dadushka*."

I'll probably end up learning more Russian than she learns

English, I thought. I had six more sessions with Mrs. Menina before I could pass my course.

Back at the university, I heard horror stories about other students' tutees, many of whom didn't want to learn. One kid even told his tutor, "I did the work. It was stupid." Stupid. The same thing I thought about this course. Then I thought of Mrs. Menina with her eager smile and her marbled notebook filled with pages of English words. I was ashamed.

The following week, during our conversation practice, I pointed to a brightly painted doll sitting on a bookshelf. "Pretty," I said.

Mrs. Menina smiled. "That is *matrushka*."

"*Babushka?*" I asked, confused.

"No, *matrushka*," she said, giving me the doll.

I admired the pleasant-faced wooden figure and then handed it back. But as I did, it broke in two in my hands. I gasped. "I'm so sorry! I broke it!"

Mrs. Menina and her husband burst out laughing. "Is meant to open," they said. "Look inside!" I found a smaller doll, a little sister to the first. "Again!" they urged. I got the picture. I opened doll after doll until I got to a solid wood one at the center. I lined the seven of them up in size order on the table.

"Wonderful!" I said. "But now we must start on our reading." I opened a copy of *Curious George* (I figured by this point Mrs. Menina might be able to handle a children's book), and we began. When we got to a page that showed the little monkey in medical garb, Mrs. Menina looked wistful.

"I was doctor," she said.

"You mean you went to the doctor," I corrected. She looked confused. Villiam cleared his throat.

"Fira was chief of pediatrics in Russian hospital," he told me.

"Wow," I said, slack-jawed. "Tell me about it."

"*Nyet,*" Mrs. Menina spat.

"Oh, c'mon. You were a doctor?"

She shook her head. "No. No more. I am in America now. So I must . . . learn . . . English," she said, gesturing so emotionally that she knocked over the dolls on the table.

Taken aback, I reached over to put the *matrushka* back together. While driving home, I wondered, *Why was she so upset?* I'd be proud if I had been a doctor. Mrs. Menina had had nearly everything taken away: her country, her culture, her language, family and friends, a prestigious job. She'd even lost a leg. But she refused to look back. Instead, she faced her future humbly, opening herself to learning new things. *She's solid at the center*, I thought. *Like a* matrushka. *Not hollow like me.*

I went to the next class with a new determination, seeing it not as a chore, but as a challenge, an opportunity to learn new things. "You know what?" I told Mrs. Menina during our next session. "You are a *babushka matrushka.* A grandmother with lots of good things inside."

She beamed, catching my tone if not my exact meaning. "More books?" she asked.

"More books," I replied. And together the teacher and her student read.

Making Way

by Dave Browning

U p here in northern Michigan, it snows—a lot. Even though I own a car-repair shop, during winter most of my business comes from plowing. In December 2007, a big—no, make that huge—storm hit. I headed out in my truck at nightfall and twelve hours later, I was still plowing, my only companion the DJ on my favorite radio station. "Hope everyone's being careful out there on those roads today," the DJ's voice blared. "We just got word that the Father Fred food pantry in Traverse City is in desperate need of donations. You can take any nonperishable food items to . . ."

Father Fred's is in the "big city" about an hour away. If Father Fred's was running low, I could only imagine how our own local food pantries were faring. My community is a group of four small towns with no real industry. Most people here are retired and struggling to make ends meet. The snow kept coming and I kept plowing, but I couldn't stop thinking about those food pantries, about families, neighbors even, not having enough to put on their tables at Christmas. *What can I do to help?* I wondered.

"Hey there, Dave," one of my clients called, pulling into the driveway I'd just plowed for her. "Drive looks great." She set her groceries down and rifled through her purse for my payment. "Do you mind if I mail you a check? I don't have the cash on me."

"Sure," I started to answer, but her grocery bags gave me an idea. "Tell you what," I said. "The radio said food pantries are down on donations. Why don't you just give me a few canned items I can take over to the pantry?"

"Sounds like a bargain to me," she said. She went back into the house and brought out a whole bagful. I loaded the bag in the cab of my truck and went on in the swirling snow. I made the same offer to my next client and the next. Plowing is three-fourths of my winter income, but my wife and I would find a way to do without it. It was those hungry families I worried about.

By the next afternoon, there was so much food in my truck I could barely squeeze in. Feeling pretty good, I went to drop off the groceries at my church's food pantry. Just a dozen cans of vegetables, a box or two of rice and some pasta sat on the shelves. There wasn't enough to keep a family of four fed for one week. I handed my bags over to the volunteers, my heart sinking. What had seemed like a big contribution just a minute ago in reality barely made a difference. *I'm just one guy,* I thought. *I want to help, Lord, but I can't fill these empty shelves by myself.*

I got back into my truck and headed to my next customer. On the way, I saw Doug, a fellow snowplow driver out on the job. "Hey, buddy," Doug called to me, rolling down his truck window. "How's it going?"

"Actually, I feel kind of bad," I replied. "The radio said the food pantries are hurting. I stopped by the one at my church and they had nothing."

"Sure is tough times around here," Doug agreed.

"I'm giving clients a discount if they donate food. But I don't know if it'll be enough." I paused. Doug is a good guy with a big heart but not a huge wallet. *Ask and ye shall receive, right?* I thought. "You wouldn't be interested in helping out, would you?" I asked.

"You mean, plow for nothing?" he said, eyebrow cocked.

"Not for nothing, just a little less than usual. Besides, we all have accounts we do for free. It's kind of like that. Just something to help," I said, my voice and my resolve faltering. Who was I to ask my friend to give up his hard-earned income? "Never mind," I said, and started rolling up the window.

But Doug didn't drive on. He looked at me and sighed. Then he said, "Sounds crazy, but what the heck. I can probably bring in more than you anyway."

The next two weeks, just about every snowplow driver in the area got in on our competition, giving discounts to their clients in exchange for food donations.

Right before Christmas I went back to my church's pantry. The shelves were crammed with cans, boxes, toiletries, even diapers. I caught the eye of one man who was there with his family. I knew they were hard up that winter, and I figured they were there picking up some groceries. But then I saw him handing over ten cans of soup to a volunteer. I couldn't believe it. Everyone was giving.

I thought I couldn't make a difference by myself, and I didn't. But I was shown that together, as a community, we could. And we did.

Sole Survivors

by Mona Purdy

It was one of those moments. A simple question changed my life. "When are you coming back?"

I was getting over a divorce, raising my kids—Morgan, Hannah and Christopher—who were all under five. I made a decent living as a hairstylist, had a nice home. But I felt guilty about the family breaking up—so I spoiled them. I took them on exotic vacations, shopping sprees for name-brand shoes, whatever they wanted. I overcompensated a bit. It was my way of showing them what I thought love was. But what kind of example was I setting?

In the spring of 1999 I went to Peten, Guatemala, to run a half marathon. As I was running, I spotted a group of kids dipping their feet in sticky black goo.

"What's that?" I asked a fellow runner.

"They put tar on the soles of their feet because they have no shoes," he said. "Barefoot, they're susceptible to lacerations and dangerous bacteria from the soil. They think the tar protects them."

I stared down at my hundred-dollar running shoes. *Do people really live like this?* I hated to stub my toe. These kids walked miles barefoot on gravelly hot roads.

During the flight home I couldn't shake the image. How could these kids play like kids are supposed to? I thought of my own children and how much they had. All because I felt guilty. Now another kind of guilt tore through me. *Maybe my priorities haven't been right. How can I help these children?* The answer came suddenly. What did Americans do with shoes? Threw them away—usually in good shape. And kids? They outgrew shoes—and fashion—almost as fast as you could buy them. I knew what to do—collect lots of shoes and take them to Guatemala. I told my idea to friends, neighbors, my kids—anyone who'd listen. I got some funny looks but I also got shoes. "Here, Mom, I'm almost too big for these," said my seven-year-old daughter Hannah, handing over her favorite black Mary Jane shoes. I was so proud of her! Before long my garage overflowed with all kinds of shoes—till eventually they spilled onto tarps on the lawn.

Around Christmastime I flew back to an orphanage outside of Guatemala City. I trudged up to the entrance where a nun stood in the doorway. "I have boxes of free shoes for you," I said.

"Please, come in!" she cried.

I nearly choked on the thick air. *Such poverty. Can I really make a difference here?* Just then, children crowded around me. Most were barefoot. When they saw the piles of sneakers and sandals, they lit up! They giggled as they combed through each box.

"These shoes may be their only Christmas gifts," said the woman. We made sure each child had a pair and left the rest to be distributed. I figured that was it—my good deed. I said good-bye and made my way outside. Then I heard a voice—the woman.

"Wait!" she shouted. I turned my head. "When are you coming back?"

There it was. The question that shook me to my core. *Lady, this was a one-time thing,* I thought.

"We need help," she said. "We always need more."

Again, on the flight I couldn't shake the image of those kids. Back in Chicago I told my friends, "We've got to keep doing this." I dubbed the organization Share Your Soles. Everything from boots to sandals and slippers, even rollerblades and soccer cleats, poured in. The project outgrew my house. A local real estate business, CenterPoint Properties, heard about us and donated a warehouse. We got more volunteers and got organized. Sneakers were washed and bleached, dress shoes were polished. Gently used shoes were best. Share Your Soles grew so much that American Airlines offered to fly us to distribution sites around the world for free! We were able to send thirteen thousand pairs to New Orleans Katrina victims and fifteen thousand to Sri Lankan victims in Thailand.

I love delivering shoes, and sometimes I bring my kids along. It's my new way of spoiling them—by showing them how blessed we really are to be able to help others. Whether it's bringing winter boots to American Indian reservations, sandals to Africa or sneakers to Central America, my kids love seeing the excitement on the face of a child getting a pair of shoes. It beats anything I could buy them.

The shoes we take for granted can have a profound impact on a child's life: They can be a form of transportation, a means for education (some kids aren't accepted to school without shoes) and a source of self-esteem. A pair of shoes can mean all that. They can change a life.

Share Your Soles has distributed over 350,000 shoes. Everyone from Boy Scouts to handicapped children to people of all faiths volunteer. I ask them the question I was asked: "When are you coming back?" I know now when you look outside yourself, you can change lives, even your own.

Where Bluebirds Sing Again

by Frank Newell

February 15, 1986. I brought my coffee out onto the front porch of my wife Peggy's and my doublewide and took a look around. Down in the southern part of North Carolina, where I was stationed with the military, spring was under way. But up here it was just getting started. A touch of warmth was in the air, the grass had a tinge of green, and the buds on the trees were starting to swell. It was the kind of day where you look around and realize it won't be long till spring and summer are back—and everything's going to be okay after all.

So why didn't I have that feeling now?

I'd been coming back to Warrenton for that things-are-going-to-be-okay feeling since I was a young man. I grew up on my family's four-hundred-acre farm. As a kid I spent my time cutting wood, hauling hay, and milking Dad's cows. As hard as the work was, I loved every minute of it. At ten o'clock, after hours of hard work, I'd hear the same sound, the happiest one I know on this planet: bluebirds singing.

Bluebirds nested on our farm. In mid-February every year without fail, they returned from down South where they migrated for the winter. They liked the holes where the knots had turned into hollows in the wooden fence posts Dad put up. Bluebirds are territorial and need at least one hundred feet between their nests. That's about twenty fence posts and, sure enough, every twentieth post on our property would have a bluebird nest built into it.

While I worked our fields, the mother bluebirds would work too, collecting breakfast for their chicks. Bluebirds are insect eaters. Bugs—with a modest supplement of wild berries—make up their entire diet (which makes farmers love them even more).

Sometimes, just for fun, I'd hammer together a slat house, using scraps of wood from my dad's workshop, and put it up for a bluebird to nest in. I'd even help out the mothers by popping a juicy worm or a caterpillar into the mouths of the chirping babies. The mothers seemed to trust that I meant them no harm. It was small payment for all the happiness they gave me in return.

But lately, when I came back to Warrenton on leave, that happy feeling was getting harder and harder to come by. Part of the reason was easy enough to find: I would be leaving the military before too long and was suffering from a classic case of retirement jitters. What would I do when I didn't have my job to fill up my days? Was my life over? Did God still have a purpose for me?

The other reason was just as obvious. Warren County had changed a lot in the years since I'd been away. Clear-cutting had taken so many trees that there was much less habitat for wildlife. That included the bluebirds.

"It's a housing problem mostly," a local wildlife official had explained to me. "With all the clear-cutting that's been going on down here, hardly any trees are left for bluebirds to nest in." I told the official about how the birds used to nest in the fence posts on our farm.

"Those are gone too," the official said. "Most farmers today use

151

metal posts. They're cheaper and last a lot longer, but there are no cavities for nesting in them, so they're useless to the birds."

Those words came back to me now. It was after ten o'clock on a morning in the middle of February, and not a single bluebird was singing. By this time the air should have been full of their distinctive, velvet-soft warbling, but there wasn't a note to be heard. Would I even enjoy life back here in Warrenton now that it was so changed from the natural paradise it used to be? No wonder I felt so empty inside. Again I wondered if God was done with me. I wished a couple of bluebirds were around to cheer me up. My thoughts were suddenly interrupted by a familiar sound. Sitting on the branch of a dogwood just a few feet away was a gorgeous, bright cobalt male bluebird. He was chirping and twittering his head off. But he didn't sound happy—not the way a bluebird does when it's singing for the pure joy of it. Nope, this bird was upset about something. And I couldn't shake the feeling that he was trying to tell me what that something was.

I'll bet you're looking for a place to live, I said, half to myself. Of course! That's it! I got up off the stoop and headed around back to my workshop. I hunted up some scraps of wood and hammered them together just like I had when I was a kid. Nice and simple: a square with a little hole in front that wasn't too big or too small, about the size of a tennis ball. I nailed the house to a post in the front yard and—saying a quick prayer—stood back to see what would happen.

A moment later, the bluebird was back. And this time he had company: a female, not as brightly colored as the male but beautiful all the same. The two birds fluttered and fussed around outside the house for a minute, bobbing their heads and flashing their bright blue wings. Then, one after the other, they entered.

I went back around to my workshop and knocked another house

together, then another, and put them up—keeping them far enough apart for comfort, of course. By the following week, just as I was leaving Warrenton to go back to work, most of the houses were full of bluebirds.

That was the day I officially said good-bye to my retirement jitters. I started spending every moment of my back-home vacation time building and setting up bluebird houses. Other folks got involved. One day we hammered up several different models and left them out for the bluebirds to examine. The differences were minor—a slightly smaller entrance hole or a slightly different type of baffle tacked around it—but the bluebirds could tell the difference. They picked the same model every time. It was kind of like a bluebird focus group. (We still run these tests every now and then to see if the birds' tastes have changed.)

We used that design from then on. Our birdhouses started going up all over Warrenton. Soon, requests started coming in from other towns in North Carolina and then from all over the country.

In 1998, two years after I officially retired, I set up a birdhouse factory of sorts just outside of Warrenton.

"Frank," Peggy said one day, "I hate to say it, but you need to start charging for these birdhouses or our whole retirement's going to be gone before we know it." I realized she was right. Charging a few bucks for each birdhouse would also ensure that we could keep the supply coming. Today, we've shipped out more than 75,000 houses to just about every state in the country. That purposeless retirement I'd prayed to God to save me from never showed up. A new purpose for my life did. As a matter of fact, I'm working full-time as a wildlife rehabilitator.

Even the very smallest creatures in God's world count to Him. And it's our pleasure—and our obligation—to lend a hand.

People Come First

by Steven Bigari

Breakfast time at McDonald's is always loud. Cars stacked in the drive-through, Egg McMuffins slinging over the counter, line cooks calling out orders.

The morning I sat down for coffee with my boss, though, the McDonald's I managed in Colorado Springs wasn't nearly loud enough. Actually, all eleven restaurants I ran for owner Brent Cameron were hemorrhaging customers—and money—for a very simple reason: our closest competitor, another fast-food giant, was offering a slew of menu items for fifty-nine cents each. Fifty-nine cents! Brent, a former McDonald's VP who had bought a string of franchises after retiring, had called me a few days before. "Steve," he had said in his calm, Abraham Lincoln-like voice, "I'm looking at the balance sheet here. Let's meet for breakfast, and you tell me your plan."

I'm a West Point graduate. I showed up with three plans. We slid into a booth. I pulled out some charts. "Okay, Brent," I said, "we're getting killed on menu pricing. But we're also taking a bath on costs. We give our employees up to three weeks' vacation—no one in fast food does that. Same with sick time. We give way too much.

And we've got to stop letting employees eat for free. Eliminate those benefits, and we immediately save several hundred thousand dollars." I looked up triumphantly. To my surprise, Brent's face was rigid.

"Come with me," he said, dragging me into a doorway on a quiet side of the restaurant—one of those vestibules for keeping cold air out. Both doors closed and we were encased in silence. Brent raised a finger and, nearly shaking with anger, said, "Plan? You call that a plan? Balancing your budget on the backs of your employees? Listen, Mr. Manager with a comfortable salary and health care, you may think these benefits are line items on a budget, but they're all these workers have. If anyone's going to lose vacation here, it's going to be you. Now, we're going back to that booth, and you're going to come up with another plan."

I followed him back to the table. I'd gotten yelled at a lot in the Army. But as I presented another of my plans—slashing prices on some key menu items—I couldn't figure out why I felt so stung. Brent was a man of faith. So was I—I thought. *Am I missing something here, God?* Had I been treating my employees like line items? That didn't sound very Christian. Then again, my faith didn't always enter the equation when it came to business. Should it?

"Now that's a plan," said Brent, after studying my price-reduction charts. "Let's implement it. No more talk about benefits. You take care of your employees, they'll take care of you."

So we dropped prices, and restaurants began filling up. The employees worked harder than ever. I pitched in alongside them on the line, bagging burgers and expediting orders. As I worked, I thought more and more about the people beside me.

There was Susan on the closing shift, a single mom whose two kids sometimes waited for her at the restaurant—tough finding childcare, I figured. Michelle, who worked days, was dedicated—

but so shy! Always looked down when I talked to her. I had no idea why. It was like that with every one of my four hundred employees. They were hard workers, good people. But something about them seemed to shout, "My life is a struggle!"

Sales rose, and I happily reported to Brent that we were overtaking, even surpassing, our competitor. One day, though, I got a worrisome phone call from one of my assistant managers. "It's Susan," he said. "You know how she brings her kids? Well, they've been coming more and more late at night, helping behind the counter, and customers are starting to complain. They're only six and eight. Do you think you can talk to her?"

I sat her down the next day and gently explained about child labor laws. "I'd be happy to help you find a good babysitter," I said.

She looked at the table and then outside at the parking lot. "You see that old car out there?" she asked quietly, pointing to a beat-up clunker in the lot. "That's where we're living right now. I brought the kids in because it was getting cold in the car. I'm sorry, Mr. Bigari. It won't happen again."

I sat back and let out a breath. I thought I'd been getting to know my employees. But this was a new level. "Susan, look," I said haltingly. "I apologize. I didn't understand. We're going to get you help. I don't know how, but we will."

That day, I began making phone calls. Food banks, child health centers, state agencies. Anyone I could think of whose mission it was to help the poor. *The poor*, I thought. *What do you know about the poor?* Not much. I had grown up middle class. I made very good money managing restaurants. The poor, to me, had always been someone else's problem—probably their own fault anyway, I had thought. But now I wondered. What was that verse in Matthew? "As you did it to one of the least of these my brethren, you did it to me." The least of these. Was that my employees? It was—in a way.

The people at my restaurants wanted to work. But they only made so much at McDonald's. And it took so little to set them back. A bad divorce. Health problems. Car trouble. The deck was stacked against them.

To my surprise, the agencies I called all got back to me—and offered to come to my restaurants to tell my employees about everything from job seminars and credit counseling to emergency clinics and health insurance for kids. We scheduled a Sunday, brought in some play equipment and a volunteer band and set up booths where government employees, including the head of public housing for the entire city of Colorado Springs, spent hours giving advice, administering immunizations and signing people up for programs they were entitled to.

By the end of the day, Susan got a subsidized apartment and Michelle learned about government-sponsored health insurance for her family. I was in the parking lot, ready to head home, when Michelle tugged at my sleeve.

"Mr. Bigari," she said, her eyes raised halfway to mine. "I don't know how to say this, but—these past few years have been really hard for me. My girls have learning disabilities and my mom has health problems. I don't have a lot of self-confidence. I didn't think I had the strength to face all these things." She looked at the booths ranged around the restaurant. "I can't tell you what it means to know these people are on my side. To know you're on my side. I just wanted to thank you."

I mumbled, "You're welcome," and said something about this not being the last time I helped out workers.

It wasn't. In fact, over the following months and years, I added more benefits. Small loans in a crunch. Help with housing or kids' healthcare. And events like the one that helped Susan and Michelle. I began calling my efforts McFamily Benefits—though it's a toss-up who benefited. The more I helped my workers, the harder they worked for me. Just like Brent promised.

It's been nearly twenty years since Brent made that promise. A lot has changed. Brent died in 1996. I bought his restaurants and ran them just like he told me—caring for employees. I brought my faith to work with me. As I did, I came to understand deeply why Jesus commands us to help the poor. It's not simply pity. It's because God knows that most people who are poor—more than two-thirds of the poor in America, thirty-nine million people—are working poor who could thrive if they only had a little help with obstacles they can't always overcome on their own.

Just ask Susan and Michelle. After getting her apartment, Susan eventually saved enough to buy a house, went back to school and now works as a nurse. Michelle stayed with McDonald's. She became an assistant manager for me until I asked her to head up a call center I designed to centralize drive-through orders. One day, thirty McDonald's executives toured the center to see how it worked. Michelle answered detailed questions about equipment and software, schedules and statistics. I watched as she talked nearly nonstop for two hours. She was poised. Informed. Confident. And she looked every one of those executives straight in the eye.

More Than We Know

by Gary Willing

I threw my duffel bag into my truck and started off on the two-hundred-mile drive from my apartment in Marietta, Georgia, to my family's South Carolina home. I was looking forward to relaxing, spending some time thinking about where my life was headed.

Lately I had been wondering what I'd accomplished in my twenty-five years, what I really had to offer in the grand scheme of things. It wasn't easy waiting tables to pay the rent so I could pursue my passion for music. I played bass guitar in a band. We had landed a regular gig, but I still couldn't quit my day job. "Just follow your heart," my schoolteacher mom had always told me, but I wondered if that was enough. I wanted to contribute something, to make a difference. How would I know if I was on the right path?

The sky was a blanket of white on that unusually nippy summer morning. I was glad I had foregone my usual driving sandals in favor of new woolen socks and hiking boots. After merging onto I-20, I pushed back my baseball cap and set the cruise control, humming along with the radio. At least the long drive would give me some time to try to sort out the answers to my questions.

As I drove, I found myself gazing at the mist shrouding the tree-tops and the rolling hills in the distance. There were few other cars, and the road was long and welcoming. I could feel the tension seep out of me.

I was making good time, and halfway through my journey it looked like I'd be able to make it to an early lunch with my family. I approached a hill and accelerated. As I reached the crest, I saw brake lights ahead and hit my own brake pedal hard. A bus had stopped. A car as well. *Oh great, a delay*, I thought. Then I spotted an overturned van on the highway and injured people lying all over the road. I reached for my cell phone—my eyes riveted to the scene—and dialed 911.

"Send help quick," I said to the woman who answered. "There's been a terrible accident."

"Where is it?" the dispatcher asked.

"Uh . . . I don't know," I said, feeling utterly useless. "Somewhere on I-20. Please hurry."

"Sir, drive down to the next mile marker and tell me the number, so we can locate the accident."

"Okay, I'll try, ma'am," I said. I pulled onto the shoulder and sped alongside the road, searching for the tiny green sign. "I see it!" I almost shouted into the phone. "It's 146."

Help is on the way, I told myself. *Now what?* I had watched countless rescue shows on television about heroes who had helped people out of disastrous situations. But I had no first-aid skills, nothing to offer the accident victims.

Mom . . . she always knows the right thing to do. I picked up the phone again and called her. "I just passed a horrible accident on the road. I called 911. I don't know what I should do now," I poured out.

"Gary, go back—maybe you can help someone," Mom said.

She was right. I at least had to try to do something. I exited and got back on the road going the opposite direction, my heart hammering. I was in uncharted territory—what did I know about this sort of situation?

By that time, a few more drivers had stopped to help. I got out. The air smelled of radiator fluid and it was eerily quiet—except for the moans of the injured.

Two guys in military fatigues were administering IVs to the most critically hurt. Some people were getting blankets out of a car, and I rushed over to give them a hand. My arms full of jackets, pillows, and blankets, I hesitated before turning to face the victims. *I have to do this, but how?*

I started moving among the injured. They were mostly young women. I draped blankets over them, barely able to look at their bruised, bleeding faces. I questioned the ones who were conscious and slowly pieced together what had happened.

They were cheerleaders from the State University of West Georgia, on their way to a camp in Myrtle Beach, South Carolina, when a tire blew out and their van flipped over several times. Apparently, all thirteen passengers had been thrown from the vehicle.

A dark-haired girl was sprawled on her stomach, right over the highway center line. I knelt beside her. "Where are you hurt?" I asked, covering her with blankets.

"My back," she managed.

"Help is coming," I assured her. I started to get up, glancing at the wreckage strewn around me and then down at her.

"Please don't leave me," she said. I lay on my side so we were face-to-face and she couldn't see how badly her friends were hurt.

She tried to push herself up. A warning bell went off in my mind. I remembered reading somewhere that moving a seriously injured person could aggravate the injuries. "No, no, lie still," I said.

"But I've got to get off the road," she said. "I'll get run over." She tried again to get up.

"The road's been blocked," I said. "You're safe." She looked confused. I had to get her mind on something else. "What's your name?" I asked.

"Haley," she said. "Haley Black."

"Where are you from?"

"Gainesville, Georgia," she murmured, closing her eyes. I knew from all those rescue shows that I shouldn't let her fall asleep.

"Haley, Haley, wake up," I said, reaching out to squeeze her hand. Her eyelids flickered open and then closed. *Oh, God, what do I do?* I thought, wanting to call Mom again for advice. Suddenly I thought of Haley's parents. She probably wished they were here. They would want to know what had happened. I was debating whether to go back to my truck to get my phone when I spotted a guy nearby with one in his pocket. I borrowed it and returned to Haley, whose eyes were still closed. "Haley," I said loudly, "would you like me to call your parents for you?"

She blinked a couple of times and mumbled a phone number. I dialed it and broke the news of the accident to Haley's parents. I told them she was awake and talking, and that I would stay with her till an ambulance came.

"Please let us know where they take her," her father said, his voice shaking. "And tell her we'll be with her soon." Then he hung up.

"Your parents will be on their way."

"My back really hurts," she said.

"Haley," I said, "I know this might not make sense, but that's a good sign—the fact that you can feel the pain." That seemed to reassure her. I picked some shards of glass out of her hair and asked her questions to keep her awake—about her classes, her hobbies, what kind of music she liked—anything that came to mind.

"My feet are cold," she murmured. "I don't know how I lost my socks." I thought of the warm, new ones I'd put on that morning. It wasn't much, but it was something I could give her. I took them off and carefully pulled them on her feet. *I wish I could do something to really help her,* I thought. *Where is the ambulance?*

It seemed like hours went by as I desperately made conversation to keep Haley conscious. I kept my hand firmly over hers as she shivered, even under all the blankets. At one point, when she complained that her nose itched, I reached out to scratch it for her—just so she wouldn't move.

At last sirens sounded in the distance. It had been about twenty-five minutes since my 911 call. "Help's here, Haley," I said, getting to my feet to look for the emergency vehicles.

She tugged on my pant leg. "Don't leave me," she pleaded.

I stayed with her while the paramedics put a body-and-neck brace on and strapped her to a gurney. The closest town was too small to handle such a crisis, so the first ambulances were taking only the most critically injured. I stood beside Haley's gurney, holding her hand until an ambulance came for her.

"I'll tell your parents where they're taking you, Haley!" I shouted above the hubbub as the back doors of the ambulance clanged shut. Slowly, I walked back to my truck.

Later that day, talking to her parents, I learned that Haley had suffered a chipped vertebra near her neck, a broken back, and a head wound requiring nine stitches.

While I was with my family, I couldn't stop thinking about Haley. *How did the surgery go? Would she be okay?* At last I decided I had to know how she was doing. I drove to the hospital in Augusta, Georgia, where she had been admitted.

When I got to Haley's room, her parents rushed over to hug me. "Thank you so much, Gary," her mother told me. "You probably saved Haley's life. The doctors say that if she had lost consciousness out there on the highway she could have died—or been paralyzed for life if she had tried to get up." I shook my head, stunned. "As it is, she'll be in a body brace for a few months, but after that the doctors think she'll be fine."

Haley smiled at me groggily. I took her hand in mine and squeezed it. "Thank you," she whispered.

I didn't do anything, I thought. Yet God had made it possible for me to help Haley simply by being there.

I still worry about my path, but I also have a new faith that I will have the strength to handle whatever lies ahead. I now think we all have more to offer than we know. Whatever I have I can offer with all my heart. And sometimes that alone is enough.

The Boy Who Needed Alex

by Lori Shaw

My yellow lab Alex, a certified therapy dog, tugged at her leash and trotted down the elementary school hallway, eager to get to the kids we'd been visiting the past couple months. She stopped at our usual classroom. I straightened her red scarf and opened the door. But there were no kids. Just the teacher. *That's odd*, I thought.

For years I'd prayed for the chance to raise a therapy dog, and Alex was a natural. A whip-smart, energetic pup, she breezed through obedience training. Her attentive amber eyes could melt the hardest of hearts. She became certified at just a year old. Deep in my heart I knew Alex was meant to do good in the world. When one of her instructors told me about Dog Tales, a volunteer group that visits schools and libraries with therapy dogs, encouraging folks to read, it sounded perfect. Alex loved kids, so I signed her up. Our assignment was the local elementary school. From our first visit, the kids bonded to Alex. Every time we came back, the students couldn't wait to sit and read with Alex.

But that day, with our regular class missing, I wondered if we could help at all. I worried about Alex. She needed to do her therapy work. "I'm so sorry," the teacher said. "I forgot to call you. The kids are out working on a project today."

Alex sat next to me and whined. "Could we visit another class?" I asked.

The teacher thought for a moment. "There is a class that would enjoy seeing . . ."

"Perfect!" I said. She led the way down the hall, and Alex and I followed. Then Alex stopped short in front of another door. "C'mon, girl," I said, tugging on her leash. But my normally obedient dog wouldn't budge. She wanted to, no, *had* to, enter this classroom. The teacher asked the class if they'd like to meet Alex. Then she waved us in. It was a small class, maybe ten kids. "Hi, everyone," I said. "This is Alex . . ."

Before I could finish, Alex made a beeline for a boy who was sitting on the carpet, his head down. She snuggled up to him and put her chin on his shoulder. The boy quietly put his arm around her.

I read a story to the kids. With each turn of the page, I caught a glimpse of the boy stroking Alex's coat. She never left his side. *That's funny.* Usually Alex makes her rounds and visits with all the kids. After we said our goodbyes, the teacher walked over. "May I please speak to you in the hallway?"

"Of course," I said, following her.

"I know you have a schedule, but could Alex visit us each week too?"

"We'd love to," I said. Then I saw tears in her eyes. "Did I say something wrong?"

She shook her head and pointed to the little boy. "He's been depressed for months. We've tried everything, and we just can't break through to him. But it looks like Alex has."

Alex and I kept going back to that classroom. Each week that little boy brightened a bit more. Today he's a happy fifth grader, who still gets visits from Alex and me.

Who could've known Alex would make such a big difference in a child's life? But that's what happens sometimes, isn't it? We ask God to give us opportunities to help, and He leads us to where we're needed. Or rather, He led my dog.

Instrumental

by Steve Baker

I've loved music all my life. In fact, music saved my life. When I
came back from Vietnam in the mid-1960s, I was stunned and
directionless. For four years I'd run clandestine combat missions
into North Vietnam. I'd seen unforgettable things, endured unforgettable pain. Then I came home to protests and people cursing our
soldiers. I became angry, a drinker, stumbling from job to job.

There was only one constant: music. As a kid in Grand Rapids,
Minnesota, I had picked up guitar early and played in a high school
rock band. My dad even helped cart our gear around. In Vietnam I
yearned for a guitar—any guitar, no matter how cheap—to strum
on worn-out evenings and sing songs with my buddies. The music
would have made such a difference, given us such an island of
peace. As it was, I didn't find that island until I got home. Even in
the depths of my alcoholism, I reconnected with my guitar and
played it in Southside Chicago blues joints. The gigs gave me something to look forward to—and a community of other musicians,
guys who knew how music plumbs the bottom of your soul. I shud-
der to think where I'd be if I hadn't come home to that.

Eventually I married and straightened myself out, quit drinking and landed a job with my dad's long-haul trucking company in northern Minnesota. I jammed with local bands on weekends and saved money until, in 1990, I had enough to make music my life. I opened a window-front store in Grand Rapids, and later moved it to a small town called Fergus Falls, population 13,471. I sold guitars, mandolins, banjos, ukuleles, pianos, trumpets, violins, flutes and anything else you could squeeze a note out of. I didn't get rich, but I did get to see the expression on kids' faces when they took their first strum on a guitar and realized they could make a carved piece of wood produce beautiful, healing sound.

That sound, in fact, was on my mind a few years ago when my stepson Marte, who was serving with the National Guard in Iraq, sent an e-mail to me, mentioning that he wanted to learn a new skill with all the downtime he had. I looked around my shop and spied a shapely acoustic guitar hanging on the wall—a perfect gift for Marte, whose birthday was coming up. My wife Barb and I packed the guitar in a box, surrounded it with Styrofoam peanuts and addressed it to Marte in Baghdad. The post office made us repack it—the box was too big—but the guitar arrived unscathed. And, on his birthday, Marte called, unable to contain his excitement. "It's beautiful!" he exclaimed. "I can't wait to learn to play."

And just like that, vivid memories of Vietnam, memories I'd buried, came back. I remembered my longing for a simple guitar, the lengthy days in the jungle when a few notes of music would've meant so much to my buddies and me. It all became real again, how hard life can be in a war zone.

A couple of days later I got an e-mail from a friend of Marte's. "That guitar you sent Marte is amazing," he wrote. "Any chance I could buy one myself? Music would really help to ease the stress around here." He included a credit card number.

Definitely! I thought, and ordered an instrument exactly like Marte's, packed it (the right-sized box this time) and shipped it off.

A few weeks went by and an e-mail showed up in my in-box. "Dear Mr. Baker," Marte's friend wrote, "I can't thank you enough for the guitar. You wouldn't believe what a hit it is—mine and Marte's. Guys are all over us for a chance to play, and the music is making everyone so happy. The only downside is that everyone wants one now, and of course most soldiers can't afford one. It's very frustrating."

I stared at my computer screen. Frustrated didn't begin to describe my feelings. *Those soldiers should have music. They need music. Why doesn't anybody do something about this?*

Just then my friend Don poked his head through the door. "What's up, buddy?" he said. Don is the sales rep for the local radio station. Sometimes he comes in to talk business. Most days he drops by to sip a soda and chat.

"Listen to this e-mail," I said and read it aloud. "I don't know what to do."

Don looked around my store, an expression of disbelief on his face. "Don't know what to do? Steve, you own a music store. Let's raise money and send those boys some instruments. I bet the local VFW Post would do a dinner for us." I looked at him and then at my rows of instruments. All that music sitting there, waiting to be played. And all those soldiers, far away, waiting to play it.

"Don, I've never raised a cent in my life," I said. "How do you even do that?"

Well, Don knew what to do. As he predicted, the local VFW Post offered to host a meatball dinner for us. We raised nine hundred dollars and I even persuaded a guitar-company sales rep I knew to give me a discount. Soon, Barb and I were boxing up fifteen guitars addressed to Baghdad. I had goose bumps driving them to the post office. That was about two years ago. Since then we have shipped more than 550 instruments to Iraq—everything from your basic guitar to bagpipe chanters, Native American flutes and a 1956 military band trumpet that was donated by a woman who told me that her dad would have wanted his favorite instrument to go to a soldier. Word about us spread on the Internet, and e-mail from soldiers poured in. Barb recently quit her part-time job to pack boxes in the back room of Fergus Music.

We're not making any money. In fact, we can barely keep up with costs—the postage kills us. But then we receive an e-mail like this one from a soldier stationed in Baghdad: "Dear Steve and Barb, thank you so much for the new guitar. It couldn't have come at a better time. I was so down, I was just walking around in a daze, thinking about home, and then somebody told me that I had a big package. That box saved the day for me. I don't know how to thank you." Thank me? E-mails like this do more than thank me. Each one is like a letter from my long-ago self—a closing of old wounds and a renewal of the promise that has sustained me for all these years. The promise that, no matter where you are in life, even in a war zone, a carved piece of wood can produce beautiful, healing sound.

Rescue on Mt. Alice

by Stephanie Millane

The view was spectacular, and Heidi and I paused to take it all in. High up Mt. Alice, above the tree line, nothing but sky and a 1,500-foot drop stood between us and the vista of the lush, evergreen Godwin Glacier; the small, rocky Chiswell Islands in the distant bay; the glaciers glimmering in the afternoon sun. It had been a steep hike, quite a workout on our day off as guides for an Alaskan kayak tour company, but it all felt worth it. I sat down to rest, gazing toward the ice-and-snow field that covered part of the trail back down. "Looks like we could just slide to the bottom," Heidi said. I laughed. It sure sounded like fun but too dangerous with all the rocks around. Better to take it slow, we agreed. *We wouldn't want an injury up here*, I thought. What would we do if something happened? It's strange, but for someone who has spent as much time in the outdoors as I have, that question was always on my mind.

It was our first time up Mt. Alice, but Heidi and I weren't new to these mountains. I'd spent the past ten summers here in Seward, Alaska, living the rest of the year in Alta, Utah, where I worked at a ski shop and skied the backcountry trails on weekends. Heidi guided hikes in both seasons and was searching for a job at a national park where she could put her degree in environmental science to work. We both loved Alaska's unspoiled beauty, especially on our vacation days when we were able to travel the remote trails by ourselves, alone in the quiet, sacred wilderness.

I'd had a ten-day course for my Wilderness First Responder certificate, a requirement for my job. But it was one thing to take a class, wrapping a dummy's plastic leg, and another to handle a real-life crisis. I knew what to do, but could I do it under pressure?

I pulled my backpack on and we started our descent, Heidi leading the way. Most accidents happen on the way down mountains, and Mt. Alice could be a bear. Even today, sixty-five degrees and sunny, snow and ice made parts of the trail treacherous. I kept checking my footing. Heidi pulled far ahead of me, rounding a large boulder.

I turned the corner and heard a loud shriek. There was Heidi, sliding down a snow chute about seventy-five feet in front of me, sitting up, her feet first. What the heck was she doing? She zoomed to the bottom and slid off to the side, flailing her arms desperately to slow her breakneck descent. Only then did I realize her slide wasn't a stunt. I held my breath. Reaching the end of the chute, Heidi bounced into the air and crashed into a large rock. She hit it with a loud, sickening thwap. I rushed down to her, nearly losing my footing. "Steph, I think I broke my leg!" she yelled. *Is she messing with me?* No, the pain on her face was real.

I knelt beside her, gulping air. The combination of exertion and altitude caused my heart to hammer against my chest. Heidi clutched her leg just below the knee. Her foot dangled at a ninety-degree angle. A leg shouldn't look like that. I reached out and palpated it. Her scream echoed throughout the mountainside.

Think, Stephanie, think! What could I do? My worst nightmare was coming true. Heidi quieted. Was she slipping into shock? I tore my cell phone from my pocket. No bars—reception was spotty up here. I squinted into the distance. Nobody within sight. I closed my eyes. *God, I know I can do this if only I can calm down and focus. Take away my panic.*

My heart and breathing slowed. Suddenly my training course came back to me. The checklist. "Heidi, do you feel light-headed? Nauseous?" I asked.

"No," she said softly.

Keep the leg elevated. "Okay, this may hurt," I said. I lifted her leg, grabbed her pack and slipped it underneath. Heidi sucked in her breath. "All done," I murmured. "I'll be back."

I walked away to find a signal on my cell. About forty yards from Heidi, I got a bar. I called our co-worker Cody at the base of the mountain. He could reach us faster than any rescue team from town. "It's me, Stephanie," I said. "Heidi broke her leg. We're on the Lookers Right Ridgeline at about three thousand feet. I'm calling 911, but we need help, fast."

"I'll hike up right away," Cody said. I hung up and then dialed 911.

"We'll send a helicopter as soon as we can," the operator said. "Should be there in a couple of hours."

Heidi was in a lot of pain. I held her hand. Her chest rose and fell erratically, her face was pale. *Something's not right*, a voice inside me said. Carefully, I slid off my friend's shoe. The bone ends were pushing against her skin. The leg was broken in pieces. I pulled off her sock. My whole body went numb. Her foot was totally blue. The blood wasn't circulating. The limb was dying, fast. I knew that Heidi couldn't afford to wait for the helicopter. The bone had to be set, now.

Again I felt the panic. Again I said a silent prayer. I would have to set Heidi's leg. Now. My hands quivered as I laid them on Heidi's ankle. If I didn't set the bones right, there could be serious nerve damage; the leg might need to be amputated. But if I didn't try—she would lose the leg for sure. I steadied myself. "Heidi, just stay still, I've got to set the leg," I said. "It'll hurt, but it has to happen."

"No, no," Heidi begged, as I started to turn the leg into place. I heard the bones grinding together; I felt them sliding. Heidi let out a wail. "Heidi, I'm sorry!" I shouted. If the break was clean, the bones would slide together naturally. Suddenly, I felt the bones lock into place. "Stop right there!" Heidi shouted. Slowly her foot turned pink again.

The phone rang. "Ow!" Heidi cried out. The leg had shifted when I let go. She needed a splint. I put the phone down. Rocks, maybe I can use them. I dug out two large rocks and placed them on either side of the leg, wrapping an ace bandage around it to keep it steady. It wasn't something I had been taught, but it stabilized Heidi's leg.

The phone rang again. "Search and Rescue," the man said. "It's gonna take us about three hours. Can you hang on?" I looked at Heidi, breathing calmly now. "I think so," I said.

My breathing steadied too. I thought about all I'd done in the past half hour, things I didn't think I could do. I'd asked God for help but it was as though He'd told me: "You're the one who can handle this." And I did. The skills had been there. I just needed calm and focus.

The helicopter finally landed, and the medic looked at Heidi's leg. "Smart," he said. "You've got it in traction. I don't think most people could have figured that out on their own." I didn't think so either.

Moments *of* Acceptance

Britches the Blue Heeler

by Reldon Bray

Mom, who suffered from congestive heart failure and lived alone, was having another one of her rough days. While I sat with her at her house that afternoon, I buried my head in the local newspaper rather than make her expend her energy talking. I turned to the classifieds, hoping to find something worthwhile in the dogs-for-sale section. I needed another dog to help me work the eighty head of cattle my wife Rose and I keep on our farm. My eyes flew right to the listing "Blue Heeler for Sale." Also called Australian cattle dogs, blue heelers are ideal ranch workers. They're born to herd, and they do it real well. Ann, the dog we had, was the same breed. I called the number in the ad.

I found out that Britches, a two-year-old, belonged to a boy whose parents had moved into town. Blue heelers need daily exercise and lots of space to run. Britches didn't have that anymore, so the boy's folks had decided to find a better home for the dog rather than coop him up. It was a tough but fair decision. I made arrangements to see the dog and then hung up.

"Sounds like an ideal mate for Ann," I said to Mom. I described Britches.

Mom nodded and then rasped haltingly, "It'll be hard for him to part with that boy, though." She paused to catch her breath. "You know how blue heelers can be one-person dogs."

I looked away. I hated seeing Mom struggle so hard to breathe. Despite the best of care and my constant prayers, each day she seemed a little weaker. Still, she remained cheerful, and I kept telling myself she'd get better soon. "Reldon," she spoke up, "the sooner that dog gets back to work, the better."

Seemed Mom always knew just what to say to me. Though I didn't get why she had to be so bad off, work was something I understood. I promised I'd go check Britches out that day.

When I saw the dog pacing around his little backyard, bluish head held high, I felt sorry for him trapped inside the fence. I made arrangements for the boy and his uncle to bring the dog to my place to see what he could do. The next day I watched Britches follow simple commands, cutting cattle from a small herd and guiding them into holding pens. I bought him on the spot.

After the boy and his uncle drove away, I gave Britches a pat on the head and called him to follow me. Instead, he plopped down on the ground, tucked his head close to his chest and refused to budge. I was barely able to get him to the house.

Eye contact is an important part of training a dog, but Britches refused to look directly at me. Nor would he follow a single command. "That dog doesn't even blink when I call his name," I complained to Mom.

"Poor fellow misses his boy," she said. Then she urged me to bring Britches to meet her.

"Up!" I commanded Britches that afternoon, trying to get him into the back of my pickup. But he refused to obey, even though I'd seen him follow the same order when given by his boy. Finally,

I had to lift the dog onto the pickup's bed and tie down his leash for fear he'd bolt. In Mom's driveway I unfastened the leash and commanded, "Britches, down!" He went through the plop, tuck, refuse-to-budge routine. I tugged gently on the leash, saying, "Come, Britches." No use. I pulled harder, but he resisted me with all his strength. "Who's training whom here?" I snapped at the dog.

I almost had to drag him inside. Mom was sitting on the couch, looking pale and tired. "Come here, Britches," she said, stretching out her arms. He went right over. Her hands were shaking badly, but she still managed to scratch him behind his ears. "What a fine fellow you are!" she praised. Britches wagged his tail.

"I'll be darned," I said. "That dog won't even look at me."

"You just have to give him some time, Reldon."

"Well, I've never seen such a stubborn dog," I told her. "He's never going to accept me."

"That dog's got a lot of adjusting to do," she said. "Just keep working with him, Son. He'll come around."

Maybe she's right, I told myself. After all, he does seem to respond to her. I took Britches with me every day when I went to visit Mom. He'd run over to her when she greeted him and then stretch out in front of her, perking up to look right at her face every time she spoke. Still, the only thing he'd do for me was walk through Mom's front door. Mom was real tickled by my frustration but kept assuring me the dog would come around.

I wondered about that. And I worried about Mom. She was getting so weak that she could only talk for short periods before needing a rest. One day in December I stopped in front of her spare room. Something struck me as different. Then I realized: This was the first holiday season the room hadn't been crammed with gifts and homemade treats for Mom's friends and family. Now it was too neat, too empty. I turned away quickly and went to fix Mom and me a simple lunch.

After I helped Mom to the table, we sat and bowed our heads. I thought about how many times we'd gone through this ritual together, how few times we might have left. I kept my head down longer than usual after Mom's breathless "Amen" so I wouldn't lose it when I looked at her again.

The rest of that day was quiet. We talked when Mom felt up to it, but mostly we just sat together. I answered the phone a few times. Always it was Mom's friends checking in. After one call I said, "You sure do have a lot of folks praying for you to get well, Mom." I forced a smile and added, "Including me."

I had to lean close to hear her reply, which was barely a whisper. "Some things you can't change, Son. God doesn't always answer our prayers the way we think he should."

Driving home that day I couldn't get those words out of my head. I gripped the steering wheel so hard my fingers turned white. *She has to get better, she just has to.* After I parked, I sat in the truck, staring at the mountains. "Oh, Lord, help me," I prayed. "I know Mom's telling me she's not going to be here forever, but it's so hard to accept that. Help me come around."

Britches's barking from the truck's bed startled me. I went around to untie his leash. I reached over to scratch him on the head, but he retreated. It was the last straw. Pulling my hand away, I slumped against the truck and wiped my tears with my sleeve.

I had months' worth of unspoken sadness in me, and I don't know how long I sat there crying before I felt a gentle bump against my leg. Britches. He was looking right into my face. His tail wasn't wagging, and his ears lay low, but his eyes locked with mine. "We're quite a pair," I said to the dog. "You lost your master, and I'm losing my mom. What are we going to do?"

It was the first time I'd gotten a good look at his eyes. They seemed to me to be filled with misery and longing. *Is that the way I look to you, God?* I wondered. I stooped to stroke Britches's tense body. "You are without a doubt one of the finest dogs I have ever had the pleasure of meeting," I said softly. When I leaned my cheek against his silky head, he didn't pull away. "Good boy," I whispered. "I know how hard this change is, believe me," I told him. "I'm going to keep working with you. You'll come around." Britches relaxed, and for the first time in weeks, so did I.

Then his tail thumped against the ground. I felt a comforting warmth, despite the biting December wind. "Come on, boy." I headed toward the house. A few paces back, Britches followed.

The next morning I had to move some cattle down to the barn. I got Ann and decided I'd give Britches a shot at it too. At the truck I called, "Up!" and Ann hopped right in. Britches stood his ground. I was disappointed, but I tried not to show it. Instead I knelt beside him and said, "Britches, I know you know what 'up' means. Fine, you're still getting used to me. But from now on, we've got to help each other. Pretty soon you're going to be the finest working dog in the state of Arkansas." His tail thumped a bit more than it had the night before.

I stood. "C'mon, Britches, I know you can do this. Up!" He jumped into the bed of the truck.

By the time we reached the back pasture both dogs were leaning forward, bright-eyed and eager. I called, "Down!" and they leaped from the truck and raced toward the herd. They circled to get the cows moving and then weaved in and out to round up the stragglers. Britches zigzagged behind one headstrong cow, nipping at her heels, and I thought, *Mom was right. This is going to work out just fine.*

Mom died two months later. For a while I couldn't stand to be around people. By then Britches was always by my side. During the months that followed he was the only earthly comfort I had, and all the more so because of what Mom had said: "He'll come around." And whenever I watched Britches dash across a field to cut off a straggling cow, I found myself coming around too.

Grandma and the Paper Girl

by Ella Duquette

I squinted against the afternoon sunshine, looking out the window for the paperboy. Ever since a stroke had weakened my legs, I hadn't been able to get around so well. I depended on the paper to keep me up-to-date with a world from which I often felt disconnected. When the paper came late, I got edgy. Finally I saw someone coming down the street. A girl, no more than ten or eleven years old, hurled a rolled-up newspaper toward my screen door. It landed with a thud.

"Just a minute," I called out the window. "Where's the usual carrier?"

"I'm the carrier now, lady," she said, hands on her hips.

"Well, the old one used to bring the paper in to me."

"Oh yeah? Well, I can do that." She came in and plopped the paper onto my lap, and I got a better look at her. Frayed shorts and a cropped top—and it wasn't even summer yet. She tossed back her shoulder-length red hair and blew a huge pink bubble.

"I hate bubblegum," I said.

"Tough beans," she said. I gasped. This snippy little thing needed to be taught some manners.

"The children around here call me Mrs. Lee, after my late husband."

"Well, you can call me Kristin," she said with a sassy tilt of her head and bounded down the steps.

Just what I need, I thought. Nothing was easy anymore. Simple tasks like dusting and doing laundry were an ordeal these days. And baking, which I used to love, was far too much trouble. My husband Lee and most of my friends had passed on. Lately I had found myself wondering why I had been left behind. It was clear to me, anyway, that if young people today all acted like that smart-alecky paper girl, I had been too long in this world.

Kristin's attitude didn't much improve over the following weeks. But I had to admit she never missed a day or forgot to bring the paper inside to me. She even took to sharing some small talk when she stopped by. She came in from a wicked rainstorm once and pulled the paper out from under her coat. "H— of a day, huh, Gram?" she said, handing me the paper. I could feel the muscles in my jaw tense.

"Do you talk like that just to shock me?" I asked. "And I'm not your grandmother."

"I just talk like all my friends."

"Not in this house, you don't," I shot back. "In my day you'd have your mouth washed out with soap."

She laughed. "You'd have some fight on your hands if you tried it, Gram," she said.

I threw up my hands. *Why do I even bother with you?* I wondered, as she strutted down the street.

But she started coming by after her paper route and other times as well, chitchatting happily about school, her friends. Each time she left, it was as if a radio had been turned off. One day a bundle of newspapers slipped from her hands onto the floor and she uttered a dirty word. Instantly she clapped a hand over her mouth and said, "Oops! Sorry, Gram."

Well, she's learned something, I thought, smiling secretly.

I dug out some of my old photographs and outfits, thinking she might like to see them. She never tired of my stories of growing up on a farm, how we had raised our own food and washed our clothes by hand. *All this girl needs is some pushing,* I thought. *Why else would she keep coming back when I'm always fussing at her over her clothes or talk? Is this why I'm still around—for Kristin?*

She showed me her report card when I asked one afternoon. "This is awful," I said.

"I do better than lots of kids," she snapped.

"You're not 'lots of kids.' Have a little pride in yourself."

"Oh, Gram, you make such a big deal out of things," she said. But I kept after her about her grades. A short time later, Kristin gave up her paper route and shifted her visits to after school. I didn't ask why she kept coming to see me because—though I wouldn't have been caught dead admitting it—her visits had become the highlight of my days.

Once she told me, giggling, about some of her friends who had been shoplifting. "That's nothing to laugh about, young lady," I said. "It's stealing, plain and simple."

"Well, I didn't do it."

"All the same, you could be guilty by association. Your reputation goes with you all your life, you know."

"Oh, Gram, stop preaching."

"If you don't like it, there's the door," I declared. But she didn't leave. In fact, we spent more time together. Still, we had our moments. Like when she baked a cake and then sank down on a chair without laying a finger to the mound of dishes. "Come back here and clean up after yourself," I ordered.

"No way. I'm not putting my hands in that sink. It's gross." She had just polished her nails—a ghastly purple.

"Tough beans!" I blurted. She laughed. *Mercy*, I thought. *Now I'm starting to talk like her.* But she did the dishes that day, and many others. I taught her how to bake fresh bread and my famous apple pie. It was wonderful to smell those familiar aromas coming from the kitchen again.

One Sunday, Kristin stopped by. "You didn't go to church dressed like that, did you?" I asked. She glanced at her shorts and T-shirt.

"All the kids dress like this."

"I've told you before, Kristin, you're not 'all the kids.'"

"Well, I suppose you think I should wear one of your old outfits, complete with hat and long white gloves!" She flounced out the door, only to come back a moment later. "I'm sorry, Gram," she said, giving me a quick hug. "Forgive me?" How could I not? Making up with her seemed as natural as making up with one of my own daughters after a fight. Gradually, Kristin started dusting and cleaning up around the house, without the slightest hint from me. She even did my laundry. It chafed at my pride to let her do things I had done for myself all my life—but she was insistent. And this was the same girl who just a short while earlier wouldn't put her hands into a sink of dirty dishes!

"How about I set your hair?" she asked one day. "My mom taught me."

This was too much. "I'm not so old and helpless that I can't take care of myself."

"Oh, don't be so stubborn. Come on, Gram," she wheedled. For the first time, that nickname didn't annoy me. I gave in, and she proceeded to work several different lathery formulas into my short locks, not letting me look in a mirror until she was done. I had visions of my hair dyed the same awful purple as her fingernails. I was amazed to find it soft, shiny and still blonde.

"You're good at this," I said, and Kristin beamed.

I was even more impressed when, shortly after graduating from eighth grade, Kristin brought me a scrapbook filled with certificates of academic achievement. "See, I told you you weren't like everybody," I said, hugging her. "You're special." It was wonderful to see she valued my approval. But the best part was seeing she was pleased with herself.

I still didn't think much of her study habits. She insisted on keeping the television on when she did homework. I couldn't fathom how she could concentrate with that racket. But then there was a lot I couldn't fathom about Kristin's world. "Gram, do you know there are eight girls pregnant in the freshman class?" she told me. I gasped. "And that's nothing," she continued. "In some schools they have police guards and metal detectors, and just about everybody smokes, drinks and takes drugs."

I shuddered. *It's so different nowadays. How can I help her deal with all these things I know nothing about?* Then I thought of how far Kristin had already come, and I knew the best thing I could do was to keep being there for her, as she always was for me.

One evening recently she brought over a cake mix. "I'm going to bake us a super-duper double-chocolate cake, Gram," she announced.

"No way," I said. "Shortcuts won't make a cake as good as from scratch."

"Oh, come on, Gram. It's easier this way."

"Don't 'Oh, Gram' me, young lady. Easier isn't always better and in this house—" She broke into laughter—the laughter I had come to know so well—and in a moment, I joined in.

Kristin shook her head and took my hand. "I don't know what it is, Gram," she said. "We hardly ever agree on anything, and you make me so mad sometimes. But I always come back. I guess I must love you." Who would have known that when I looked out the window for the paper carrier that afternoon five years ago, I would end up finding my best friend?

"We're Losing the Baby!"

by Maggie Baxter

Whatever is the matter with me?

It's a beautiful evening in early spring—and there's no reasonable explanation for why I've abruptly canceled my plans to go away for the weekend. As I've just explained with some embarrassment to my friends (who have now left for a retreat without me), I simply have a strong feeling that I'm needed at home.

I run through a mental checklist of what might be compelling me to stay. My family is in good health. My older daughter Lisa called earlier in the day to wish me a good trip. My younger daughter Katy is expecting a baby, but it's not due for three more weeks. Still, even after the twilight's silver-blue mist lures me outside on my deck, I can't shake this uneasiness. Somehow Katy keeps entering my thoughts.

Katy is twenty-two years old and about to be a mother herself, but I sometimes feel as though she's still my baby. Right now things aren't too good between us. A few weeks ago we exchanged angry words after a mix-up about a get-together we'd tried to arrange. "You never have time for me anymore," she said, and I resisted the impulse to say the same. Katy and I had always been close. But lately we just haven't been connecting. In fact, I've been worried that the space between us is widening.

The cool quietness of the night helps to calm me. Before going inside I take one last look overhead, staring up at the panorama of stars glittering in the vast darkness. Suddenly, so clear they seem almost audible, words come to mind:

> In every thing by prayer and supplication with thanksgiving let your requests be made known unto God. And the peace of God, which passeth all understanding, shall keep your hearts and minds through Christ Jesus.

Why have I thought of these words now? I'm still wondering even after I go inside. When the phone rings, I reach for the receiver and hear Katy's voice, tight with pain: "Mom, I think I've started labor. It might be a false alarm. But can you meet us at the hospital?"

It's ten o'clock when I get to the hospital. Katy is in labor, and she's already in the birthing room, which looks almost like a bedroom with its rocking chair and comfortable recliner. There too are Katy's husband Mike, her big sister Lisa, and Mike's parents. We're all allowed to stay with Katy throughout the baby's birth.

Katy's IV is started, and a blood pressure cuff is strapped on. The fetal heart monitor is inserted. A machine alongside the bed now sounds with every beat, and a rapid beep beep beep fills the room. As Katy's labor becomes more intense, Mike and I take turns as breathing coach. "Katy, focus on the far wall . . . breathe in . . . hold it . . . breathe out . . ."

Two AM. Nurses and technicians come and go, checking machines, checking Katy. We joke, trying to keep Katy distracted. We can see from the rise and fall of lines on a screen that the contractions are fiercer and more constant. Katy asks for something for the pain.

By three o'clock in the morning the anesthetic finally works. While Katy catches brief snatches of rest, I watch the monitor that shows in numerals the beats per minute of the baby's heart—155. The rhythmic beeps lull us. A nurse comes in to suggest we all go downstairs to get some coffee. "Nothing much is happening here," she says, smiling at Katy's quiet form.

Our sleepy group straggles toward the door. But as I pass Katy's bed, she says, "Mom, don't leave me."

"Honey, what's wrong?" I send the others on.

"The contractions seem to be different," she says. I squeeze her hand and tell her to rest. "I'll wake you if anything happens," I tease.

I watch the machines. The contractions are less intense but lasting much longer.

And there's another change. Up until now, the digital readout of the baby's heartbeat has remained steady, never varying more than ten beats with each reading: 150 . . . 145 . . . 140 . . . But now, after each contraction, the beeps are further and further apart . . . 125 . . . 120 . . . The baby's heartbeat is slowing . . . 95 . . . 90 . . . 80 . . .

Katy's eyes open wide. "Mama, something's wrong!" 70 . . . 65 . . .

Two nurses rush into the room. I hold Katy's hand, hoping my grip doesn't indicate my panic.

. . . 40 . . . 30—

The beeps stop. No numbers flash on the screen; it's completely blank.

Reeeeeeeee . . . One long shrill wail fills the room. Suddenly white uniforms are everywhere.

"What's happening?" Katy's voice is jagged with fear as a nurse pulls an oxygen mask from the wall and slips it over Katy's mouth and nose. "Breathe," the nurse says firmly. More people crowd the room; there's a clatter of extra equipment being rolled in and set up.

Tense voices ricochet around us. "Is her doctor in the hospital?" "Who's on call?" "Better set up for C-section." And then I hear words that I hope Katy does not. "Tell the doctor to get here fast," someone calls out. "We're losing the baby!"

"Mama, pray! Please pray!" Katy's words are muted but distinct behind the oxygen mask.

I'm frozen with terror; I try to do as Katy says, but it's hard with all these strangers rushing around me. "Katy, honey, I am praying." I lean closer to reassure her.

"I mean out loud!" Her hand twists frantically in mine.

I'd laugh if I weren't so scared. Katy's been known to roll her eyes when I even talk about praying, much less bow my head to say grace in a restaurant. She's often told me in great embarrassment, "Puh-leese, Mom, don't pray in front of people."

But now she repeats her request. "Pray out loud," she begs. I know I've got to keep her calm. But how to pray, what words to use?

In every thing by prayer and supplication with thanksgiving . . .

"Thank you, God," I say, "for this baby you've created, this little one we are so anxiously awaiting. Thank you for the hospital and the nurses." My voice starts off weak and unsure, but as more reasons for thanksgiving come to mind, my voice becomes confident and strong.

The piercing alarm fills the room, fills our ears, tries to fill our hearts.

"Louder, Mama!"

Let your requests be made known unto God . . .

"God, we want this baby. But we also want what you want. Help us through this, God, please! Be in the hands and hearts of the good people working here." Katy nods as I pray over the wailing of the alarm.

*And the peace of God, which passeth all understanding, shall
keep your hearts and minds through Christ Jesus.*

With each word, I see that Katy is relaxing, that the tension and
fear are leaving her body, and leaving the baby's body too. "Thank
you, God," Katy murmurs.

The alarm stops. There's complete quiet. And then we all hear
it . . .

. . . beep . . . beep . . . beep . . .

. . . 30 . . . 40 . . . 45 . . .

The baby's heart beats again . . . 70 . . . 75 . . . 80 . . .

No one speaks. Everyone listens to the blessed sound of that tiny
heartbeat until it is healthy.

A soft cheer goes up in the room. The doctor pats Katy's arm.
"We'll keep an eye on you, but I think you're going to deliver this
baby normally. And soon."

Our unsuspecting family appears, bewildered by the crowded
room. When I follow the doctor into the hall and ask what happened, he shakes his head. He can't explain what caused the crisis.
And he has no idea why it reversed itself. "There are some things
we'll never have answers for," he says.

Six hours later, baby Caitlin is born. But since she's been
deprived of oxygen, her skin is a dark blue-gray. All eyes watch as an
oxygen mask is used again, this time on the baby. I hold my breath
and then watch in wonder as a pink glow suffuses the tiny body. A
cheer goes up in the room once more: The baby is healthy!

A few minutes after that, a nurse hands a blanket-wrapped bundle to me. In the early morning light, I look long and wonderingly at
the exquisite, wide-awake face of my new granddaughter.

"Mom?" Katy stretches her hand toward me. "I'm so glad you
were there. I still need you, you know."

"Oh, Katy," I say. "I still need to be needed."

Trusting some inner instinct, I'd been home for Katy's call. And as we trusted in the power of his promises in a time of crisis, God had been there for us.

Ah, me and Katy and Caitlin. Yes, as the years pass, there will be moments—many moments—when we do not connect.

But then will come the times when we're completely connected in ways that pass all understanding.

Grounds for Peace

by John Wallach

The news had only one story that February morning in 1993. In our home outside Washington, DC, my wife Janet and I sat staring at the TV screen. A car bomb had exploded beneath the World Trade Center in New York. Commentators speculated that the terrorist act was the work of Muslim extremists. As a journalist I was used to covering stories like this. Although I wasn't reporting this one, I couldn't escape the terrible irony for anyone in the media. A terrorist's aim is to spread fear; reporting his action means he succeeds. Fear, in turn, leads to hate—which invites terror in response. It was a vicious cycle. I asked myself again as I had so often, *Can people ever stop hating?*

I remember the first time the question came to me. I was just six years old, lying awake in my bedroom in Scarsdale, New York, wondering at the fates that had let my parents survive and me be born. German Jews, they were taken from their home in Cologne to a death camp. They'd escaped, made their way to Nazi-occupied France, been caught, reimprisoned and escaped once again. A daring French priest guided them across the Pyrenees to Spain, from which my parents finally made their way to America and New York.

Two years later I was born. Even at age six I understood how rare our good fortune had been. A million Jewish children, I was told, had been burned in the ovens. What a "million" was I couldn't have known—only that hate could do unthinkable things.

Can people stop hating? As I grew older, the question grew more insistent. One of the reasons I became a foreign correspondent was a desire to learn about other people—and help them learn about one another. If we knew one another, would we go on hating?

Janet is also a writer, and in 1987 we accepted a reporting assignment in the Middle East. We lived for months with ordinary Palestinian and Israeli families. We shopped with them in the street bazaars, ate with them, played with their kids, went with them to synagogue or mosque, observed their decent, hardworking daily lives. And were struck by how alike they were. How much they had in common . . . far more than the differences that fatally divided them. Yet because they never knew one another, zealots could sow fear and hate.

Another thread was woven into the pattern when Janet and I sent our younger son to a summer camp in Maine. There, Mike was thrown in with boys from different backgrounds. At first, the usual misunderstandings and frictions existed among various groups. But the camp experience had a way of erasing these tensions. Bunking, swimming, eating and canoeing together led to bonding across cultures and classes.

All this, I think, was at work in my subconscious when I rose to make a toast at a Washington dinner party honoring Shimon Peres, then Israel's foreign minister. The Egyptian ambassador and a representative of the PLO attended, and I'd been included as part of the press corps. After dinner I stood to salute the peace efforts being explored by both sides. Then, without any intention of doing this, I suddenly heard myself saying, "I'm planning to hold a camp this summer for teenagers from the Middle East. I'd like to invite each of the governments represented here to send us fifteen of your brightest youngsters. Perhaps in a casual setting we can sow some small seeds of peace."

The surprise on the faces before me was nothing compared to my own astonishment at the words that had come out of my mouth. The delegations hastily conferred. No one wanted to appear to be against peace; before I knew it, Seeds of Peace was born. Fearing the governments would back out, I called a press conference the following morning. By afternoon the news was out: Israel, Egypt and the PLO were cooperating on a peace camp!

At first I carried on with my job for the Hearst newspapers. I was staying up nights to work out the endless details of getting the idea off the ground. We contacted Mike's camp and found that we could book the facilities later that summer after the regular season was over. Of course, this took money. We raided our savings, raised funds from family and friends to reserve the camp. The different governments chose the kids who would attend; we asked only that they be top students, proud of their heritage and proficient in English. Future leaders were who we wanted.

The last week of August 1993—six months after the World Trade Center bombing—forty-five boys arrived at the camp. In the bunkhouses they were assigned cots side by side with those they'd been brought up to regard as mortal enemies. At first the kids were edgy and the chaperones appointed by each government overprotective. But before long, the youngsters were sharing universal camp experiences, such as lost sneakers, swapped jeans, mixed-up towels, awful camp food. ("American breakfast cereal is much too sweet!") Bottom line, these were teenagers! Soon they were swapping tapes of favorite pop singers, playing baseball and soccer together, even attending each other's worship services. Before my eyes, my old question was being answered. In one small group, in one small place, antagonists were discovering that the enemy has a face.

But I soon learned personally some of the hard steps on the path to peace: the ancient, intractable conflicts of history and culture. Listening—really listening—to the other side, turned out to be the toughest and most important skill required to build peace. We enlisted conflict-management experts to guide "coexistence classes" that became the heart of the camp program. Every day the campers met in the big hall for a minimum of two hours, encouraged to confront the volatile issues. Who has a moral right to the land of Palestine? Who should govern Jerusalem? The boys were asked to share personal tragedies, too, the death of a family member —perhaps at the hand of relatives of the kid in the next chair. The facilitators laid down only three rules: No violence. No insults. No interrupting. A pencil was passed from hand to hand; only the boy holding the pencil was allowed to speak.

By the end of the two weeks, the kids had formed friendships unimaginable back home. A Hollywood producer heard about the project and offered much-needed funding—if the governments relaxed their boys-only policies to include girls. A little to my surprise, all agreed.

We were off to a promising start. We extended the camp period to three and a half weeks and soon were holding three sessions every summer, hosting close to two hundred kids at each one. With the camps taking more and more of my hours and energy, I decided to devote myself full time to Seeds of Peace. It was a scary step, but I'm convinced that God has a plan for every life, and I believed that this was part of His for mine.

In February 1995, I left Hearst. We sold our home, and with fifty thousand dollars and a staff of four, became a year-round nonprofit organization devoted to waging peace. A Palestinian-American friend of mine, George Rebh, designed our camp T-shirt: green and white, with three youngsters holding hands, their shadows forming an olive branch.

How fragile, though, was that little sapling! Bad news from home was sure to provoke episodes like the one that occurred during the fifth year of the camps in 1997. It was July 30, eleven days into this particular session. The kids were having breakfast when one of the Israeli girls received a phone call from home and came back to the dining room in tears. Arab terrorists had set off a bomb in the central vegetable market, the Mahane Yehuda in downtown Jerusalem, causing many deaths and injuries. Panic swept the Israeli campers, fearful for their families. I asked everyone to assemble in the big hall. Instead of milling about, as they had the day before, the kids huddled in groups, Jews on one side of the room, Arabs on the other.

I told the kids this was a test for us all, exactly the kind of terror Seeds of Peace was formed to combat. "These are the situations," I said, "when it's most important that we go on talking to each other. Let's see if we can make the sound of peace louder than the noise of war." Reluctantly at first, they did talk.

"I think the Israelis will hate us so much," said one Palestinian boy, "that they won't let Jewish kids come here again." Back and forth they went. Arab and Jew, each side clearly convinced that the other was the aggressor in the long conflict and itself the victim. But out of the morning's exchanges slowly emerged the realization that when violence occurs, both sides are victims.

Another Palestinian boy expressed it in a shaky voice: "I am crying because we are human beings and the people we killed were human beings too." Tolerance and understanding won out that day. But with every killing back home, the camps threatened to erupt in hostility. Some day, I feared, an eruption would blow the program apart.

By the fall of 1999, we'd sponsored peace camps for seven summers, graduated more than two thousand youngsters, had an annual budget of three million dollars from private donations and were also holding camps in Europe and Asia to bring together Serbs and Albanians, Indians and Pakistanis, Greeks, Turks and Cypriots. In volatile Jerusalem itself, we'd opened a year-round Seeds of Peace Center, a five-thousand-square-foot building dedicated to coexistence.

Then, in the summer of 2000, the Maine camp nearly self-destructed. This time it was an Arab who'd been killed—and he was the cousin of one of our own campers. The Palestinians demanded to hold their own funeral to coincide with the one back home. Such funerals are occasions for emotional anti-Israeli demonstrations. Because free expression of feelings was at the very heart of our program, we had to allow the funeral to take place. The grieving, angry boys and girls gathered in an old frame building near the dining room. From where I stood outside, gazing at the serene vista of woods and lakeshore, I could hear their sobs and shouts and the sound of pounding drums. At last I was permitted to enter. Some of the kids were in tears, some praying, some calling for revenge on the Israeli campers. Would this be the end of everything?

One boy made sure I was looking and stripped off his Seeds of Peace T-shirt, threw it on the floor and stomped on it. Other campers followed till half the kids in the hall were grinding their shirts into the pine floorboards. *Can people stop hating?* I'd never been less sure than at this explosive moment when everything I'd worked for was being rejected. Almost without thinking, I started to pull my own Seeds of Peace shirt over my head. "You're right and I'm wrong. If *peace* is just a word on a T-shirt, I don't want to wear mine either!" The kids stared. For a long moment the room was silent as one small experiment in peace hung in the balance.

Then the Arab boy whose cousin had been killed picked up his shirt and slipped it on. Another youngster retrieved his. Then another and another, until all had put their shirts back on. For that one moment, at least, I had the answer to my question.

Not Alone

by Ricki Distin

I sat in my dining room, the big table piled with paperwork: hospital forms, insurance claims, coverage statements. All a medical and legal paper trail for my twenty-year-old son Danny, leading back to that day when everything about his life and mine changed forever. One minute he was joyriding with some friends out on a twisty country road. The next, a quadriplegic and brain-damaged, almost every trace of the strong-willed, energetic, even exasperating boy I loved gone. Or almost. Danny had been out of the hospital a while now. He used a special wheelchair sized for his six-foot-two frame. Our house bustled with caregivers; a nurse's aide, a speech therapist, an occupational therapist, a physical therapist, all seemingly trying to resurrect as much of the old Danny as still might exist inside his broken brain and body.

In fact, it was those caregivers who had me going through all that paperwork that afternoon. They had started saying ominous things. Danny, six weeks shy of his eighteenth birthday the day of the accident, was an adult now, off our insurance and covered by Medicaid. "We'll have to discontinue our visits if your son doesn't show more signs of improvement," the therapists told me. "Insurance just won't cover it anymore."

I told them that I would figure something out, like I'd been doing all my life. Lead, follow or get out of the way—that's what my husband Denny said my motto could be. I'd had a chaotic childhood—alcoholic parents—and I'd basically raised myself. Who else could I count on to keep everything under control? Denny complained that he couldn't do a single chore without me following behind him to do it all over again. Well, I liked the beds made a certain way. Given Danny's condition, wasn't it obvious that we needed more order and structure around this house?

Now I needed a solution. I'd kept things going so far by quitting my job to coordinate Danny's team of caregivers. What would we do without them? More than that, what did they mean, "If your son doesn't show more signs of improvement"? Were they saying that Danny would never improve? I didn't want to believe that. All of our efforts couldn't be for nothing. Surely we could bring him back a little. Surely life wouldn't go on like this forever.

I concentrated harder on the papers. So little money! So many expenses! Denny pastored a small church and worked full-time for the telephone company. No way could we afford to pay caregivers out of our own pocket. I tried to beat back the despair that began to envelop me, beat it back like I had since I was a kid.

The phone rang.

"Ricki?"

It was Missy, the occupational therapist. Actually, she was more than a therapist. She was my friend, my rock in all the fear and uncertainty of caring for Danny. She'd even started attending our church. I felt that she was destined to be a part of our lives. When she spoke, though, her voice sounded apprehensive.

"Ricki, I have some bad news. The home-health people talked to us today. They told us that they're not going to pay for any more visits with Danny. They can't justify it. They say that Danny has reached a plateau."

Silence on the line. "Ricki?"

I said something, kept her on the phone long enough to get a few more details and thank her. Then I hung up.

From the living room, a television hummed. Danny was in there with his grandmother, Denny's mom. I thought back over the long, tiring day. Up at seven. Raise the electric bed. Feed Danny through a tube in his stomach. Transfer him to a shower chair and bathe him. Shave and dress him. Wheel him to the porch for speech therapy. More feeding. Recline his wheelchair for rest. Transfer him to the physical therapy equipment. Back to the wheelchair to watch TV. In an hour or so he would sit with us at dinner. Then we'd transfer him to bed, get him positioned and say goodnight, until we awoke in shifts to give him medication through the night.

Plateau. Such a pretty word for such an unhappy thing, one identical day after another stretching as far as the eye could see.

I stared at the paperwork, trying to focus, trying to keep down something black and suffocating inside me. A solution, a solution. I needed a solution. The panic rose higher.

Pray, Ricki. The day of the accident, a trauma doctor had told us that Danny's head injury was so severe that he wouldn't live twenty-four hours. Denny and I had prayed in the intensive care unit, reaching through a tangle of tubes and wires to place our hands directly over our son's motionless body. *Just save his life,* we'd pleaded. *That's all we ask.* The vital signs on the monitors had changed almost instantly.

Why wasn't God answering my prayers now?

Denny came in, home from work. "What's wrong?" he asked instantly.

Was it that obvious? "Missy called—" I didn't finish the sentence. Couldn't. I sobbed on our great big dining room table, a converted pool table actually, from back in the days when the kids always seemed to have their friends over, before the accident. I felt Denny's arm around my shoulders. I sobbed, sobs that seemed to come from my toes. Finally I lifted my head, wondering what kind of mess my face looked. I told Denny what Missy had said. "Oh, Lord, what are we going to do?" I cried.

Denny held me. Like a good pastor, he knew when to let silence do its work. When he finally spoke, I was calmer and able to hear. "Ricki," he said, "I know it doesn't sound good. But maybe it's not as bad as it seems. Missy's not giving up on Danny. No one's giving up on him. It's just how the system works. At least they've been here long enough to teach us how to do everything. Let's try not to panic. God's gotten us this far. I know he'll get us to whatever we need to do next."

I sat up, wiping my eyes and trying to let Denny's words sink in. "God's gotten us this far." How far? I couldn't help wondering. Not far enough! Not as far as we needed. Not as far as I needed. I was the one who'd be home with Danny all day. I was the one who'd need to keep it all together, keep everything under control.

I stopped and looked into Denny's eyes. He regarded me calmly, like he always did, almost like he knew the storms my heart generated and knew just as well how to outlast them. Control. What exactly did that mean? What had I spent this past hour—no, my whole life—obsessing over?

I thought back to all of the years I'd tried to shape and direct Danny. From wailing infant to mischievous youngster to rebellious teen, he had made his own way anyway. What about his recovery? Had all my management of the paperwork and the caregivers changed any of the medical facts? Goodness, I hadn't even been able to make a dent in the way my husband tucked in the sheets. Instead, all I had succeeded in doing was hurting his feelings.

Who was next on my list to take charge of? God? Dear God, from now on you'll be taking your orders from me. Love, Ricki. It sounded so ridiculous that I almost laughed out loud.

And yet how true. What I really dreaded was God taking control of me. It was one thing to believe in God—and I had, with my whole heart. It was another thing to surrender to him, to give up everything—my will, even my own son—to his total care. What might he do? Anything! He might tell me to stop staring at medical forms because Danny's healing had gone as far as it ever would. He might remind me that I had prayed—that in fact I had already surrendered at Danny's hospital bedside when I begged for my son's life, no matter what. Danny, broken, helpless Danny, was an answer to prayer. A miracle I didn't understand yet. And just maybe God would show me reserves of strength and courage I never knew I had.

I felt something inside me release, change, like the end of struggle and the beginning of acceptance. A picture came to mind of someone drowning, thrashing so hard that the lifeguard couldn't get a hold to pull him from the water. I stopped thrashing. I threw my arms around Denny's neck and held him tight.

A few minutes later we went into the living room. There was Danny, his face so sweet and soft, staring at the television. We sat with him for a while, letting the afternoon change itself to evening. Finally, I got up to fix dinner. Soon it would be time to get Danny ready for bed. We would transfer him and prop him up with pillows.

We'd read some Scripture, pray, put on a little music and wish him goodnight. One evening, like so many others.

Today, twenty-one years later, I marvel at how many such evenings we've had. Not long ago someone asked, "Do you ever laugh?" I wanted to say, "Come to my house!" There, anyone can see those blessings God so improbably promised. Like Missy, who remains a dear friend and a faithful member of our church. Or Connie, another friend we were able to hire as a part-time nurse's aide, with the help of a government program. Or our Friday movie nights, when Danny's older siblings, Christy and Chip, now both married with kids themselves, come over and everyone piles on the living room floor, snuggling up, with Danny in the middle, to watch a video. I think they've stayed nearby in part because of Danny. He's kept us close. Taught us how to love. And taught me that sometimes the most transforming change of all is surrender.

When Daddy Decided to Splurge

by Roberta L. Messner

A friend was going to look after my dog Muffin while I went into the hospital for some surgery. On the way to her house I stopped to see my mom and dad, Muffin trotting in after me as though she were a regular member of the family. A Benji look-alike, she'd been my soul mate for seven years. From the first time I'd spotted the wiry-haired stray hiding in the briers by a chain-link fence, we'd been inseparable. I'd always tried to give her the best life I could.

"Muffin will be just fine while you're gone," Mom assured me.

"I can't believe you're not putting that mongrel up at the Hilton," Dad commented. "The way you spoil her! Giving her that fancy-dancy stocking full of dog biscuits at Christmastime and taking her everywhere." I steeled myself against his words. That I spent too much money on Muffin was an old issue. That I should be saving for a rainy day was an even older argument. "I've always told myself," Dad went on, "that I'd be better off if I were Roberta's dog."

I just hugged Muffin a little harder and tried to ignore Dad's remarks. But even after I left, they stung. I dropped Muffin off at my friend's and drove on to the hospital, still thinking of what Dad had said. Why did his criticism hurt so much? I was a grown woman with a successful career as a nurse. Why did his approval matter? It was as though I were a little girl again, trying to make my daddy proud.

A child of the Depression, Dad had had to be careful with money. He'd worked as a telegraph operator on the railroad and supplemented his earnings by selling old pocket watches at flea markets. A horse trader, people called him. When I was barely out of diapers, I picked up his jargon. He loved to tell about the time he tugged on my pigtails and asked if I'd take a five-dollar bill for my Tiny Tears doll. I took a long look at her pink bottle and packet of tissues and shot back, "I want more, this here's a rare one!"

By the time I was ten years old, I was doing odd jobs in the neighborhood, hoping to match Dad's industry. I hosed off porch furniture, waxed floors and starched the curtains in a neighbor's guest bedroom. With the first dollar I earned, I put aside ten percent for church, but the next ten cents I took straight to Broughton's Dairy. There I bought a double-dip cone of lime sherbet, Daddy's favorite, and climbed the steep iron stairs of the telegraph tower where he worked. I tapped on the screen door and hollered, "Surprise!" I just knew he'd be pleased. "I bought this for you with the money I've been making." Lime-green sherbet dripped down my fingers as Daddy tapped out a Morse code message.

Finally he looked up and smiled. But as he took a lick of soupy sherbet, he cautioned, "Don't be squandering all your hard-earned money on ice cream now. You should be putting something away for the future." All the way home I fought back tears. Wasn't there anything I could do to make him happy? When I was a little older, I took up the violin so I could join in when he pulled out his fiddle. Then I studied piano. My first recital, I knew how proud he'd be of the way I played "The Londonderry Air." But at the last minute Daddy couldn't come. He had to work overtime. We needed the money. For a rainy day.

After I studied nursing and pursued my RN career, I became something of a horse trader myself, going to flea markets, collecting antiques. No matter what I bought, Dad was able to take the wind out of my sails when I told him the deal I'd made or how much I'd managed to save. With Muffin, though, I never cut corners. She deserved the very best. In the hospital after my surgery, I kept thinking of how happy I'd be to see her again. It was then that I received word Muffin had jumped the fence in my friend's backyard and raced off. No one could find her. Lying in my hospital bed, I prayed that whatever happened, she would be safe. Still, when no news came, I was frantic.

The morning my mother drove me home from the hospital, all I saw were dogs. Dogs playing, dogs barking, dogs running to greet their masters. But no wagging tail awaited me when I got home. "I'm so sorry, Roberta," Mom said, tucking a blanket around me on the sofa. "Your father is worried too."

Yeah, right, I thought, scrunching miserably into the pillow. Later, I got up to make a cup of tea, and the phone rang. The caller said she'd seen the ad about Muffin and wanted me to know she'd just lost her little pooch and knew exactly how I felt. *The ad?* I wondered groggily before stumbling back to rest.

The next night I got more calls. One man who worked at the Waffle House asked for a better description of Muffin. Before hanging up he added, "Your dad must think the world of you to go to all this trouble." *Why did he say that?*

Another caller said, "The dog your father described to me is here, I'm sure of it." What were they talking about?

The following day, a co-worker drove me around to check on the leads I'd received. None of the shaggy mutts people had found were Muffin. One was a hundred miles away, but I knew how Muffin loved to jump into any open car door, so I felt compelled to investigate.

Alas, the "female dog with matted hair" turned out to be a male cat. "I felt so bad for you I guess I got carried away," the stranger admitted.

Then my sister called. "I found Muffin at the pound!" I was beside myself with relief as I went with her to investigate. But I knew at once when I approached the cage that the thin, mangy dog wasn't my Muffin. "Just call her name," my sister urged. "Maybe she's lost weight."

"Muffin!" I cried. And from the saddest corridor in the animal world, fifty-six dogs of every description howled in unison. With that, my heart just broke. All those animals longing for a home expressed my own longing for my dog. It was as though my loneliness had found a voice.

By then I had given up, but when one more person called, absolutely certain he had my dog, I allowed myself to hope one more time. A friend drove me to the end of a muddy hollow, where a man stood with a yelping, stubby-tailed orange dog much bigger than Muffin. "She just has to be yours," he insisted as the huge dog pawed my skirt.

"I don't think so," I said sadly. The man looked at me woefully.

"Lady," he said, "I've already promised my grandkids a trip to Disney World with all that reward money your father's giving."

I was stunned. "Reward?" From the man who always accused me of squandering money on Muffin? The thrifty father who wanted me to save for a rainy day?

"I got the ad right here." He pulled out the beat-up newspaper he had jammed in his back pocket. "See, this one." He held out the want ads and pointed to an item he'd circled. I took the paper, read it once, then twice, blinking hard to clear the tears that blurred my vision. The ad was clear and to the point. "Please help me find my baby girl's lost dog," it said. "$1,000 reward."

"Thank you, anyway," I said in a wobbly voice. "Do you mind if I keep this newspaper?"

Mom and Dad visited me that night. "Daddy," I said, "you and I have some things to talk about."

That's when Mom spilled the beans: "He's been looking everywhere for Muffin. He gets in the car and drives all over, calling out the window. And he's been telling people to call and to pray for you." I couldn't believe my ears. Now I had to ask him about the biggest surprise of all.

"Daddy," I said, "what about the reward money?" He shuffled his feet.

"Well," he said, "I figured it was the only way that dog could be found."

"But a thousand dollars? Daddy, that's so much money! You've never splurged like that. What about always saving for a rainy day?"

Daddy fixed his eyes on a crack in his brown leather shoe. "Sweetheart," he said, "the day you lost your little Muffin, I felt the biggest downpour of my life. You were so sad, I would have given anything to get your dog back for you. I'm sorry she hasn't come home."

I thought of all the scrimping and saving Dad must have done to put away a thousand dollars and how quick he was now to give it up for me. The years suddenly faded, and I was once more the girl who had learned bargaining from the best horse trader in the business. You can't put a dollar figure on love, but Dad had come up with "a rare one" of his own. Nothing was too much for my happiness. "Thank you, Dad," I said, my voice breaking.

This story has a bittersweet ending. Muffin never turned up, but my prayers that she was okay did a lot to comfort me. Eventually, Dad took me back to the pound, and I brought home one of those howling mutts that was yearning for a home. It wasn't a replacement for my lost dog—nothing could take the place of Muffin—but this was a new dog to spoil to my heart's content. I named her Cleo, and we had many happy years together. And from that point on, Dad and I had an understanding. He can complain all he wants about the money I spend, and I can spoil my dog as much as I want.

Love can express itself in many different ways. I realize that when I was young, Daddy worked hard to be a good provider, saving for a rainy day. Then, as now, he was sheltering his baby girl and giving me love the best way he knew how.

150 Pounds Later

by Jane Shukitis

I've got pictures!" My sister Kim sang out, waving a plump packet as she breezed in the front door. A few weeks earlier she'd gotten married. I had been her matron of honor. It was a beautiful wedding, outdoors with a Hawaiian theme. But, boy, did I dread what I'd see in those pictures—what I did my best to avoid seeing almost every day of my life.

Kim spread the photos out on my dining room table. I oohed and aahed at how beautiful she was in her gorgeous wedding dress—as radiant as a bride can be. "Doesn't Mom look great?" I said. My husband George looked wonderful, too, in a Hawaiian shirt and orchid lei. Then there was me. The lady in the tent. No matter how big my smile, no matter how strategically I tried to position myself behind people, no matter how lovely the fabric of my dress, no matter how beautiful my flowers, I was the "heavy" woman. My arms were huge; I had at least three chins. There I was, all 282 pounds of me, preserved forever in photos that would be handed down for generations.

It would be one thing if I could just go on a quick diet and lose the pounds. But this was how I had been for years. A size sixteen in my own wedding gown, forty pounds added that first year of marriage, more weight gain with each of my two children. I put on seventy pounds with my second child. The doctor was concerned. I was concerned. I was a registered nurse. I knew the health risks obese people faced: diabetes, high blood pressure, cardiovascular disease. I saw it all the time on my job.

Other people went on diets, lost weight and kept it off. I'd go down ten pounds and then balloon right back up. The grapefruit diet, the high-protein diet, liquid diets, nothing worked and I couldn't stick with anything for more than a few months. I'd always think about how everyone else was eating things I couldn't—and how unfair that was. I'd been teased about being fat ever since I was a child—but I managed to be a success in other areas of my life. George and I had been married and in love for more than twenty years. Our two children were grown and doing great. I'd moved from direct-care nursing and was now a senior executive for a large healthcare system. I could organize a meeting, deliver a PowerPoint presentation, manage a multimillion-dollar budget. I just couldn't lose a pound and keep it off. Why? Why was it so hard?

Kim left a few photos for me to keep. I hugged her and said thanks, but I wanted to burn every one of them. As though that would somehow solve the problem, that all at once I would never worry again about fitting into an airline seat or dread having my picture taken. I could be disciplined in my life—in college, nursing school, at work—but not when it came to my weight. I sank down next to our bed, the wedding photos scattered around me, and got on my knees. In desperation I prayed, *I just don't want to live like this anymore. I've got to do something. Help me, Lord!*

I signed up for the Weight Watchers program—again. I knew Weight Watchers well—my mom had used the plan for years. I had never lasted very long in the program. But if I was serious, I needed a system, some structure. I knew I needed the support of a group.

I practically crept into that first meeting. There were women there in all shapes and sizes. Some were plus size, others were so slim they could have just come from the gym. "All I really need," I overheard one woman say, "is to lose ten pounds." Ten pounds! No one would even notice if I dropped ten pounds.

The moment I really dreaded was the weigh-in. I was glad to get tips on healthy eating and to learn the system of figuring out what you could eat by counting points—that was all good—but I hated walking to the back of the room and getting on the scale. I was sure everyone was watching me. Only two of us would see what the scale said, but I could imagine it screaming out the number for all to hear: "282! 282!"

I didn't dare tell anyone that I was going to a weight-loss program. If I failed—and I always failed—I didn't want anyone to know. Better to keep it a secret. Then keeping it a secret had its own pitfalls. One day at work, a colleague celebrated her birthday with a sheet cake in the conference room. "Here," she said, handing me a jumbo slice, "take a piece with a rose. I know you love that." I barely managed to smile and shake my head. The food points on that one slab of cake alone would be more than I could afford to have all day. My heart raced and I practically ran out of the room.

George, of course, knew I was dieting. "I'll help you," he said. Because he gets home before me, he often makes dinner for the two of us. "Show me how to count points," he insisted. So I taught him how the Weight Watchers system worked. One afternoon I was fighting a ferocious battle against surrendering to a sugary snack. Just then George called. "Honey, how many points do you have left today?" His telephone call got me back on track.

Still, I wondered if I was going to make it, even as the weight came off, one slow pound at a time. Doubt was my biggest enemy. I never felt this way when I was going to college or getting my nursing degree. Then again, I'd never faced such a daunting goal before. I wanted to get down to 155 pounds if I was ever going to look at myself in the mirror again or be in someone's wedding photos.

I remember one meeting—I'd been so good all week, eating George's perfectly calibrated meals, never sneaking or snacking— and at weigh-in I expected to be rewarded with a good number. At least a few pounds. I looked at the scale. Something was wrong! The woman shook her head slightly. She wrote down the number. I'd gained four pounds that week! How? I was devastated. I couldn't even stay through the rest of the meeting. I picked up my purse and drove straight home, crying the whole way.

I knew that fluctuation was a very normal part of weight loss. At the time, though, it threw me into crisis. It made me wonder how my husband could stand it, how he had tolerated my weight and my unhappiness about it for all these years. What did he see in me? Why did he still love me? I felt so unlovable! This is the hardest thing you have ever done, Jane, I told myself, harder even than earning a nursing degree or learning how to be a good manager. All those achievements had been external things. This, I now knew, was something deep inside of me. Something that I had to face.

That next morning I got up early, leaving my husband still in bed, and went into the kitchen to read my Bible and think and pray. In the quiet of the morning, with the sun just coming up over the trees outside, I thought of George and all of his love and support. He didn't see me the way the wedding pictures showed me. He loved me as I was, yes, but also for all the potential he saw in me, all the good he'd always encouraged in me. Listening to the birds out-side and seeing the sun glinting off the trees, I realized that's just the way God sees me too. His love is without conditions, as mine is for him. A voice seemed to whisper in the morning stillness, *With me you can do all things. My love makes anything possible.*

It was a turning point, the turning point. I made God a real partner in my weight loss. I woke up early in the morning and asked for His help. I went on long walks outside—I'd never been one for much exercise in the past—and kept up the prayers. In all my efforts in the past, I felt so alone. Not now. I'd shared my secret. For the first time I could feel how much God wanted me to succeed. The weigh-ins, what people thought, none of it mattered much anymore. What mattered was that losing weight was bringing me close to God, and that felt better than any success I had ever experienced.

In just four years—four amazing years—I reached my goal. I was down to 155 pounds! I felt great and was ready to celebrate. But I wanted to see if I could lose a little bit more. I kept up my exercise, the prayers and the meetings. In six months I went down another twenty-three pounds! For the first time in my life I was wearing a size-four dress. Size four! It seemed almost impossible. And I've been able to keep that weight off—150 pounds gone for good.

I am happier, healthier, I'll live longer and have more years with George and my children. Yes, I am thinner. But it's not just about being thin, at least not for me. It's about being a whole person, the complete person God wants me to be, wants you to be. He is here to help us. It is the one thing I will never doubt.

Peace Process

by Jim Hinch

The day I met the women of the Faith Club, I sat in my kitchen and read the newspaper over breakfast. The headlines were sadly familiar. Fifteen bystanders killed in Iraq. Attacks and counter-attacks in Palestine. The one-year anniversary of subway bombings in London. I looked out the window. It was a brilliant summer morning in New York City, where my wife and I were expecting the birth of our first child a few months later. Outside, the air hummed with street noise—honks, squeals, a medley of languages. I listened and thought about the baby. *What kind of world will greet it?* I wondered. *A world like my city, where people of all backgrounds live and strive together? Or one like the headlines, consumed by sectarian strife?* I noticed a front-page photograph: Israeli armored personnel carriers streaming into the Gaza Strip. Jews, Muslims, Christians—the fighting seemed never ending. Where was the hope?

I stuffed a pen and notebook in my shoulder bag and boarded a crosstown bus to an elegant apartment building on New York's Upper East Side. A doorman escorted me to an elevator, which stopped at the second floor. I knocked at apartment 2A. Voices burbled inside, the door opened and there stood three women in dressy clothes, smiling nervously. One was blonde, with a vaguely patrician air. Another wore a halo of generous curls. The third, who introduced herself as Ranya Idliby, had long, straight, light brown hair and a gentle handshake. "Welcome to the Faith Club," she said. "Can I get you some coffee?"

I took a seat beside a table arranged with a plate of wafer-thin cookies and a vase of pink and orange roses. Ranya introduced her friends, Suzanne Oliver and Priscilla Warner—members of the Faith Club, a religious discussion group the three women had founded after September 11, 2001, when many Americans were asking urgent questions about faith. I had come to Ranya's apartment to write a story about the club, a seemingly straightforward assignment. But, as Ranya served me coffee in a polka-dotted cup and saucer before settling herself beside her friends on a pair of small sofas, I wondered exactly how to proceed. Ranya was a Muslim, the daughter of Palestinian parents who, as children, had fled their homes near the Sea of Galilee and Jerusalem when the nation of Israel was founded. Priscilla was Jewish, a native New Englander who had lived in New York for decades. Suzanne, the blonde woman, was a lifelong Christian, raised in Kansas City. If the headlines I had read that morning were any guide, these women shouldn't even have been in the same room, much less best friends. But there they were, chatting and laughing as if their faiths had never disagreed. *What exactly was going on here?* I wondered. *How had these three women achieved what the rest of the world could only wish for?* I asked them that, and they replied with a laugh that they hadn't always been so friendly. When they first met, they had been living in what Priscilla called their "comfort zones," embracing mostly stereotypes about each other's faith and the assumption that a discussion group would be like a college class—informative, maybe, but hardly life-changing. They certainly hadn't expected to become friends. In fact, they wouldn't have met at all if it hadn't been for the people who often bring women together—their children.

After September 11, Ranya's daughter Leia, the only Muslim in her kindergarten class, began coming home with awkward questions about religion—such as what Muslims should celebrate at Christmas. At the same time, Suzanne, whose daughter Anne was Leia's classmate, was asking questions of her own. Neither woman had answers. To her embarrassment, Suzanne realized she knew next to nothing about Judaism and even less about Islam. Ranya, raised a Muslim, wondered whether she even fit her faith anymore. She had graduated from Georgetown University in Washington, DC, with a degree in international politics and, long before moving to New York with her husband Sami, a businessman, had given up trying to juggle modern American life with regular Muslim worship. Now, though, pressed by Leia, Ranya began a frantic search for information about her faith. To her surprise, she discovered that, although Muslims, Christians and Jews appear to be intractably at war, they all worship the same God, the God of the Old Testament. Muslims even believe that Mohammed, in a vision, had stood at the Temple Mount in Jerusalem, praying with Jesus and Moses. Elated, Ranya decided to try to put together a short children's book about commonalities between Christianity, Judaism and Islam— something to answer Leia's questions and help other children learn about their faiths. One day, at the school bus stop, Ranya casually mentioned the book project to Suzanne, who jumped at the idea. A mutual acquaintance suggested the two women get in touch with Priscilla, a writer of children's books, who lives with her husband

and two sons in a suburb north of New York. A few weeks later, all three sat on a gray velour sofa in Ranya's light-filled living room, drinking jasmine tea and admiring the view of a ninety-four-year-old Catholic church with stained glass windows across the street.

The room was cozy, but the initial meetings quickly grew contentious. Priscilla blurted to Suzanne that Jews sometimes suspect Christians of being anti-Semitic, blaming Jews for Jesus' death. Ranya told Priscilla that many Muslims think Jews use the Holocaust to justify Israel's territorial expansion. Suzanne and Priscilla confessed to Ranya that they had long held stereotypes about Muslims as oil-rich potentates, terrorists and fanatical oppressors of women. "Right off the bat, it was much more complicated than I had assumed," said Suzanne.

When conversation swerved to Israeli-Palestinian relations, Ranya and Priscilla struck up a heated argument. "We raised our voices, interrupted each other," Ranya said. "I was saying, 'You think this!' She was saying, 'You think that!' We stopped eating. It was very serious." Suzanne tried to mediate, but the other two told her to butt out. When it was time to go, they walked out of Suzanne's apartment, where they had met that day, into a gloomy rain, and continued arguing all the way to Ranya's, several blocks away. They stood outside the door for a time and then looked at each other. They were soaked, their hair plastered to their faces. "We can't part angry," Ranya said at last. "Do you want to come inside for some tea?" They went upstairs, dried off and calmed down.

I interrupted this story. "Wait, what on earth prompted you to patch things up like that? Did you come to an agreement about the issues?"

No, the women said. That was the secret of their group. When they started, they promised always to give honest answers and never to shy away from difficult topics. Their resulting differences strengthened both their friendship and their faith. "What kept me coming back was a search for truth," said Suzanne. "I wanted to understand them in their faiths and resolve their truths with mine." As each woman learned about the others' beliefs, she came to understand her own better. And the straight talk helped everyone feel comfortable when asking difficult questions—about good and evil, God's presence in pain and the right way to live in a world full of conflict.

Priscilla, who had begun the meetings skeptical about religion, was inspired by Suzanne to pray regularly and develop a personal relationship with God. Ranya, who struggled to reconcile her faith with television images of extremists, grew more confident in believing that the God of Islam is a God of peace and mercy. And Suzanne, after learning the common origins of Christianity, Judaism and Islam, realized that all three are founded on the same idea: "Love God with all your heart and mind."

Of course, more than talk brought the women together. They cooked for each other—Ranya's chickpea salad with sesame paste and pine nuts, Suzanne's jasmine green tea, and Priscilla's constant supply of gourmet cookies. Suzanne often came to meetings with her toddler Teddy, who made everyone laugh by shimmying beneath the coffee table and dragging out Ranya's son Taymor's Spider Man toys. Priscilla's sister was diagnosed with breast cancer and Suzanne shared her own grief at the sudden death of her sister four years before. Priscilla invited Suzanne and Ranya to a Yom Kippur service and defended Ranya when a man at a post-service dinner confronted Ranya with questions about the Palestinians.

The children's book did get written about nine months after the women's first meeting. But it never found a publisher. By that point, though, the three women didn't care. "This is now my family in this city," said Ranya, laying a hand on Priscilla's.

"I can't think of anything I wouldn't share with them," said Suzanne.

"I've had dear friends for forty years," said Priscilla. "But I know these women in a completely different way."

These days, the women seldom argue. Their main focus is on helping others do what they did. They wrote a book about the formation of the Faith Club, which did get published. And they promote it—along with the basic idea of meeting and befriending people of other faiths—with missionary zeal. "When the other is a real person, you learn to appreciate them," said Suzanne, pointing to a verse in Acts: "Truly I perceive that God shows no partiality, but in every nation, anyone who fears him and does what is right is acceptable to him."

Ranya mentioned a similar verse in the Koran that states: "Those who believe, the Jews, the Christians, any who believe in God and the Last Day, and work righteousness shall have their reward with the Lord."

Priscilla said that before she met Ranya and Suzanne, she had found faith difficult to talk about—in more than two decades of marriage, she could remember only a single conversation with her husband about God, lasting all of three minutes. Now, she even talks to her sons about the Faith Club. "We've been to a sacred place I haven't been with anyone else," she said.

I wanted to stay and hear more, but the day was wearing on. I finally got up to go, and Ranya gave me a box of Middle Eastern candy to take home to my wife, who happens to love Turkish Delight. I shook hands with the three women, rode the elevator down to the lobby and walked out into a sunny New York afternoon. I boarded the crosstown bus and thought again of my unborn child, who, one day, would come home asking me knotty questions about faith. The headlines, of course, would always be there, new and tragic every day. But so would the Faith Club, three firm voices in a world of conflict. I settled the candy box on my lap and looked out the window. The city rolled by—noisy, diverse and completely at ease.

CHAPTER

7

Second Chances

A Love for the Land

by Larry Lewis

Once I had loved farming, but now I was ready to quit. I was forty-six, raising about six hundred acres of corn, soybeans and hay—and I was dead tired. It was the same treadmill most farmers are on. Pay thousands of dollars for seeds, chemical fertilizers and pesticides. Work till you drop. Come home smelling like a house tented for termites. Then watch as weather or a bottoming commodities market washes it all away. "Get bigger or get out," the agribusiness companies said. I didn't have the money to get bigger. And I didn't know what to do if I got out.

Farming was in my blood. My dad had farmed before he became a postman, and my grandfather and uncles owned small dairies near our house in southwestern New York. From the time I was old enough to handle a pitchfork, I was out baling hay, tending cows and driving a tractor. In high school I practically lived on my grandfather's farm. He had heart trouble and needed help with his four hundred acres. The farm was beautiful—a few neat fields and a wide expanse of rolling green pasture. High Up, my grandfather called it. I'd wake early and listen to the farm stirring. My grandfather would already be weeding the garden before we went to milk the cows. He farmed the old-fashioned way—hard work and common sense. No fancy technology for him. Just love of the land and an honest, flinty, Depression-era determination to be self-sufficient.

I was determined too—to live just like him. I majored in agriculture in college and gradually built up my own farm near the small town of Penn Yan, in New York's Finger Lakes region. I worked hard and raised my boys to farm too. But, by the mid-1990s, I was beginning to wonder if I'd made the right choice. My barns weren't full of the simple tools my grandfather had used. They were stacked with artificial fertilizers so potent they literally burned the soil away. After planting, I spent most of my time spraying pesticides. The companies that sold the chemicals assured farmers they were safe. But a few years before, my neighbor Klaas Martens, who farmed fourteen hundred acres of corn, soy and red kidney beans, had lost all movement in his right arm after a blocked nozzle exposed him to a big dose of pesticide. To top it all off, grain markets seesawed every year. My boys and I could go heavily into debt buying equipment and chemicals, work our tails off—and still lose money. One day, talking to Klaas, I confessed I was near despair. "Farming is all I've ever done," I said. "But it's killing me. I feel stuck."

"Well," he said slowly, "you could always go organic." I laughed. After Klaas's pesticide accident, he and his wife, Mary-Howell, had gradually weaned themselves off chemicals and begun selling their grain to organic dairies. Every chance he got, Klaas preached the virtues of organic farming. He and Mary-Howell were no hippies—they went to church and planned to enroll their kids in Future Farmers of America. And I had to admit, their fields didn't look half bad. But—organic? It sounded like farming on the fringe to me. "Try a few acres," Klaas said. "What can it hurt? Think of it as . . . old-fashioned."

My ears pricked up at those last words, and I agreed to give it a try. I started with thirty acres of red kidney beans, which had done well for Klaas and Mary-Howell. I tilled the soil, planted the seeds—and watched with alarm as, almost immediately, weeds began thrusting up. Ragweed, pig weed, velvet leaf—the field was carpeted with tenacious invaders, all leaching nutrients from the soil and robbing seedlings of sunlight. I panicked and thought about the pesticide in the barn.

"Don't worry," Klaas said. "Weeds are inevitable. You're not going to have those perfect-looking fields you get with chemicals. Run a cultivator to cut some down, and when the beans start coming up, they'll shade the soil and out-compete the weeds. You have to keep on top of it and check the field constantly. But trust me, it'll work." Run the cultivator. Check the fields. This was a lot more involved than spraying some chemicals and waiting for harvest. Klaas told me I needed to prime the soil too. Artificial fertilizer kills off most of what makes soil naturally good for plants—worms, composting vegetable matter—and replaces it with synthetic nitrogen and other nutrients. Plants get what they need, but the soil goes dead, to the point that, after a while, nothing will grow in it without more chemicals. Klaas told me I could add ground-up limestone and gypsum to get the balance of acidity and calcium right, and rotate crops to give the soil in each field a chance to rest and recharge. "You'll get worms going in there pretty soon," he said. "Then you'll have soil plants love." *Hmm*, I thought. *Old-fashioned is right. What a lot of work!*

Neighbors came by and saw the weeds sprouting amid the kidney beans. Farmers are sensitive about the look of their fields the way some women are sensitive about their figures. "Are those kidney beans I see in your ragweed field?" they joked. Embarrassed, I mumbled something about worms and life-cycles.

Then the beans came in. They were beautiful. And the price!

Organic produce, I discovered, can fetch more than twice as much as conventional crops. "I'm going organic," I told Klaas. It wasn't just the money. It was the satisfaction that came with having produced a crop naturally, the old-fashioned way. Maybe this was how God wanted His land to be cultivated.

The next year I kept my same crop mixture—corn, winter wheat, soy beans and various kinds of hay—but planted each without pesticides or artificial fertilizers. The work was intense and nonstop. Grain planting in April. Corn and soy in May. Harvesting grain and winter wheat in summer. Then the hay harvest, followed by corn and soy. Not till November, when I planted the following year's winter wheat, could I rest. There wasn't rest for my mind, either. With chemicals, the year is more or less predictable—except for weather. You plant, spray, harvest. Organic farming requires vigilance and perfect timing. Some grains are planted early to shelter later grains from weeds. Fields must be repeatedly cultivated. I couldn't even use poison to kill the rats that fed on my seed supply; I had to trust my cats.

Driving home one late summer evening, watching the sun slide below the lip of a valley, I realized I was exhausted. I had been up since five that morning, doing a little bit of everything. Dragged the cultivator through fields on my thirty-year-old Ford 5000 tractor. Weeded. Tested corn by biting kernels to see if they were dry enough to harvest. I could have complained. But as I passed a clover field bathed in rich golden light, I realized I was happier than I had been for years. Yes, I was worn-out—but worn-out the way I had been after a long day on my grandfather's farm. The clover field appeared in the rearview mirror, and I thought, *My fields don't smell like spray anymore. They're lovely.*

Three years later, my farm was officially certified organic. I practically had to turn customers away. Organic dairies were springing up around New York, and they all needed grain to feed their cows. Around that time, Klaas and Mary-Howell bought an old mill in Penn Yan and began grinding organic grain. Customers came calling from New York, Pennsylvania and Ohio. It seemed farmers couldn't grow fast enough and the Martens couldn't grind fast enough to keep up with demand.

It used to be every transaction with a customer, especially the big agribusiness companies, was merciless bargaining. Now I was working with friends, people I saw in town whose kids I knew. They were fair, and it was Mary-Howell saying hello when I called the mill. In the winter, when fields were dormant, she and Klaas invited organic farmers in the area to meet once a month to trade advice and help newcomers. The gnawing need to get bigger, the insecurity and competitiveness of my old farming life was all gone.

Not long ago, I was talking to one of my neighbors, a Mennonite farmer named Eddie Horst who milks forty-eight cows and grows the organic grain to feed them on fields down the road. Eddie's wife and eight kids all work on their farm, too, and the day I visited, he and one of his older boys were repairing a barn. They put down their hammers, and we talked for a while about how, in many places, kids are leaving farms, seeking a life that's not all dead-ends. "Not here," said Eddie, who even puts his littlest ones to work gathering eggs.

"Mine too," I said. My youngest son, Matthew, who's twenty-six, farms with me and will probably take over when I retire. I thought back to 1996, when I was ready to quit—how I'd laughed at Klaas's organic proselytizing. In some ways, I guess I have ended up on the fringe—less than one half of one percent of all US farmland is organic. But if that's the fringe, I like it. It's farming the way I remember. Season to season. Father to son. And, best of all for me, grandfather to grandson.

The Talking Cure

by Cheri Fuller

My husband Holmes stood at the kitchen door. "I think I might have found a job," he said.

I looked up from the dishwasher. The news was wonderful, and wonderfully unexpected. But something in Holmes's voice gave me pause. He sounded tentative. "It's in Dallas," he concluded. "Temporary architectural consultant for a construction company. I just got off the phone and I think they're going to make me an offer."

I stared at him. "Dallas?" He nodded. My spirits fell.

Holmes desperately needed work. His last construction project had ended a month and a half before, taking the bulk of our income with it. But, Dallas? That was more than two-hundred miles away! A four-hour commute. And the job was temporary, so there was no point in picking up and moving.

Holmes muttered something about the pay being good and then retreated to the family room.

I sighed. He was the strong, silent type, not given to sharing his feelings. I knew his difficulty finding work depressed him no end. But how I wished we could talk! Not disappear behind books and magazines or glued to the TV.

I finished loading the dishwasher and walked to the family room. Holmes was in his chair, reading. I curled up on the sofa with my laptop. My mind burst with questions about the job, about what Holmes was thinking. But I knew there was no point in asking. Either our conversation would stall or we would end up arguing about our money worries.

We sat, silent, while the clock ticked. It was an all-too-familiar scenario, almost as if we had grown afraid of talking, as if any conversation would lead us back to that dreaded subject, our finances. No, better not to talk. Finally we got up to go to bed. "Goodnight," we mumbled into our pillows.

The next morning, after doing my devotions on the sunporch, I found Holmes brushing his teeth. "Maybe my sister and brother-in-law would let you stay with them," I ventured. Much of my family still lived in Dallas, where I had grown up. "You could come home on weekends."

Holmes nodded. Minutes later he returned from a quick phone call. "I start Monday," he said.

Monday morning Holmes hoisted a suitcase into the trunk and backed down the driveway. I waved until I couldn't see the car; then I went back inside. Closing the door, I realized with a stab of guilt that I wasn't all that sorry to see him go. It wasn't like his departure changed much. The house was just as silent with him there. We never went out. The days when he'd come home with yellow roses "just because" were long gone.

I kept busy. I did some writing on my computer, e-mailed some girlfriends, took a walk and then stretched out on the sofa with a novel. That afternoon our daughter, who lived down the block, came over with her kids. The house felt lighter without the tension between Holmes and me. But I was restless. It hadn't always been like this.

I couldn't stop thinking about better days in our relationship. How cared for I'd felt on our first date at Baylor University when Holmes held the car door open and then gently took my elbow walking into the old Beacon Theater in Waco. We'd shared a bucket of popcorn. When the last few kernels were left, our fingers brushed and my face flushed. Moments later, Holmes reached over and cradled my hand in his.

I remembered raising our three children together. Holmes getting started in the building industry. We'd had our share of financial ups and downs over the years. But nothing like this. Somehow our marriage seemed to be suffering more this time around.

Once, when we were living in Maine and the housing market had stalled out, Holmes ended up taking a night shift at a printing plant. I worked as a substitute teacher and we squeaked by on savings. Still, we'd had good family times. Our schedules let us spend days with the kids picnicking, bicycle riding, taking trips to the beach. Maybe that was it. With the kids grown and gone, there was no longer a buffer between us. Maybe we were experiencing some fundamental flaw in our relationship. Something we'd never acknowledged before.

The next morning I sat on the sunporch with my Bible. I came across a passage in Romans: "Love one another with genuine affection, and delight and honor one another." The simple words went straight to my heart. Affection. Delight. Where had it all gone? *Lord, help us love each other like that again.*

That night Holmes called to check in. Maybe it was because he was on the phone, not sitting in his chair, but he actually talked. "Job seems pretty good," he said. "I'm getting to work on houses." I told him about my day. He filled me in on the latest news from my sister's house. "I better go," he finally said. "Got to get up early tomorrow." He paused. "I miss you, Cheri."

I caught my breath. "I—I miss you too," I stammered. We hung up.

The next day I puttered around the house, strangely eager for Holmes's phone call. When the phone rang, I jumped for it. We talked even longer that time. And not about money for once. This time I didn't hesitate telling Holmes I missed him. He answered right back.

Friday arrived. Holmes would be home that evening. I turned on my computer after lunch to check my e-mail. I about fell over. There in my inbox was a message from my husband, who almost never used computers. "I'm learning e-mail for the job," he wrote. "Can't wait to see you tonight. Love you, H."

I stared at that e-mail. What was going on here? I believed in answers to prayer, but this was uncanny. Something was different. Something had changed in our relationship without my realizing. Was it the distance? Was that why I felt almost giddy contemplating Holmes's return that evening? I could hardly work the rest of the afternoon. Finally, I abandoned the computer and got started on dinner. I made Holmes's favorite—meat loaf and mashed potatoes. While the meat loaf baked, I shook out a tablecloth and lit a scented candle. I went to our bedroom to change. I chose a green sweater I knew Holmes liked. Then I went to the window and watched for his car.

He pulled into the driveway. I glanced in the mirror, ran my fingers through my hair and threw open the door. There he was. With a bouquet of yellow roses.

I hugged him—when had I last done that?—and practically skipped into the dining room. We ate, talking the whole time. Holmes's job wasn't so different from some of the other projects he had worked on, but he now had a week's worth of news about it. He wanted to hear about my days too. Somehow, we found all kinds of things to discuss that we hadn't talked about on the phone.

Holmes came to the end of something he was saying. We were silent a moment. I gazed at him across the table, admiring his kind, thoughtful face in the candlelight. All at once it struck me. The missing ingredient in our relationship this past week was money. Our separation after all these years together pushed even that worry aside, as if a light had been shone on what was truly important about our marriage.

Holmes's going to Dallas had exposed a flaw in our relationship. Left to our own devices, rattling around the house together, all Holmes and I had been thinking about and arguing about and stressing about was our shaky finances. It took a break in that routine—a break from that all-consuming fear and worry—to bring the rest of our marriage, all that was good and godly in it, into focus.

I reached over and took Holmes's hand. Genuine affection. It felt wonderful.

Our money troubles didn't evaporate overnight, but we finally learned to discuss them in a way that didn't drive us apart. Besides, you'd be surprised what a good—and inexpensive—time you can have eating breakfast together on your porch, watching the cardinals and finches alight on the bird feeder. Or browsing in the bookstore at the mall and later sipping coffee in a café.

Or, my favorite, catching a matinee. That's what we did that weekend. We drove to the multiplex, sorted through myriad options—so different from the little Beacon Theater back in Waco!—and bought tickets. Settling into our seats, I reached for some popcorn. Holmes's hand brushed mine. I glanced at him, feeling my heart quicken. Holmes glanced back at me, smiling. The movie started and we leaned in close. We were still holding hands when the lights came up.

Faith Factor

by Robin Hinch

Nearly four years after joining Episcopal Church of the Messiah in downtown Santa Ana, California, I felt almost like a full-fledged member—emphasis on almost. I attended every Sunday, happily settling into the all-redwood sanctuary built more than a century before. I baked and brought food for coffee hour, hosted small group dinners and went to classes. I drove elderly members on errands and served as clerk to the vestry.

The only thing I didn't do? Believe in God. Well, I sort of believed in God. I wanted to believe in God. But I wasn't exactly sure what I believed. About a lot of things. Including myself.

For years, I'd been my ailing husband's caregiver. When he died, I wasn't sure who I was anymore. But I would soon find out. When I'd stumbled upon Messiah while writing a story for the *Orange County Register*, where I was a reporter, I'd been a devout skeptic. Something about the church had moved me, though, especially the rector, Father Brad. He was conducting a memorial service for a homeless woman. He'd opened the church to all the woman's friends, most homeless themselves. He made a point of hugging and talking to each one. It made an impression on me.

I began attending, and in the years that followed, my life changed almost unimaginably. Overweight since childhood, I had surgery and lost 210 pounds. My husband, severely disabled by a stroke, died, ending decades of caregiving. I neared retirement age. My older son got married, moved to New York and had a baby. My younger son graduated from college and launched his career.

You'd think such changes would have strengthened whatever spark of faith drew me to Messiah. And they did—to a degree. Still, as I neared my four-year anniversary at the church, I remained unsure about myself and my beliefs. All my life I'd been defined by need. My husband needed care, so I cared for him. My boys needed me. I needed to make people accept me, an overweight woman, so I bent and contorted myself whichever way they wanted. Robin the Rescuer, I called myself, always there to do whatever people needed, whatever would make them glad to have me around. I wondered—just why was I at Messiah? Because I believed in God? Or because all those church activities gave me a dose of acceptance, something to do, someone to be? Was it Robin the Believer baking muffins for coffee hour or Robin the Rescuer?

One Sunday I fell into conversation at coffee hour with a woman named Peggy. I didn't know Peggy well. She was quiet and low-key, about twenty years younger than I. She happened to mention what she'd be doing the following weekend: skydiving, jumping out of a plane at 12,500 feet.

I practically spat out my coffee. "Peggy! You—you skydive?" I took a closer look at her. Nothing, not her understated clothes, her slender frame, said adventure woman.

She nodded. "Every weekend. I love it. It means so much to me. Have you ever thought about it?"

Again I choked. "Oh no. Not me." One thing in my life had most emphatically not changed: my mortal dread of heights. Even as a child I wouldn't let my own father twirl me by the arms—what my grand-daughter calls "doing dizzy." I cowered at stepladders. Skydiving! That would be the day.

A few weeks later Peggy invited me to a party. I was still trying to reconcile the thought of her skydiving when, walking into her house, I found myself in a room full of divers—all Peggy's friends. Peggy, I learned, owned her own parachute, knew how to pack it and was learning to jump in formation.

"Robin, you've got to try it," one of her friends said. Again I laughed. "No, I mean it," he insisted. "Everyone says they're afraid of heights. The minute you're out of the plane you forget all that. Why do you think we do this every weekend? It's like nothing you've ever experienced. It is a total sense of freedom." His tone was almost reverential.

I talked to more people. They all said the same thing, in the same awed voice. I assured each one of them I would never, ever jump out of an airplane. But I couldn't help noticing—I was the one asking questions, wanting to know more. I caught myself. *Robin, you are in your sixties. A few years ago you were too overweight to walk around the block. You're terrified of heights. You are not going skydiving.*

The following Sunday I buttonholed Peggy at coffee hour. "Why do you skydive? Your friends—the way they talked, they were starting to persuade me!"

Peggy smiled, then paused, as if searching for the right words. "Well, I'll be honest. The first time I jumped, I was scared too—until I went out the door. Then it was this incredibly spiritual, moving experience. I felt like God was there with me and I could see all of his beautiful creation. It was a gift."

She stopped, and I realized I was tuning out everything else in the room.

"The airfield's only an hour and a half away," Peggy continued. "You can come anytime and just watch. I have a video I can send. I definitely don't want to pressure you."

Weeks went by. I retired from the newspaper and suddenly had a lot of time on my hands. Skydiving began cropping up more and more in my conversation—much to the horror of my friends and family. "Mom!" my older son Jim exclaimed one day on the phone from New York. "You hate heights! You want to jump out of an airplane and break your leg and wreck this good life you've got now? Listen, if you're serious about this, tell me. I will fly out there and talk you out of it. I mean it." I heard him. But what I found myself thinking was, I'll call him after I jump.

Peggy's video came. Watching it, I peered closely at the airplane. It looked like an airplane. Nothing too scary. One by one the divers tipped out of the hatch. So quick! *You'd hardly notice,* I thought. Then they were in the air, jumpsuits whipping in the wind. I looked up, out the window. It was a warm, dry southern California morning. Perfect skydiving weather. I went to find my car keys.

The airfield was in Riverside County, surrounded by patches of farmland and subdivisions. A propeller plane with shark's teeth painted on the nose ferried divers up and then returned to the runway for more. This being a weekday, Peggy wasn't there. I watched divers glide in for a landing. At first just tiny pinpricks in the sky, they slowly descended until I could see their limbs, the colorful chutes. Gently, without fuss, they stuck their legs out and skidded to a halt on a strip of grass. Several immediately repacked their chutes for another dive.

Not quite deciding anything, I went into the office and signed some papers. I was given a jumpsuit and watched an instructional video. A young man shook my hand. "I'm Adi Blair. I'll be your dive partner." Dive partner?! Novice divers go tandem, strapped to an experienced instructor who knows when to open the chute. Half buoyant, half dazed, I followed Adi across the tarmac to the airplane. The propellers roared. We clambered in and sat on benches running down either side of the hull. The propellers roared louder and the plane trundled down the runway. I barely noticed taking off, I was so busy chatting with other divers.

The plane rose to cruising altitude. I chanced a look out the open hatch—and that's when it hit me, like a smack. *I'm 12,500 feet in the air.* The earth, far below, looked unreal, like a toy. I was about to jump out there! My entire body seized with panic. I looked frantically to Adi. "I can't do this!"

Calmly, he edged us toward the hatch. "Yes, you can."

"No! You don't understand! I can't do this!" I began praying—hard. We were beside the hatch. "No!" I screamed.

"Would you mind bending to one knee?" Adi asked. Blindly, I did. Adi made a slight motion with his body—and we were out, free falling. I felt wind rush against me—but it wasn't wind, just air roaring past at 120 miles an hour. I opened my eyes.

Everything was changed. The world spread before us, fields, highways, hills, shading to southern California haze. The air—it was all around us. We were in it. Of it. Just like Peggy said. I felt something build in my heart—not fear; that had vanished in an instant. No, it was plainer than that. With the solidity of irrevocable fact, I knew that I was in the presence of God. Not some God conjured out of my own need. Just God, maker of the sky and everything else, holding me in his hands.

Adi pulled the chute and we jerked upright. The wind ceased and we floated in serene silence. I basked in it. I, Robin Hinch, terrified of heights, once terribly obese, had jumped out of an airplane.

Five minutes later we came in for a landing. I actually botched that part and ended up plowing ignominiously into the grass. But I got up smiling like all the other divers. Maybe more than the other divers. Did I believe in God? In this new life he'd given me, this new person I'd become? In the silence of 12,500 feet I had heard my answer.

Out of the Fire

by Andrew Carroll

The call came just a few days before Christmas in 1989 while I was cramming for my midterm exams at Columbia University in New York City. It was my dad phoning from Washington, DC. There had been a fire, he'd said. No one was hurt, but our house was destroyed.

Not until I returned home a few days later and saw the damage firsthand did the enormity of the loss sink in. Everything was gone: books, clothes, stereo equipment, high school yearbooks, family photos, my grandfather's silver watch and, worst of all, the personal letters I had been saving in the back of my closet.

None of the letters were war-related or written by famous individuals, but they were of great sentimental value to me. The only historically significant letters I had were from a close friend who had been living in China during the student uprising at Tiananmen Square. His descriptions of what it felt like to be in Beijing—the young people defying the tanks, the short-lived euphoria—were an irreplaceable piece of history. Now they were literally up in smoke.

After the fire, I began talking with other people about their letters and asked if they had favorites. A dear friend of mine, Anne

Tramer, mentioned some letters her grandfather Erwin Blonder had mailed home during World War II. Erwin had fought in the Vosges Mountains in France with the 141st Infantry and served in an especially dangerous position. "Don't tell Mom or Shirley," he wrote in a candid letter from a foxhole to his brother and father, "but they've made me a forward observer."

"And you know what?" Erwin later recalled. "My dad kept that secret to his grave. No one ever found out about my wartime job until I read that letter out loud to my wife Shirley at our fiftieth wedding anniversary.

"Grandpa never talked about the war," Anne told me. "We never knew that side of him until he read that letter." *We never knew that side. . .* These words sparked my desire to seek out more letters. I began scouring flea markets and yard sales. I spoke with antique dealers. I also talked to veterans and active-duty troops, who told me about how important mail was to their morale on the battlefront. They described letters they dreaded receiving (a "Dear John" message from a sweetheart) or the ones that were agonizing to write (condolence letters to the families of fallen comrades). I was shocked to learn, however, that many veterans were throwing their letters away.

In the fall of 1998, I wrote to "Dear Abby" and told her about my effort to collect and save these letters—the Legacy Project, I called it. She agreed to mention it in her column. I figured I'd get a couple dozen responses. Thousands was more like it. Day after day, they filled my post office box.

"Dear sir," began one note attached to a bundle of letters, "I am a widow, eighty-five years old, and my husband and only son have passed. My husband served in Patton's Third Army. There is no one I can give these letters to, so you may have them." Another woman sent me letters from her husband who now had Alzheimer's. He couldn't remember anything, but his memories were captured in what he had written as a young man in uniform. And they were as vivid as the day he had lived them, decades earlier.

While it was difficult to read about the harsh realities of war— the separation of loved ones, the brutality of combat, the loss of innocent life—I was inspired by letters filled with tremendous faith. "I went to church tonight," wrote Capt. Molton Shuler to his wife during the Korean War. "Let me paint you a picture of the 'church': a grassy hillside surrounded by mountains. And a rugged-looking chaplain—crew haircut and all—dressed in fatigues, standing by a podium with a red velvet cover and brass candelabra minus candles, all placed on a couple of ammo boxes." After describing the Mass itself, Shuler wrote, "Only a couple of times in my life before this evening have I felt God's presence in such a way."

Faith was also present on the battlefield. Lt. James R. Penton wrote to his mother about a nun he'd seen tending a small farm in France in 1944: "All morning long, as the whine of artillery kept the rest of us in our holes, that nun moved serenely about the skeleton of the burned-out barn, milking the swollen cows, feeding and watering the chickens, collecting eggs. . . . I know that our most argumentative and skeptical atheist was duly fascinated and impressed by that display of power and force of that sister's faith— and complete fearlessness."

Some of the correspondence is from more recent conflicts. Not long ago, I received a copy of a hand-written letter from twenty-four-year-old Sgt. Justin Merhoff, who was awaiting possible deployment to Iraq. He wrote to his grandfather Hugh Merhoff, a veteran of World War II: "Dear Gramps . . . you are the reason I am in the army today. You instilled in me the values that you learned during your service, and it has made me a better soldier. Most important, it has made me a better person."

To date, I've received more than eighty thousand letters from every war in American history. I had to rent a second apartment to hold them all. All of this correspondence is a tangible connection to our past and contains hard-earned wisdom about resilience, sacrifice, gratitude, integrity and courage. These letters have inspired me like nothing I've ever read.

When I think back on the fire, I realize that what seemed to be the worst moment of my life was actually a blessing. Even though I had lost everything when our house burned down, the experience ultimately gave me something much more important and enduring: It renewed my faith. And because of this, I know that no matter what battles I encounter in life, there is *always* reason for hope.

To learn more, visit www.graceunderfire.us or read my book *Grace Under Fire: Letters of Faith in Times of War.*

A Burden to Share

by Jan Bono

I grabbed the railing and hoisted myself up three steps to the community hall. Gasping for breath, I lumbered into a room where a dozen people sat in folding chairs. One was empty, but I figured it would collapse under my weight. "Have a seat here," said a large woman on the sofa along the wall. People moved over to make room for me. Plenty of room.

I was forty-five years old, five foot six—and weighed 396 pounds. The only clothes that fit me were size 60 blouses and voluminous elastic-waist pants. My shoes all had Velcro straps; I couldn't reach my feet to tie laces. I had recently bought a new full-size car because it was the only one whose steering wheel I could fit behind. I was miserable. Yet I couldn't admit it to anyone. I couldn't even talk about it.

The meeting started right on time. People introduced themselves and told why they were there, how many pounds they'd lost and what they'd eaten that week. Then it was my turn. I forced out the words. "I'm Sylvia," I said. "This is my first time at a support group. I don't really have anything else to say." My name wasn't Sylvia, but I was too ashamed to let anyone know who I really was. Besides, I was used to keeping secrets. I was always telling people that I was trying to lose weight. "It's not my fault that nothing works," I declared. What I wouldn't admit was that my life was devoted to eating on the sly.

As far back as I can remember I loved to sneak. Mom made big batches of chocolate-chip cookies for our family of six and stored them in bags in the freezer. I'd take a bunch and hide them in my room. Whatever was bothering me—however sad or bored I felt—gorging myself always helped, as if I could fill up a sense of emptiness inside. Even when I was a child, my eating was dishonest. Later in college, studying for exams, I'd devour my way through rolls of raw cookie dough. Or polish off a bag of chips and then start in on the candy bars I'd stashed in the back of my desk drawer. I hid food like an alcoholic hides booze. Marriage didn't help me cope any better with my problem. When I went through a painful divorce, my weight crept up . . . 200, 250, 300 pounds. Only food could fill the void.

I taught middle-school English and social studies, and I hated overhearing kids mutter "fatso" and "whale" behind my back. I slipped deeper into depression, which was worsened by failed diets and bouts of overeating. Finally, I started counseling sessions with a therapist in the spring of 1999. "Do you watch what you eat?" my counselor asked in our first session. "Yes," I said. Actually, I was watching it go into my mouth. I would stop in a restaurant for a meal, drive to the other side of town and have another meal—then head home and have a third. That way, I convinced myself, nobody would know just how much food I was really consuming.

"You need to talk to some people who struggle with overeating," my counselor suggested. "There's a group that meets every Saturday downtown."

"I'm not a joiner," I said. "I can change by myself." But the truth was, I refused to imagine my life any other way. I left the counselor and headed for a drive-thru where I picked up several value meals plus extra orders of fries. "For my co-workers," I lied to the boy who handed me the three bulging bags.

The next week my counselor laid it on the line. "I'm not going to see you anymore," she said, "unless you attend a group. And you've got to go to at least twelve meetings." That's why I was sitting on the sofa at the support group, feeling more uncomfortable by the minute.

"I've had some bad moments this week," the woman next to me announced, "but with God's help I managed to keep track of my calories and eat three sensible meals a day." God's help? I was sure God couldn't help me.

"I was feeling down," a man said, "but I realized overeating wouldn't change anything, not really. So I called a friend to go to a movie instead." But food did change things for me. It was my friend.

I clapped along with everyone else, but deep down inside I had a terrible feeling. Not me. These other people might be helped by all this "sharing." Maybe they were even losing weight. But me? I was a hopeless case. As soon as people realized my secret, they would turn away. Even these folks. Especially these folks, who certainly didn't need a loser like me dragging them down. And all this talk of God. What would God want with someone like me? I left the meeting and drove straight to the grocery store. On the way home I wedged a pint of Ben & Jerry's between my knees so I could eat as I drove.

"I went to the meeting," I told my counselor.

"Did you talk?" she asked.

"Sure," I said. I wasn't exactly lying, but I wasn't being honest either. All I'd promised was to attend twelve meetings. The weeks went by, and the most I ever said to the group on Saturday morning was "My name is Sylvia" and "I don't feel like talking today."

The eleventh Saturday approached. I was nearly home free. That Friday in school, I had lunch with the other teachers and made a production of having only half a turkey hero. "I'll eat the rest for lunch tomorrow," I announced, thrusting it back in its brown bag. Easier to finish it off between classes in my room when no one was looking. I headed down the hall for class, moving slowly through the student throng.

"*Moooo. . .*" came the taunt of some boys behind me. The sound seemed to echo in the hall. I pretended I hadn't heard. An image stormed through my mind of me sharing this ugly humiliation with my support group. I blotted it out; I could never talk about something like this, never bare my soul. I thought of the sandwich in my bag and how soon I could get to it.

Saturday morning the leader said, "Today we'll talk about hope." Hope? Vaguely I heard the others talking. Round the circle they went. Then it was my turn. Waves of despair I'd been suppressing for years surged up and nearly took my breath away. In a flash it all came pouring out.

"I don't have any hope," I began. "I can't even remember what hope feels like." I blinked frantically to keep back tears. *Go on*, a voice inside me said. *Go on.* Somehow I knew I needed to do this, to accept, acknowledge and feel the pain. I grabbed a tissue and continued. "I have no hope of ever being a normal size again. I have no hope at all. . . ." I was shaking. I started to sob so hard I couldn't say another word. I motioned for the next person to go ahead and take her turn.

The meeting ended. I dodged the hugs and headed to my car. I drove out in a spray of gravel. *I'm never going back. I've made a fool of myself. There is no hope for me. God, even if You are listening, You're wasting Your time.*

On the way to the grocery store I stopped at the post office to pick up my mail, a little surprised that anything would get between me and a meal. Among the bills and catalogs was a thick envelope from a friend I'd taught with but hadn't heard from in months. Inside was a pretty card on which my friend had written: "Here's something for you to hold on to." I pulled the tape off the small package she'd enclosed. A flat polished rock of white-and-purple marble dropped into my hand. Engraved on it was a single word: HOPE. I gripped it tightly in my hand. I drove home and put the rock in the center of my dining room table. I didn't want to eat at all, as if that tiny stone were a great rock that stood between me and my compulsion. It was Day One of my recovery.

The following Saturday I went back to the meeting. Number twelve. I wasn't ashamed to speak. I couldn't afford to be ashamed. "I'm determined to lose this weight," I said. "With God's help and your encouragement, I know I can do it." I had already begun planning. I would set up what worked for me. Only three meals a day, no snacking in between, yogurt instead of ice cream, hold the cheese and mayo and consume half the portion, maybe less. I couldn't exercise yet—I could barely even move—but foresaw the day when I would get up every morning for a brisk walk. "I can do it," I announced. "I'm not alone." I took a deep breath. What I'd said was scary, but I'd made my commitment out loud, and I wasn't backing down. "I have something else to tell you," I said. "My name's not Sylvia. My name is Jan. And I'm really glad to be here."

The Girl in the Poster

by Franco Barlettai

What would I have done without that advertisement? It seemed to stare back at me in almost every Tokyo subway car I squeezed into. A man and a woman in traditional Japanese clothing, posed somewhat stiffly against a lush, parklike backdrop. The man had thick blondish hair, and even though the woman wore a crimson kimono and an ornate headdress low over her soft features, she too was clearly Western. And beautiful, so beautiful, like a dream. What was the ad for? I couldn't understand the Japanese words, but it didn't matter. I was mesmerized by it.

I never settled in Japan the way I had in other far-flung places I'd lived in since I left my native Italy at the age of nineteen. Maybe you saw the Bill Murray movie *Lost in Translation*. I felt a lot like that. I'd never been so aware of my foreignness, so much so that I began to feel foreign to myself. It wasn't just the little cultural differences. (I'm a big guy, so I had to get used to bending way down to use the bathroom sink and ducking through doorways, for instance.) It was the feeling of being so alone, even in the teeming crowds of Tokyo. The situation had even put a strain on my marriage. This was supposed to have been an adventure. Now I longed for something familiar.

I was born in a mountain village in the soft, green heart of Tuscany. My parents ran a bakery, so naturally I learned to bake. But there were few opportunities in our little town, so I used my skills to get jobs at hotels and restaurants all around the world— England, Swaziland, the Bahamas. I had stayed in New York City the longest, fifteen years in all, working at some of the best Italian restaurants in Manhattan. In 1991, I was offered the job of chief pastry chef for a new Four Seasons Hotel in Tokyo. My son was grown and the opportunity seemed too good to pass up, so my wife and I moved to Japan.

I worked out of a kitchen on the fourth floor of the Four Seasons Tokyo at Chinzan-so hotel, facing a beautiful park with a five-tiered pagoda. I watched cherry blossoms carpet the ground in spring and runoff from autumn rains fall like gauzy curtains from the intricately carved eaves of the pagoda. Japan was truly lovely, but I felt homesick for America. My subway ride home from work was just four stops, but it could get so packed my feet barely touched the floor. Occasionally an exhausted businessman dozed off on my shoulder. I'd keep my eyes fixed straight ahead on that ad. I suppose it came to symbolize that familiar world I yearned for.

A trip to Florida to see my son play in a tennis tournament convinced me: It was time to come home to America. Florida seemed like a good place. I loved the beach and I wanted to settle down. So in 1993, we moved to Tampa and I opened a bakery like my parents had owned years before in Italy. But things didn't settle down. My marriage fell apart. I found myself living hand to mouth for the first time in years. I'd invested every penny I had into Delizie Italian Bakery. Each day, I set out rows of breads and cookies, cakes and pies. I stood at the door in my jelly-stained apron and handed out samples. Slowly, customers came. By December 1995, I'd hired three workers to help me in the shop and had dozens of holiday orders lined up.

Then in early December, for various personal reasons, all three of my employees left. I was in real trouble. I had to fill those orders, but there weren't enough hours in the day to bake and run the shop. One night I pulled a batch of my pine nut cookies out of the oven and glanced at the wall clock. Nearly midnight. I still had another twenty next-day orders to fill. I stared at the phone. *No, Franco, you must not cancel*, I told myself. I grabbed some dough and began hand-rolling a batch of my pencil-thin breadsticks. I couldn't keep this up by myself. The Help Wanted sign had been up in the window for two weeks and no one had come yet.

An elegant woman entered the shop the next day. "May I help you?" I asked, assuming she wanted to place an order. To my surprise, she responded in fluent Italian, like sweet music to my ears. Her name was Frances, she said, and a friend of hers who was one of my customers had told her I could use some help in the shop. I came out from behind the counter and shook her hand. "How is it you know Italian?" I asked.

"I lived there," she said, looking at me with her clear blue eyes, blue as the gulf waters off Tampa Bay. "I loved Italy." She smiled. And for a moment I couldn't take my eyes off her.

"Well, I'm happy you are here now. Can you start right away? Stay out front here while I am baking?" She went to work straightening the pastry display, organizing order forms and taking care of customers. We didn't say much. We didn't have to; she just seemed to know. We worked in a quiet rhythm, and the baking felt almost effortless to me.

That night I slept well for the first time in weeks. She was waiting for me at the bakery door in the morning.

"Good morning, Franco."

"Good morning, Francesca." She laughed at the Italian version of her name and followed me inside. The customers chatted with her as she boxed their orders. That's how I picked up that she'd been widowed for several years.

At the end of the day I handed her a basketful of my breadsticks. "Thank you!" she said. "My friend said they're out of this world."

"No, thank *you*, Francesca." I held the door open for her. "You have saved my life!"

I asked myself who this woman was who'd walked into my bakery like an angel. I wanted to know all about her. We both lived alone, I learned as our days in the shop together passed, both had grown children, both had lived all over the world. She was as much a vagabond as I! She'd had sadness too. She had loved her husband deeply, and his death left a profound wound. Yet it hadn't made her bitter or broken. She was beautiful all the way through. Still I hesitated asking her for a date. We were both healing, trying to get on our feet again. I wanted to be cautious.

Finally I invited her to lunch at the Don CeSar hotel. We talked until it was time for the waiters to get the dining room ready for dinner. We went down to the beach and walked slowly past the pink hotel towers shimmering in the sun, slowly, as if we were trying to stop time from passing. Finally we rested on a log in the sand. Francesca turned to look into my eyes. She started to speak and then stopped. I pulled her close and kissed her.

Loving Francesca turned out to be my greatest adventure of all. She surprised me at every turn, and never more than that afternoon two months into our relationship. I was at her apartment when I noticed a large scrapbook lying on a shelf. "What's this?" I asked her, taking it down.

"Oh, just old stuff I saved from when I was a model." She perched on the couch beside me, the warmth of her shoulder against mine. We flipped through the pages. A picture flashed by. Just a glimpse. Could it really be? I felt a rush of recognition, enough to make my head spin.

"I know that picture!" Francesca turned to me, and all at once I saw that face and her face come together as one. "You're the one from the train," I said. "In Tokyo."

"I am?" she asked, laughing. "Oh, that. I was so young! The other model and I wondered what we'd gotten ourselves into. It took hours to get my clothes and makeup on."

My eyes flitted between hers and the book. "So it was you!" That mysterious lady from the poster, the one who'd had such an inexplicable hold on me, was sitting right there on the couch calling me Franco and giggling at my shock. It felt so completely . . . familiar. We were in the same world at last. I grabbed Francesca's hands and told her the story—how lost and alone I'd felt in Japan. Until I saw her picture.

Francesca shook her head slowly. "I can't believe it was still up in the trains. I must have done that shoot fifteen years earlier, at least."

"What was the ad for?"

"Oh, you couldn't understand it?" She gave me a good long look, her eyes glimmering. "Franco, that ad was for a wedding chapel."

It wasn't too long afterward that Francesca and I had our own wedding. No fancy costumes or ceremony for us, just two people who'd found each other at the right place, at the right time in life. I am just a baker. A baker who married the woman of my dreams.

Meet Forrest Hump

by Brent Thackerson

The camel's dark oval eyes were glazed, the lids only half open. He lay on the ground in his pen, his mangy flanks quivering with each labored breath. That November morning, Roger, our animal director at Boys Ranch Town, a 145-acre farm for troubled boys on the outskirts of Edmond, Oklahoma, had come to me, worried. "I can't get him to stand," he said. "He's rubbing holes in his skin by dragging himself around." Now I watched anxiously as the vet I'd called looked the camel over. Despite arthritis and wobbly joints, the exotic creature had become an integral part of our program since he was donated to us a couple of years ago, teaching the boys the responsibility of caring for an animal, and even starring in the scene with the wise men in our annual drive-through Christmas pageant. He was as friendly as a great big puppy, and the boys loved Forrest Hump, as they called him. Finally, the vet finished his examination. "Your camel has progressive, degenerative joint disease," he said. "He's not going to get better. The humane thing would be to put him down."

I sank down on a hay bale. I'd made a lot of tough decisions as campus administrator for the ranch, but this was the most painful.

Put him down? What would I tell the boys? *Yes, Lord, I knew this day would come. But these boys have lost so much—homes, parents, siblings. Must they lose their beloved camel too?* Yet, in my heart, I knew it would be cruel to let Forrest suffer. I found Roger and broke the news. "Isn't there another way?" he asked.

"I'm afraid not," I said. "Tell the boys when they come to the barn this afternoon. Give them some time to get used to the idea; then arrange for the vet to come back. We can't have Forrest suffer any longer."

I busied myself with other matters. As administrator, I wasn't with the boys at the ranch every day, but one of my duties was deciding who would be admitted. I was considering a seventeen-year-old named Kyle. Our cutoff was fifteen. Still, his social worker had begged me to consider him. Abandoned by his parents, Kyle had spent the past few years bouncing among relatives, in and out of shelters and foster homes. Most recently, he'd lived on the streets—sneaking into a trailer at a construction site after dark to catch some sleep. He had no idea what a normal life was like and didn't trust anyone. "I think he'll turn around at the ranch," the social worker said.

I relented, but regretted it a few days later when Kyle's house parent gave me a call. "He won't listen to anything I say," she said. I went down to the cottage to check on Kyle. I marched in to find clothes everywhere, trash all over the desk, his bed unmade. "Kyle, you must clean your room," I demanded. He stared down at the floor, his baggy clothes seeming to swallow him up. "I don't want to," he said. I gave him a lecture. But he didn't acknowledge a word. Finally I walked out, spent. On my way back to my office, a prayer stormed through my thoughts: *Lord, did I make a mistake? Is there any way to reach a boy like this?*

The reports of his bad behavior kept coming. "Kyle won't do his chores." "Kyle verbally threatened one of the other boys." I was walking through the ranch one day when I heard a commotion outside my office. "Leave me alone!" I heard Kyle shout. The scowl on his face and the way he wrenched away from his house parent said it all. He'd been teasing a younger boy and wasn't taking the reprimand well. "This place is stupid," he yelled. "I don't know why I'm here!" I shook my head. In the eleven years I'd worked at Boys Ranch Town, I'd never given up on a child. I always had faith that with love and proper discipline, any boy could change. But Kyle . . . he seemed to have as little chance at recovery as Forrest had.

Forrest . . . how long had it been since I'd checked on him? I'd been so occupied with Kyle. I drove up to the barn to see if Roger had taken care of things. A group of younger boys was huddled in Forrest's pen. They were hand-feeding him and urging him to drink from a pail of water. It was heartbreaking. I hated to tell these kids to give up. But they had to know when it was time to quit. I confronted Roger. "I know," he said, "but the boys are praying every night that Forrest will get better. I've never seen them pray with such conviction. They believe God is going to heal that camel."

"Roger, it's not fair to let them get their hopes up," I said, irritation rising in my voice. "Call the vet. If you don't, I will." I walked away feeling angry. I hated to give up on Forrest, but what good would it do to hold out false hope? The vet himself said our camel had no chance of recovery. I'd already made one dreadful mistake with letting Kyle in. I wasn't going to blunder again when it came to Forrest.

The Christmas pageant was coming up, always a fun time for the boys. Carloads of folks would drive through our ranch to see our boys present scenes from the Nativity story. Animals from our ranch joined in—donkeys, cows, sheep—and until this year, Forrest, the star of the show. I hoped Kyle would participate. That would at least be a step in the right direction, something to feel positive about.

At our first planning meeting for the pageant, we gathered the kids and took out an array of costumes. The boys spread out the robes and headdresses, talking excitedly about the roles they wanted to play. Except for Kyle. He slumped in a chair, arms crossed, sulking.

A few days later, I went back to the barn. I hoped Roger had dealt with the Forrest situation. But, no, there was still one boy crouched by the camel, a feed bucket at his side. Kyle. He was talking softly to Forrest in a way I'd never heard him speak before. Kyle reached out and scratched Forrest behind the ears, letting the camel nuzzle him. "Hey, Kyle, how's it going?" I said.

Kyle quickly grabbed the feed bucket and stood up. "Fine," he muttered, hurrying past me out of the barn.

Not long after, I drove by the barn. Suddenly I slammed on the brakes. An animal was walking across the pasture. *I don't believe it.* There was Forrest, standing. I got out and he wobbled toward me. "Roger!" I called. He came running out of the barn, saw Forrest and stopped in his tracks, mouth agape. The vet couldn't explain it. "Our boys just loved him," Roger said. "That's what it took."

I looked at Forrest with a profound mixture of amazement and relief. I'd thought the boys were being foolish, holding out hope for him. But shouldn't I be doing the same for Kyle? Maybe it wasn't so foolish after all. If God could help heal a sick camel, he could certainly help heal this troubled kid. So instead of giving up, I doubled my prayers for Kyle.

There was quite a crowd on the first night of the Christmas pageant. Lines of cars slowed my approach to the ranch as I drove up. I slipped the narration CD into my player. The kids looked great, I thought as I drove toward the first station: the birth of Jesus.

"They saw the child with his mother, Mary, and they bowed down and worshiped him. Then they opened their treasures and presented him with gifts of gold, incense and myrrh . . ." The manger scene was perfect. Our farm animals surrounded the small basket where the baby Jesus lay sleeping. Mary and Joseph looked on adoringly. Then I saw the three wise men in flowing robes holding their gifts, gazing at a far-off star, with their camel, Forrest, by their side. All of a sudden, I did a double take. I almost didn't recognize the boy dressed in the wise man's robes, his arm resting on Forrest, his hair cut short, mostly hidden beneath his costume wig. The last boy in the world I'd thought would volunteer for a role like this. A boy I'd thought was too far gone to help. Now I saw how close he must've been all along.

Stars Above

by Laura M.

Thanksgiving night, 1986. I pulled my Dodge Colt outside the low white Alcoholics Anonymous clubhouse, cracked the windows and gave my two-year-old English setter, Grey, a pat on the head. "Be good, girl. I'll be back in an hour and a half."

Grey was my "sobriety dog." Not that I'd been sober the whole time I'd had her, but the need to keep her fed, walked and happy was one of the few things—maybe the only thing—keeping me alive. I was twenty-six and at the tail end of ten disastrous years of drinking. I'd had my first drink young—fifteen, to be exact—and from the very start I was a blackout drinker. The older I got, the more frequent—and the more terrible—the blackouts got. Not that I was an alcoholic. I wasn't even thirty! Alcoholics were old men in trench coats, people who drank all day long. I could go for a week, even a month, without a drink.

But not without a price. The more sober I was, the more depressed I got. I'd drive over bridges and think about pulling the wheel hard to the right. It got bad at this time of year too. The dark moods were more intense—blacker—with the holiday season. I didn't know what was wrong with me. I just knew that if I didn't find my way soon, I'd be beyond help, or dead. So this Thanksgiving I'd decided to skip seeing my relatives. They'd ask too many questions, make me feel bad about where my life was going . . . or not going. Who needed that? I couldn't be alone, though. Much as I loved Grey, a Thanksgiving with only her would leave me so down I'd have no choice but to drink.

So here I was, taking a still-warm pumpkin pie out of my trunk and getting ready to have my holiday meal with a bunch of drunks. I'd been to a couple of AA meetings before, more out of curiosity than conviction. But I'd never been to one on Thanksgiving. An "eatin' meetin'" was how it was billed. How much more pathetic could you get? Above blazed the stars, but all I felt was darkness. I walked through the door hoping to go unnoticed. No such luck. "That's a nice-looking pie!" Wayne, a burly man I recognized from other meetings, practically bellowed. "Let's find a place for it on the dessert table."

Wayne guided me over and I wedged my contribution in among the other pies, cakes and cookies. Now that my arms were free, Wayne wrapped his own around me in a big bear hug. "Glad you made it," he said.

How on earth did he know how hard it was for me to make it there? I teared up. *I must really be losing it.*

"Thanks," I managed to say. "I'm happy to be here."

"Let's open with the Serenity Prayer," a woman on the other side of the room announced. Everyone stopped where they were for the prayer. I mumbled along with them, only half remembering the words: "God, grant me the serenity to accept the things I cannot change, the courage to change the things I can, and the wisdom to know the difference."

The group broke up again amidst a murmur of amens. I wondered how Grey was doing. Maybe I should go. Several more people introduced themselves. There was none of the usual holiday grilling about what I'd been up to the past year. No one seemed to expect anything of me, in fact, or cared about anything other than that I was there. *But do I belong here among all these hard-cores? Is this what I'm supposed to be doing?* My doubts didn't kill my appetite, though. I ate two helpings of turkey and stuffing and was working on a big piece of chocolate pie when Wayne introduced the evening's speaker.

A tall, elegant-looking woman stepped up to the podium. A woman who—even with the big cowboy hat she was wearing—struck me as a real lady. There was just something about the way she walked that let you know she had confidence in herself—that she knew exactly who she was. I couldn't imagine that she was an alcoholic or what she might have to say. But the woman told her story, a powerful and familiar one. Years of problem drinking. Deep, dark depressions when she tried to stay dry. Feeling confused, lost. "The holidays were the worst," the woman said. "Every time I drove over a bridge around that time of year, I wanted to drive off of it."

I felt a sudden lightness. It's hard to explain, but it was as if something shifted inside me and fell into place. In AA, people talk about identifying—hearing someone else's experience and totally connecting with it. That Thanksgiving night I experienced my first true identification with another alcoholic. That dignified, together-looking woman standing up at the podium wasn't just telling her story; she was telling mine. And as I listened to her speak, the last of my defenses fell away. I finally understood why all these people were there and I understood why I was there too.

Out front, Grey hopped to attention when she heard me approaching. I unlocked the car, got in and wrapped my arms around her. "You're going to be a real sobriety dog now," I murmured into the thick fur of her neck. I could've been imagining it, but I think even she sensed a difference in me. Above us in the crisp night sky, stars pierced the darkness, so many lights it was hard to understand why it wasn't blazing bright all the time. Inside me, it was.

Heartfelt Gratitude

Trouble at the Melrose Diner

by Richard Kubach

November 22, 1990. It was the worst possible time for disaster to strike. The day before Thanksgiving: D-day, when you run a diner with a bakery attached to it. All day long we'd been helping take orders for cakes and pies, helping out in the kitchen and otherwise dealing with the hectic rush that any good neighborhood restaurant and bakery gets during the holidays.

Not that the Melrose was just another neighborhood restaurant. Ask anyone in south Philly, and they'll tell you the Melrose is special. A legend, really. Not because we have the best food around—though I like to think we do—but because of our attitude. My dad, Dick, started the Melrose in the thirties, soon after he arrived in America, fleeing Hitler's Germany. Like countless immigrants before him, Dad was short on money and long on dreams. He wanted to start a diner that would reflect the Old World values he'd grown up with. In particular, one that followed the Golden Rule: Do unto others as you would have them do unto you. Dad lived by those words, personally and professionally.

From the day he opened it—in an abandoned diner that no one else wanted to touch—the Melrose was special. In a time when decent working conditions were not exactly at the top of most restaurant owners' lists, Dad wanted to provide a genuinely good environment for his employees. He even supplied his waitresses with orthopedic shoes! In the early fifties, when Dad got the chance to build a brand-new diner a block away, he took pains to design a space where the staff would be as comfortable as the clients. He installed central AC in the dining area . . . and piped it into the kitchen and bakery as well. What was good for people, Dad learned, was good for business.

Ever since 1973, when I came aboard full-time, I'd done my best to keep the Melrose running with those same values. We developed an Employee Assistance Plan that included psychological counseling programs. When our head baker came down with an allergy to, of all things, flour, we created a special elevated area where he could still decorate the cakes and supervise the baking without coming into direct contact with sacks of raw flour. But of late, the Melrose had been a struggle. Running a restaurant where the staff's satisfaction is just as important as the customers' is not always the most practical business model. It seemed like each new month brought with it some new expense, some incentive to cut corners and put the Golden Rule on the shelf. "Give it up, Rich," one of my friends told me. "Your dad was a great guy, but you can't run a business these days thinking like he did."

I found I was working harder, staying later and worrying more. That Tuesday night before Thanksgiving, I got home at eleven o'clock, grabbed a quick shower and was out cold by eleven thirty. The phone by my bed woke me two hours later. It was Paul Tierney, the Melrose's general manager. His voice was grim. "Richard, a water main broke. The entire basement is full of water. The power's out. We're completely shut down."

This will kill us, I thought. I staggered out of bed and put on some warm clothes.

It was past 3:00 AM when Paul and I got to the Melrose. The street was a river. Stepping down into the basement, I couldn't believe my eyes. There looked to be about three feet of black, murky water down there. Baking tins, pie boxes and fruit from our largest inventory of the year bobbed on the surface. Even one of our walk-in freezers was floating. I plunged into helping set up some pumps and temporary electrical power. As the pumps came online, the water started to go down. By 7:30 AM it was down to a foot. Maybe we can open after all. . . . Suddenly, there was a rumbling sound. The water instantly went from one foot deep to seven. We ran out into the street. "Looks like a section of the floor gave way," the fire chief told us. "We're back to square one."

There was so much water and mud in the basement now, it would be a solid week's work to get it out. Not to mention all the lost inventory and revenue. Thanksgiving would come and go with the restaurant's doors closed. We'd be lucky to open by Christmas. By then, who knew what the financial damage would be? Could the Melrose even survive?

Some employees formed a bucket brigade to aid the fire department pumps snaking down into the black mess. *One body less won't make a difference now.* I headed to my office. My eye caught a photo of Dad on the wall. Dad was just about twenty years old—a young dishwasher, new to the country, knowing only a few words of English—but his eyes were bright with hope, hope and faith that the values he'd brought with him to America were the right ones. The timeless ones. Work hard. Be honest. Do unto others. . . For fifty-five years, the Melrose—Dad's dream come to life—had survived. At least I could be thankful for that.

The office door swung open. Paul. He was wearing a huge grin. "I think we're going to make it back sooner than we thought."

"Impossible," I said.

"I called the staff and told them we'd be closed through Thanksgiving. No one wanted to see that happen to the Melrose after everything the place has done for them. Half of south Philly is on its way over. I think we can do this." Paul was right. There were waitresses, neighbors, customers—even reporters. Within the hour, the place was packed with help. It did feel like half of south Philly was there. Within hours, cakes and pies were going out the door again. Incredibly, by Friday morning we were fully operational, serving up food to a packed dining room.

Dad always said the Golden Rule worked if you just stuck with it through thick and thin. That Thanksgiving, I found out it worked both ways.

Love Online

by Susan P. Ebbert

The best part about my job as a receptionist for a printing company was the view from my desk. I worked right beside a floor-to-ceiling window looking out on green grass, plants, shrubbery and the wide blue sky. Sometimes I saw birds. When it rained, drops splashed against the window with a quiet tapping sound. Generally, my work days were busy—answering phones, filing, greeting visitors. But at lunch and on breaks, I liked to take a few minutes to check out the Guideposts online prayer board, where people describe their needs or worries and ask the readers to respond with prayer or maybe a short e-mail reply. Sitting at my desk, with the world outside just beyond the glass, I would close my eyes and pray over those requests, picturing the lives of the people who wrote them. It was a daily ritual that brought me great serenity and helped me feel connected with other spiritual people. Which was a good thing, because my life was anything but serene. I was a single mom, divorced twice, with two grown kids and a daughter still in high school. I didn't make much as a receptionist, so I worked a second job at a craft store—twenty hours on top of forty at the printing company. I often didn't get home until 10:00 PM, which meant that, on some days, I barely saw Tracey, my daughter. I woke up tired every day, and I certainly had no time to get out and meet people. Actually, that part didn't bother me so much—after two divorces, I didn't trust my instincts with men.

I did, though, sometimes ask God for a friend. Someone to take the edge off my loneliness. I guess you could say that was my main prayer request after prayers for my children.

One cold, cloudy February afternoon, I had a break at work and clicked on the prayer site. Often, the site was packed with requests, more than I could pray for individually. So my habit was to read each one and then say a blanket prayer—about all I had time for before the phone interrupted me. That day, though, one request caught my eye. "Please pray for me," it read. "I have been divorced for two years. I have no friends, no family and I'm really lonely. I've been praying about this, but nothing seems to change. I feel like God has abandoned me. Please pray for me not to lose my faith. Mark."

"I feel like God has abandoned me." My breath caught when I read those words. I knew exactly how that felt. When my second husband and I had divorced after sixteen years, I had plunged into a black depression—too deep for God to hear my cries, I had thought. Maybe I can give Mark now the encouragement I needed then. I clicked the Reply button and typed a brief note: "Mark, I know how you feel. I've been there. God has not abandoned you, even if it feels like he has. Things will get better. I don't know how, but I know they will. I'm praying for you. Susan."

The next day the first thing I saw when I turned on my computer at work was an e-mail from Mark. I opened it immediately. "Hi," it read. "You are the only person who responded to my prayer request. Thank you so much. It really means a lot to me. Please don't stop writing. I need a friend. Mark."

Oh! I thought. *This man is so lonely!* I tried picturing him. Where was he writing? In an office like mine? In a room late at night, unable to sleep? "Mark," I typed, "don't worry. I won't stop writing. Feel free to e-mail anytime you need someone to talk to. I'm praying for you. Susan." The rest of the day I checked my inbox periodically, but no e-mail from Mark. *Well,* I thought, *maybe he didn't mean it.* I had corresponded a few times with people on the prayer board, but the conversations had always petered out—like most things on the Internet, I figured. I tried not to let it bother me. But that night, driving home from my second job, the road seemed especially dark and quiet.

The next morning there was an e-mail from Mark. This one was longer, with more about him. He only wrote once a day, he said, because he had no computer at home—he used one at his local library after work. He lived in a small town in upstate New York, where he had come with his ex-wife, who was an officer in the Navy. They had been married eight years and had moved all over the world, even to Iceland. It was all that moving, he said, that wore out their marriage, never putting down roots, never starting a family. Mark had left a government job when he married and now was a clerk at a Home Depot store. He knew no one in his small town and spent most of his spare time walking in the woods and reading at the library. "I hate TV," he wrote, "especially sports. How boring!" *That's refreshing,* I thought. All my second husband had ever wanted to do was sit in his chair and watch sports. Maybe this Mark and I could be friends.

We began corresponding daily, and soon I knew a great deal about Mark, as if a complete person was forming before me on my computer screen. He told me he did sculpture in his spare time, mostly carvings of wildlife. After a few weeks, when we had traded addresses, he even mailed me a picture of a tall Viking he had carved for a NATO base in Iceland. "I want you to see that what I tell you about me is true," he wrote. Tracey saw the envelope with the photos and asked about them.

"They're from a friend I met online," I told her.

"Online?" she said, sounding skeptical. "Mom, you gave your address to a guy you met on the Internet?"

"He's just a friend," I said.

Which he was. Though I had to admit I was waking up every morning itching to get to work so I could turn on my computer and find an e-mail from Mark. We could talk about anything. Life, books, the outdoors (which Mark told me he loved, and I did too), God, church, music, the Bible. Anything. Mark's e-mails were long. And his story broke my heart. He had been an orphan, a runaway, he told me. He had basically raised himself from the age of fifteen. He felt profoundly alone. So did I, I realized—except when reading his e-mails.

"I'd love to call you sometime," he wrote after a few months. I hesitated. I could just hear Tracey, "Mom, you gave him your number?" But I did just that, and soon I was getting to bed even later. We talked an hour every day after work.

One night the question came. "What do you think about a visit?" Mark asked. "I have some vacation coming and I could drive down. I'd love to meet you." I had been hoping for—and dreading—this question. Mark had already voiced surprise at my strong southern accent—what other unflattering details would he notice in person? And how did I know I would like him? On the phone, he was so glad for someone to talk to that he sometimes barely shut his mouth. "Honey," I had to say once, "I can't get a word in edgewise with you!" Would he be the same when we met? What was I letting myself in for?

I told Mark I'd think about it, and that night I lay in bed, praying hard. *God, am I nuts for meeting this man? I've made such bad decisions before. Are you guiding me now or is this just me again making a choice I'll regret? I am so confused.*

The next day, Mark called. "Okay," he said. "Here's why I think a visit is the right idea." And he began methodically laying out reasons, reassuring me, telling me the visit would work out. "We'll just let it be what it is," he said. "No pressure." His voice was calmer, even more tender than usual—utterly open and honest.

As he talked, I felt a warm feeling slowly spread from my head, as if I'd been touched there gently, and then through my body, down to my toes. It was a feeling of peace—serene, indescribable peace such as I had never known. Before Mark even finished, I knew I was going to meet him, and everything would be fine. *Trust me*, the feeling seemed to say.

So a few weeks later I sat in my living room after work, listening intently to the silence outside my door. A knock came. I opened the door, and there he was, in jeans and a polo shirt, about eight inches taller than me, with broad shoulders and a bit of gray hair. And the most charming smile I had ever seen in my life. He gave me a hug, and we stood there, just looking at each other—the real Mark, the real Susan, right there, together. Then we started in talking—and we haven't stopped since.

We were married two years later, and we still, I'm almost embarrassed to say, e-mail every day. Multiple times. Even send e-cards. Mark has come to love my southern drawl—and everything else about me, he says. I know what he means, because that's the way I feel about him too, no matter how much he talks.

Mark told me that on those walks in the woods he had written to me about, he had actually been crying—to himself and to God, asking why he was so lonely, why God seemed so far away.

When we found each other, we found more than a good husband and wife. We found God waiting for us in our hurt, using those years of loneliness to prepare us for each other.

Mark and I had gone to that Web site looking for an answer to prayer. The answer, God told us, was really quite simple. It was us.

Remembering

by Richard H. Schneider

Frankly, I wasn't all that impressed when it was announced that a memorial for World War II veterans would be built on the Mall in Washington. As a vet, I had never felt the need for a special monument. The freedoms we enjoy in the United States are memorial enough. And reminders of war—any war—are painful. Then last May I read about the dedication, with its pomp and ceremony. Yet all I could see from the photos was a boring circle of granite columns flanked by two arches. I agreed with critics who said the design was funereal and pretentious. And why should it clutter the Mall between icons such as the Washington Monument and the Lincoln Memorial, like some kind of tourist attraction?

But something nagged at my conscience. Didn't I need to see it before making up my mind for good? My son Kit is a history buff. "Come on, Dad," he said, "we should go visit it."

All right, I thought. *But what do I need a monument for? Why should we live in the past?* So on a sweltering July day, the two of us found ourselves standing at the memorial.

"It feels like a cathedral," Kit said. It was hushed and serene, with hundreds of people quietly strolling past its columns.

I couldn't help but notice the mementos left behind by loved ones. I saw a framed newspaper article about a "Neil Palmer of Minnesota" and a wreath for "Bernie Silver, in loving memory." A fresh tribute to someone who had died more than sixty years ago. How long our memories last, how deep the pain and gratitude is! The two arches soared above us, one representing the Atlantic theater, where I fought, and the other, the Pacific. Within each lofty belfry flew four giant bronze American eagles, almost like the cherubim guarding the Ark of the Covenant. I hadn't gotten this sense from newspaper photos. Suddenly I felt someone tugging at my sleeve. I looked down to see a girl holding a notepad. "Are you a World War II veteran?" she asked. I nodded.

"I'm doing a project for school and have some questions to ask. Where did you serve?"

"France, Belgium, Germany."

"Were you in any battles?"

"Not really, except when we were caught between enemy lines in the Battle of the Bulge."

"Were you scared?"

"Like never before," I said. "Or since."

Groups of young people were interviewing people like me. They didn't have many old vets to choose from. We're dying at the rate of more than a thousand a day, or so I've been told. Good thing they were asking their questions now.

I turned to the walls and read the quotations from Roosevelt, Truman, MacArthur and part of Eisenhower's address to the troops on D-day: "You are about to embark upon the great crusade toward which we have striven these many months. . . . I have full confidence in your courage, devotion to duty and skill in battle." I remembered the letters Ike sent all of us at times of crisis. I still had mine. I joined the people crowded around bronze bas-relief

sculptures—one of a training camp, like Fort Leonard Wood where
I'd served, and one of a family gathered around a radio listening to
war news. The sculptures portrayed all Americans, from the millions who labored in factories and shipyards to the youngsters who
collected scrap metal.

"Dad, check this out," Kit said. He pointed to the eyes and nose of
a cartoon character peering over a fence. Under it were the words,
"Kilroy was here."

A vet standing nearby laughed. "Remember that?" he asked. "It
was on everything from latrine doors to ammo cases." I sure did
remember. Kilroy had the oddest way of cheering up the troops.

We walked to the Freedom Wall. It's emblazoned with four thousand gold stars, honoring the more than four hundred thousand
Americans who died in the war. I prayed for them. Names of classmates and neighbors from Oak Park, Illinois, came to me—the ones
who never returned. I gave thanks that the three blue stars that
hung in my parents' window awaiting the return of me and my two
brothers didn't turn to gold, symbolizing that we weren't coming
back.

Our day neared a close. We sat on the granite benches that line
most of the memorial. The setting sun bathed the Washington
Monument on one side of us while Lincoln looked benevolently on
from the other. *How appropriate*, I saw now. Being watched over by
one who founded our country and one who saved it. I looked at the
young people studying the inscriptions. *This isn't really for us veterans*, I decided. *It's not so we can live in the past, but so the past can
live in the future, and the sacrifices that made that future possible
will be honored.* I took a last look at the circle of columns and the
soaring arches. Not so boring. Not so boring at all.

All That Glitters

by Penny Musco

You date a man for three months and then get engaged. After a year, you marry him. By your first Christmas together as wife and husband, you think you know everything about him—from how he parts his hair to how he butters his toast. And then you go shopping together for Christmas tree decorations. And you find you really don't know him at all.

That first year together, Joe and I picked out the perfect tree. Now it was time to shop for decorations—ones that would grace our Christmas trees for the rest of our lives. We stopped at a church bazaar and found some boxes of old-fashioned ornaments that reminded me of my family's decorations. Then we headed to the drugstore for lights. Walking down an aisle I spotted a tinsel display. I reached for a box. "No." Joe said, guiding my hands away from the brightly colored red and green box. "No tinsel."

"What?" I asked him. "No tinsel?" I gave him a quizzical look, trying not to look as shocked as I felt. What was a Christmas tree without tinsel? Had I married a crazy man?

"I'm not wild about it," he said. "Never have been."

I tried to reason with him. "Honey, we have to have some tinsel," I said. "We always had it at our house growing up."

"Well, we didn't," Joe said. I argued. I kept at him for a week. At last he relented—on one condition. "We'll buy one box and that's it—forever. If you want to put tinsel on the tree year after year, you'll have to take it off the tree and reuse it."

This is the man I married? I thought. What happened to compromise? Where went understanding? Maybe he was crazy.

Still, I had married Joe for better or for worse and this was the only negative thing about him, so I acquiesced. Or seemed to acquiesce. I figured I would decorate the tree with tinsel, and once he saw how lovely it looked, he would change his mind. Well, almost a quarter century went by and nothing changed. Until last Christmas.

As usual, I unearthed the box of used tinsel from the attic. The life expectancy of a strand, I've learned, is only about one year. Strands break easily when they're stripped from spiky branches. My box of precious tinsel was almost exhausted. I showed the depleted box—its red and green now faded and dull— to Joe. "Honey," I said, "I know our agreement, but I would really like to buy some new tinsel this year."

Joe got a stubborn look in his eyes. "No," he said.

I didn't argue. This was the only blip in our wonderful marriage. But twenty-five tinsel-deprived years were enough. I took to subterfuge. *Next year I'll buy a fresh box*, I thought, *and sneak in some new strands—few enough so he won't turn suspicious.*

May was our twenty-fifth wedding anniversary. Instead of buying each other expensive gifts, Joe and I decided to throw a party for ourselves—a big one. A few nights before the party, Joe and I went out for a quiet dinner. A kind of pre-celebration, just the two of us, holding hands under the table, like we were kids. At home afterward, we sat on the couch and snuggled. I felt so close to him at that moment, so grateful for all of our wonderful years together, that I experienced a pang of guilt about my underhanded tinsel plan.

All at once Joe slipped his arm from around my shoulder and sat up. Then he pulled a gift-wrapped box from out behind him. "I thought we weren't going to buy each other presents this year," I protested. "I don't have anything for you!"

"It's for us," he said. I fumbled with the wrapping, like a child on Christmas morning. I paused when the last bit of wrapping was finally off. Slowly I pulled the lid off the box. Then I started to cry. Inside lay a glistening heap of tinsel—silver, for our silver anniversary.

"Do you know how hard it is to find that stuff in May?" he asked, a smile creeping up the corners of his mouth. "I had to go on the Internet!"

I threw my arms around him and held him for what seemed like . . . twenty-five years. Later, when I was alone, I let the tinsel spill through my fingers. *No,* I thought, *Joe still isn't crazy about tinsel, but he is crazy about me,* and said a prayer of thanks for the gift of my husband.

Some Service Dog

by Brenda Mosley

Something poked me in the face. Something cold and wet. "Not again, Toby," I moaned groggily, pushing my dog's nose away from mine. I rolled over. Just as I was falling asleep again, he nipped at my sleeve. "Toby, stop!" I commanded. He flopped down next to my bed and promptly started snoring. I didn't even care about the noise. Maybe I'd finally be able to get some sleep myself. I drifted off.

A tug on my foot. *What now?* I forced my eyes open. Toby was trying to pull off my sock. I nudged him away, glaring at him. He cocked his head and looked at me quizzically. My alarm clock hadn't gone off yet. It was only 5:00 AM. I'd been planning to get up early for my doctor's appointment, but not this early. Would this dog ever learn? Every night for weeks now he'd been waking me up. Not just once or twice. Constantly. I couldn't remember the last time I got a good night's rest. And I needed it. Living with both cerebral palsy and multiple sclerosis was debilitating. If my old service dog were still around, I might have coped, but Toby? All I'd been able to train him to do so far was fetch my slippers. Some service dog! I needed help with a lot more than that.

My old dog, a retriever named Farley, had only taken basic obedience lessons when he came to live with me. I'd never trained a dog
before, but he was so smart it didn't take long for me to teach him to
do all kinds of things around the house. Farley would bring me the
phone, get a can of soda from the fridge, take clothes out of the
dryer. He carried grocery sacks, helped me up from chairs, steadied
me if my walk got wobbly. He even pulled me in a wheelchair those
times I had to use one. For ten years he was my companion, my
partner. Together we helped other people with disabilities train
their service dogs. Thanks to Farley, I'd been able to avoid the fate I
dreaded—moving into an assisted-living center—even after my
condition deteriorated so much that I had to quit my job teaching
preschool and go on disability. He was a real answer to prayer, my
Farley. A champion service dog.

I was inconsolable when he died. What dog could ever replace
him? But I knew that if I wanted to continue living on my own, I'd
have to get a new service dog. So I went to a kennel, hoping I would
find another answer to prayer. Yet even I couldn't quite believe the
retriever I spotted in an outdoor run. *He looks just like Farley!* Long
legs, reddish fur and all. Toby was his name, the kennel owner said.
I took Toby for a test walk on a gravel path, a tricky surface for me.
He walked beside me slowly and deliberately, seeming to sense my
hesitation. *Good temperament*, I thought. The only drawback:
Ideally, a service dog is fully trained by age two, and Toby was
already four.

But Toby's uncanny resemblance to Farley . . . what else could he
be but another answer to prayer? *I bet I can teach him to act like
Farley too*, I thought. I had a good track record when it came to
training service dogs. I brought Toby home. The first thing he did
was tear through every room in the house. "Stop!" I ordered. He
paused and looked at me before bolting through the doggy door to

the backyard. Toby had been kenneled outdoors his whole life. It would take time for him to adjust to living in my house.

I just didn't expect it to take so long. Everything scared him. When the phone rang, he howled and cowered in a corner. When the dryer buzzed, he ran for cover. When the deliveryman knocked on the door, Toby jumped a mile high, barking frantically.

Toby's sole talent seemed to be napping. He would drop off right in the middle of a training session. Once I spent an entire morning rolling a tennis ball across the floor. "Fetch," I said. Sometimes Toby grabbed the tennis ball in his mouth, but he wouldn't bring it back to me. *Aren't retrievers bred to do this?* I decided to try something softer. Maybe it would be easier for him. I dropped one of my fuzzy slippers near him. "Get the slipper, Toby." Toby ignored the slipper, walked over to me, put his head on my leg and yawned. "Off," I said, pushing his head gently toward the floor. "Get the slipper." Toby curled up at my feet and dozed off.

Something in me just snapped. "Toby," I called. Loudly. He jolted awake and looked at me. I bent down. "This is a slipper!" I yelled. I pushed it into his mouth. "How could I have ever thought you were an answer to prayer!" I got up, stumbled into the bathroom and slammed the door. I stared at my reflection in the mirror. I looked drained. The MS was making me weaker and weaker. *Dogs don't respond well to anger*, I reminded myself. *You've got to try again with Toby. You don't have the strength to start over with another dog.*

I opened the door. Toby sat in the exact spot I'd left him. His tail wagged. He still had the slipper in his mouth. I didn't know whether to laugh or cry. "Drop," I said. Right away he did. "Good dog!" I patted his head. He spent the rest of the day happily retrieving my slipper. But that was all he learned in two months of training. I couldn't count on Toby day-to-day. Certainly not in an emergency. I couldn't count on him for anything, really, except waking me up at night, practically every night. *And I've had enough of that,* I thought, swinging my legs over the edge of my bed and sitting up. I eyed my so-called service dog. Toby sprawled on the floor, apparently satisfied that he'd successfully kept me from yet another night's rest.

I stuck my feet into my slippers and stood. Might as well get ready for my doctor's appointment. Prepare myself to tell her I'd made the decision I had dreaded my whole adult life. I was going to give up my dog, my house, my independence. Could she help me find a place in an assisted-living center?

Later that morning my doctor ushered me into her examination room. "Are you okay, Brenda?" she said with concern. "You look tired."

"That's because I'm not sleeping."

"Why not?" she asked.

I told her about my problems with Toby. "Maybe he's just acting out because I've been working him so hard," I said. "But I wouldn't have to if he'd just learn."

My doctor listened to my lungs and checked my nose and throat. "It might be good that Toby's been waking you."

"Good?"

"You're showing signs of sleep apnea. People with this condition stop breathing during the night. Left untreated, it could lead to a heart attack or stroke." She set up an appointment for me at a sleep clinic the following week.

Toby and I went to the clinic together. They said it was okay because he was a service dog. My bedroom for the night was connected to a control room, where observers would monitor me while I slept. Normally that would have bothered me, but I was too tired to care. A nurse attached electrodes to my head, chest and legs. I stretched out on the bed and Toby curled up on the floor beside me. As usual, he conked out right away. Well before I did. And as usual,

Toby barely let me sleep a wink. He'd get up to lick my hands and snort in my face. *He's hopeless. Incorrigible*, I thought. *At least now my doctor will know what I'm up against.*

I took Toby with me to get the sleep-test results. "Looks like my suspicion was on target, Brenda," my doctor said. "You stopped breathing fifteen times during the night. Your dog woke you every time."

Just like that, everything came into focus. *No wonder poor Toby naps so much*, I thought. *He's worn-out from trying to save my life!* He was like those dogs I'd read about who have a remarkable talent. They can sense when a seizure or a cardiac episode is about to hit their owner and alert the person.

I looked at Toby, dozing beside my chair. I leaned over and stroked the soft reddish fur behind one of his ears. He opened his eyes and started to his feet. "No, you rest, Toby, you've earned it," I told him. "Will you give me another chance? I'll be as patient with you as you've been with me, I promise." Toby licked my hand and lay down.

My doctor outfitted me with an oxygen tube to regulate my breathing while I sleep. Now Toby wakes me only if the tube slips off. It's pretty amazing how well we learned to work together once we both got enough rest. Before long, Toby could do everything Farley had done. These days, Toby and I train other dogs to help people with disabilities. He loves to demonstrate how to get a can of soda from the fridge, carry a bag and, of course, fetch slippers. My Toby is some service dog, all right. A real answer to prayer, one I didn't even know I needed, yet I couldn't live without.

Save the Hitchin' Post!

by Cathy McKinney

Friday night at the Hitchin' Post. The Velvet Tears launched into a country-and-western medley. With a whoop, folks jumped up from their burgers and fries and hurried onto the dance floor. Seemed like everyone in town was out there two-steppin' up a storm. I got some pork tenderloins sizzling on the grill and went from table to table refilling sodas. Sure I had a lot to do—cooking and waiting on tables and seeing to all our customers. But I loved it, loved being in the middle of all that small-town, down-home congeniality. It was something I'd known a lot of here in Indiana, especially after my daddy died in a car accident when I was thirteen. I cried hard and prayed even harder, begging the Lord to please somehow help us make it without Daddy. Really, it was our neighbors who got us through, coming from miles around to lend a hand and get us back on our feet again.

No surprise that when Bob and I got married, we chose this area to start our own family. We settled just outside Norman, population not even a hundred. Bob managed an egg farm, and when our two boys started school, I worked as a cook at the Cracker Barrel. The restaurant I really fell in love with, though, was the Hitchin' Post on

Norman's main drag. One day in 1998 I even asked the owner Roseanna and her husband Jerry if she needed any help. The next thing I knew, I was waiting tables and taking shifts at the Hitchin' Post grill. It didn't take long for the regulars to become my second family. Mr. Hall, who owned the sawmill, showed up every morning at seven like clockwork with his pal Danny Fleetwood for coffee and flapjacks.

"Hey, Cathy, are we gonna get some decent-sized flapjacks this time?" they'd tease me every day.

"Flapjacks are supposed to be small," I shot right back. Claire and Dick Goben (I always called him "Pappy") swung by for dinner and never left without showing me the latest pictures of their grandkids. I knew it was the weekend when I'd look up from the grill and see Bonnie and Bill Maples at their table at the edge of the dance floor, their toes tapping away to the Velvet Tears. Sometimes Pappy would convince me to get onstage with the band and sing "Coal Miner's Daughter."

I'd never had a job that was so much fun. Sure, the place was kind of run-down, and the kitchen equipment was old. Still, there was a camaraderie, a spirit here I was grateful to be a part of. That's why I didn't hesitate when Roseanna asked me to cover for her that evening in August 1999. Roseanna was at the grill frying rib-eye steak when a phone call came in. She hung up, a worried look on her face. "Jerry collapsed," she told me and another girl waiting tables. "I've got to go to the hospital."

"You go look after him," I said. "I'll take care of things here."

The place was full, but we managed to take everyone's order and get it cooked and served. I'd barely wiped the spilled coffee off the counter when another crowd started coming in. And the tables were still loaded with dirty dishes. Yikes! That's when one of the regulars who was still lingering over his coffee got up. "I'll clear," he said, without me even asking him. Another customer followed right after him and started washing dishes. We made it through the rest of the night without Roseanna.

We were all saddened to find out we would have to get along without her for a lot longer. Her husband was diagnosed with brain cancer, and she was so busy caring for him, she hardly made it to the restaurant at all. The other waitresses and I cooked up some of his favorite dishes and sent them over to the house, along with a lot of prayers. I was at the Hitchin' Post from the crack of dawn to well after dark. Slowly, I got the hang of running a restaurant. What made it easier was knowing that if I got overwhelmed, I could count on my regulars to make and pour their own coffee and, yes, even clear their own tables.

Then last February Roseanna broke some bad news. "I can't keep up with Jerry's medical bills," she said. "I have to sell the Hitchin' Post." Some people from out of town had made a good offer.

Out of town? Strangers taking over our town's favorite gathering spot? I knew Roseanna had no choice, but I couldn't help feeling upset. I could tell our customers were too. But they kept coming in. Maybe too many of them, because the septic system backed up and the buyers pulled out. Roseanna had to close down the restaurant altogether. It sure seemed like it was the end of the road for the Hitchin' Post. On February 28, I shut off the grill and hung up my apron. I sat at a table in the empty dining room and took one last look around. No folks cleaning their plates, talkin' up a storm, or doin' some dancing. The place was quiet, dark, empty. I put my head down on the table and bawled like a little baby.

Even having more time to spend with Bob and the boys didn't make me feel any better. Soon as I drove by the closed-up Hitchin' Post, the tears would come right back. The Hitchin' Post was more than a restaurant. The place was the soul of our whole town.

Couldn't someone do something to get it going again? A voice inside my head promptly answered: *Can't you?*

The next day my friend Melva Sturgis dropped by my house. "I know you've been feeling blue," she said.

As I poured her a glass of iced tea, I thought again of all those folks I'd waited on for so many months. "I feel as if I'm meant to start up the Hitchin' Post again," I said. "But the place needs so much fixing up. I don't know how I'd do it all."

"You're not alone in this," Melva said. "Plenty of folks would love to see the Hitchin' Post reopen." All of a sudden I remembered when my daddy died and so many people came to help my family without us ever asking them. Maybe it was time for me to be a good neighbor and give good folks a place to gather. Roseanna agreed to sell the building to me, and the bank gave me a loan to buy it. By June I was officially the new owner of the Hitchin' Post.

It wasn't until I unlocked the door of the place and walked in that I grasped the enormity of the task that lay before me. No question the plumbing needed a complete overhaul. The walls could definitely use a new coat of paint. There was a puddle in the middle of the floor where the roof was leaking. *What have I gotten myself into?* I heard the floorboards creak a few yards behind me. It was Danny, along with some friends. "Guys, I'm afraid I haven't had time to make coffee yet," I joked.

They waved me off. "How about we put in a whole new septic system for you, Cathy?" Danny said and quoted me a figure that barely covered the cost of the materials. "Just save us seats every morning for breakfast," he said. "And, oh yeah, bigger flapjacks."

A couple of days later another of our regulars came by and reminded me that her sons were business consultants. They wrote up a new business plan for the restaurant and didn't charge a dime. My stepdad is scared to death of heights, but he climbed right up on a ladder and tore out an old chimney so we could start renovations. Melva helped me rip out rotting counters, and others carried off our trash. One family planed yellow poplar planks and hung the boards on the dining room walls. Every day, it seemed, another person came forward to help us bring the place back to life.

One Tuesday in July Melva and I drove forty-five miles to Bloomington to get lumber for a new roof. When we got back, I swear half the town was waiting at the Hitchin' Post to help us put it on. New ceiling and exhaust fans were donated. I saved $250 to buy a sink at an auction, but when the bidding shot out of my price range, I left. I headed to my car, disappointed.

"Hey, Cathy," Helen Ayers called out, "any luck?"

"I didn't get the sink I needed," I said. "Other people outbid me."

"Well, I outbid them," Helen said. "Let's go pick it up."

At last, on August 3, 2001, we had our grand reopening. The Velvet Tears tuned up, the kitchen was humming and I ran around the restaurant with a half dozen of the townspeople setting the tables. I barely had time to tie on my apron before I heard the screen door. Folks coming in for dinner. "Cathy, how about some service?" a cheerful voice called. In half an hour the place was packed. I'd extended the dance floor over where Bonnie and Bill Maples used to sit, so I gave them a new table of honor. I couldn't wait to belt out a chorus of "Coal Miner's Daughter" for Pappy.

"Are you still servin' those little-bitty flapjacks for breakfast?" one of the guys teased.

"Tomorrow morning they'll be big as a pizza pan," I said.

That night we served close to two hundred people, almost twice the population of the town itself! I looked around the place and it hit me: The Hitchin' Post was more than a restaurant. It was the people who were brought together to help each other. In that sense, the Hitchin' Post really is the soul of our town.

A Ferret Named Polo

by April J. Miller

It was all going to be so perfect. For as long as I could remember, my father had talked about moving to Montana—Big Sky country. We'd taken many a hike amid sun-washed stretches of green grass on our visits there. It was a long way from our home in Georgia, but Dad dreamed of buying a farm in Montana and getting into the burgeoning business of raising ferrets to sell as pets. "Everyone has them out there, April," Dad told me. "They're small and skinny with big raccoon eyes—really frisky and playful. We'll get a place with plenty of room for them to run around." No, it wasn't your standard white-picket-fence-and-a-dog American dream, but it didn't matter. I'd always loved animals, and this sounded like it would be a real hoot.

Dad quit his job and went to Montana to look for a farm. I gave him his first ferret, which he named Jake. "The little guy's a handful," Dad reported on the phone. "He won't let me get into my slippers. This morning we had a tug-of-war for ten minutes." I laughed, wishing I were already there with him. I gave notice at the executive recruitment firm where I worked, looking forward to trading cubicles and reports for wide-open spaces and frolicking ferrets. Mom and I planned to sell our home and join Dad as soon as he found a place.

But within weeks Dad started suffering severe pain in his hips. When he went to a doctor, he was diagnosed with an advanced stage of cancer. Mom and I rushed to Montana to be with him. Three months later he was dead.

The new life we'd prepared for was over before it had even started. Jake was given away and Mom and I returned to Georgia alone. I couldn't understand why God would choose to take my father right when he was about to live his longtime dream.

Life held no magic after Dad was gone. It was much too painful to talk about. Mom and I would eat dinner in silence, with no plans for selling our house and running a farm to discuss, no excited phone calls from Dad. I would stop by the pet store sometimes and watch the ferrets scurry around in their pens, imagining my dad wrangling over the slippers with Jake. I could see the bemused smile on his face, hear him telling "the little guy" to let go, and felt the bitter pain of what might have been.

I couldn't go back to my normal routine as if everything were okay. Longing to hold onto some of the thrill of anticipation I'd gotten every time I'd thought of life on a Montana farm, I looked for a job related to animals. A position opened up at a petting zoo and I grabbed the opportunity. At last I'd get the chance to be outside with animals every day the way I would have been on the farm with Dad.

The petting zoo had every kind of animal from llamas to deer to foxes. But of course I was drawn to the ferrets. There were two of them, and their antics made them popular with the kids who visited. Still, even though I loved the ferrets, the little creatures were a constant reminder of what I'd lost.

Soon a third ferret arrived. He was particularly small and sable-colored, and his name was Polo. Each time I tried to introduce Polo to the two resident ferrets, they started fighting. "I guess we'll have to find a special place just for you," I said to Polo as I peered into his deep black eyes. "Don't worry, little guy, I'm going to take very good care of you."

I put Polo in a separate pen. He was sickly, so I had to take special care to feed him right, and I spent lots of one-on-one time playing with him to keep him from being too lonely. I felt at ease with him, despite his characteristic ferret hyperness. Taking care of Polo became my reason for getting up in the morning. One afternoon the zoo director told me she thought two ferrets were enough. "Could you find a home for Polo?" she asked. Could I!

That evening I brought Polo home and introduced him to Mom. She reluctantly agreed to let Polo join our household—if he stayed in my room.

My room became the ferret's romping ground. He never sat still. He'd chase me around and then hide behind a piece of furniture before jumping out at me. When I finally collapsed on my bed exhausted, he'd curl up under my chin and nap with me. One morning I awoke to find him chewing on my slippers. "If only Dad could have seen you," I said to him, remembering Dad talking about the ferret I'd given him. Again the keen pain of loss struck me. I picked up Polo. Stroking his soft fur, I felt a warmth and love that reminded me of Dad. I could almost imagine him reaching down to pet the little ferret too.

One day when I thought Polo was asleep, I opened my bedroom door. Before I knew it, a furball whizzed by my legs into the hallway. "Mom, look out!" I called. "Polo's on the loose." But he was chasing Mom around the living room. I started chasing Polo, and the three of us ran around the room, Mom shrieking, Polo chucking, and me laughing until we all fell on the couch.

Then Polo hunched his back, leaped into the air and scampered away. Mom giggled. "Guess he's made himself at home," she said.

Mom gave Polo free run of the house after that. He developed a taste for caramel corn, and many an evening he entertained us with his spontaneous games of tag and his aerial acrobatics, which we nicknamed the "weasel war dance." I felt alert again, tuned in— waiting to see what Polo would do next.

After dinner one evening, Mom and I sat watching Polo dash around the house, scattering papers and knocking over knick-knacks. "I don't think your father had any idea what he was getting himself into," she said with a quiet chuckle. I laughed too. I could picture Dad in Polo's wake, methodically putting things back in place over and over.

I came home one evening to find Polo retching. Soon after that he started losing weight and was too sick even to nibble on caramel corn. I could feel every rib in his tiny body when I held him. I took him to the vet for tests. Later that day the vet called back and told me Polo had a tumor. They could remove it, but the operation would cost more than I could possibly pay.

"I can't afford it. I'm sorry. I guess you'll have to put him to sleep," I said, unable to hold back my tears until I hung up.

I didn't go to say good-bye to Polo because I couldn't bear the thought of losing him. Instead, I went into my room, where I threw myself onto the bed.

When Mom came home and I told her the news, we hugged each other for a long time. It almost felt like I was losing Dad all over again.

I finally managed to get to sleep and was still in bed the next day when the phone rang. It was the vet. He said, "Good afternoon, Miss Miller. Polo made it through the surgery with flying colors."

"What?" I said. "But I thought he was gone."

"One of my technicians fell in love with Polo and wanted to keep him, so she covered the cost of the operation. She says you can visit him anytime."

"Polo's alive," I said quietly. *But he's not mine.* "Thank you, doctor, and thank your technician too."

I knew I couldn't visit Polo only to have to go through the heartbreak of leaving him behind. Whether dead or alive, he was still lost to me.

For days I ate little, slept a lot and didn't answer phone calls. One night while lying awake, I could take no more. *God, I miss my father,* I prayed. *I miss Polo. And I miss you.*

I went to church more, desperately seeking comfort. I started, little by little, to talk to others about my father and Polo, to let them pray for me. And I found myself mentioning Dad more in conversations with Mom.

One morning I decided to tidy up the post-Polo household. Everywhere there were reminders of the lively little creature. Ferret fur all over the sofa cushions, caramel corn stuck in the carpet and his favorite hiding places.

Other memories came back, like Dad saying, "We'll need a big place where they have plenty of room to run around. Just us, the ferrets and the big Montana sky." I could still see the way his eyes lit up when he talked about it. It wasn't so much the idea as it was his enthusiasm for it that made it special. That, and how much I loved him.

All at once I was overwhelmed with gratefulness to God, not only for the love he had put in my heart for my father, but also gratefulness for Polo, who had given me hope that there could be joy in life even after the worst thing in the world had happened.

That afternoon I got a telephone call. It was the vet's assistant who had stepped in to save Polo's life. "I've gotten a couple of other ferrets now, so if you'd like, you can have Polo," she said. "He's in great shape."

I was on my way to her house in a heartbeat. I picked up Polo and brought him back home. "Now you be careful," I said. "I just cleaned this place up."

With that, Polo scampered across the floor, launched into his weasel war dance and headed for the caramel corn.

The Old Cane Chairs

by Laura Knight Moretz

G ilbert Poplin. Chair caner." The scrap of paper with a phone number had been sitting in my kitchen drawer for months. I'd gotten it from a local upholstery shop. "Best chair caner around," the owner of the shop had said. "Not that there are too many of them left." Five of the six cane chairs that sat round our dining room table had been in my family for more than forty years. My mother had ordered them from E. A. Clore, a Virginia chair manufacturer, just after I was born. They're good, honest chairs, made to last a lifetime. Lately, though, they'd been showing signs of wear, and I'd wondered what to do about them. Our two boys—Thomas, seven, and Will, four—were as tough on those old chairs as they were on the rest of the house—and on me.

"Why don't we get rid of these things?" my husband Brian said one Saturday last August, watching as I dabbed a sponge between the frayed, ancient fibers of one of the chairs to remove a glowing pink glob of Will's spilled yogurt.

"I can't let these chairs go," I said. "I've been sitting on them all my life."

"And they look it too," Brian said. "The cane has almost completely worn off three of them."

It was true. The chairs were as worn-out as I felt after a day of chasing after the boys. I'd just offered to host a dinner for some members of our new church. *Brian's right*, I thought. *I can't seat guests on these old things.* It was either pitch them or get the worst of them re-caned. That was when I remembered the number in my kitchen drawer.

"Bring them on down," the voice on the phone said when I called. Not rude exactly. More like to-the-point. No-nonsense. Old-fashioned. *Like the chairs themselves*, I thought. I carried the three most beat-up ones out to our van, corralled the boys and drove over. Mr. Poplin's house was on the other side of town— small and green, about half the size of ours. He answered the door holding a long, thin cane. It took me a moment to realize he was visually impaired. "Bring them to the utility building out back, please," he said with that same slightly gruff tone. I pulled one of the chairs out of the back of the van and Thomas grabbed another. Will ran ahead of us into the backyard. It was fenced in, I noticed with relief.

"Why does he have that stick, Mom?" Thomas asked.

"He must not see well," I said.

"Then how will he fix the chairs?"

"Well, I guess his fingers will do the seeing," I said.

Mr. Poplin was waiting for us in back, sitting in a chair at the front of his building, his eyes looking straight ahead. Behind him, shrouded in darkness, I saw spools of twine and chairs in various states of repair. "Here's the worst of them," I said, setting the first chair down right in front of him. Then I called to Will, who was already drifting a little too far toward the back of the yard.

"I can fix this," Mr. Poplin told me, running his hand over the weave of the seat. "How many did you say you had?"

"Three," I said. "Will, come over here this minute. I mean it. Now!" Will finally came over, just as Thomas was coming round from the front with the third chair.

"That'll be thirty-five dollars a chair," Mr. Poplin said. "Write down your phone number, and my wife will call you when the job is done."

"That sounds fine," I told him.

Mr. Poplin's expression brightened a little. "How many boys you got here?" he asked me.

"Two," I said.

"Could you ask them to stand in front of me for a second?"

"Sure. Will, Thomas, come on over here in front of Mr. Poplin."

The boys obeyed, though they both were a little perplexed. So was I, for that matter.

When the two boys were right in front of him, Mr. Poplin stretched out his hands. He put one squarely on each boy's head, as if he were sizing them up like a pair of chairs that needed fixing. "About what I thought," said Mr. Poplin. Then, turning toward me, his eyes still fixed on some faraway point, he said, "Cherish these boys. They'll be gone before you know it."

Again, that same terse tone. But by now I knew how to read it. I could see what was in Mr. Poplin's heart. "I will," I said. "You can count on it."

On the drive home, Thomas was full of questions, as usual. "Why did Mr. Poplin put his hands on our heads like that?" he asked me.

"It's like I told you," I said. "Mr. Poplin's eyes don't work so well, so he sees with his hands." *And with his heart*, I thought to myself. How thankful I was for my boys, my family . . . and for all the hard, wonderful work that goes with it.

A week later, Mr. Poplin's wife called to say he was done with the chairs. They came back with a firm, hard weave of cane—looking as new as the day my mother had bought them. By the time they need caning again, Thomas and Will will be grown and gone. It will all happen before I know it, just as Mr. Poplin had said. And I will cherish and give thanks for every moment.

CHAPTER 9

Life's Surprises

Surprised by Love

by Linda Gillis

The bathroom was a mess. Tissues overflowing from the trash can. A tube of toothpaste lying open on the counter. A bar of grimy soap lying next to the soap dish. My husband Glen had only stopped by the house while I was at work to get some things and do his laundry, but he sure made his presence known. *A mess . . . just like our marriage*, I thought. We were in the middle of a "therapeutic separation." That's what the family counselor called it anyway. After thirty-seven years, marriage to Glen had become increasingly frustrating and lonely, and I thought a break would breathe life into our relationship. Instead, it only magnified our problems. I stalked out of Glen's bathroom and sat down on the couch to eat dinner in front of the TV. How had it all gone wrong?

When the last of our three children, Susan, left home, suddenly it was just Glen and me. I dreaded returning home after work to cook dinner while Glen watched stupid old adventure movies or played around on his computer. I hoped things would change when Glen retired in 2001, and we moved from Illinois to Arizona to be closer to our son Michael, his wife Jodi and our four-year-old granddaughter Mikaila. But Arizona was worse. We rarely went out.

He acted as if he hardly noticed me. He dressed like it too. "Casual" didn't do it justice. All we seemed to do together was watch old sit-coms. Glen spent his free time golfing. I spent more and more time working at a spiritual retreat center. I prayed constantly. Where had we gone wrong? Didn't God bring us together to stay together? The only relief was when Mikaila came for sleepovers. I stocked a box full of toys for us to play with. She especially loved bath time, always playing with a little green rubber frog that squeaked when she squeezed it and sprayed water.

Finally, I told Glen I wanted a divorce. He convinced me to see a counselor with him. When we broke the news to our kids, they were understandably upset. Especially our daughter Karen, still in Illinois. Glen and I met with a therapist for ninety-minute sessions every month, talking about our childhood, dating, our engagement and our marriage. Everything. It all came out, years of frustration and unspoken resentments. Especially after the kids moved out. The spark between us was gone. Yes, Glen and I loved each other, but were we still in love? It didn't feel like it. Now Glen was living in an RV, parked a few miles away at a campground. We had agreed that while I was at work, he could enter the house to get his stuff and do his laundry. But couldn't he at least clean up after himself?

I couldn't finish my dinner. I started to tidy things up in my bath-room when I spied Mikaila's little rubber frog by the tub. I picked it up. Such an ugly little thing! Those bulging red eyes, that green bumpy skin. It certainly stood out. I was about to put it away when I had an idea. *I'll show him*. I marched over to Glen's bathroom and stuck the frog on top of the toilet brush. "You might be able to ignore this mess, but you can't ignore Froggy," I said. He had to take the hint. I checked Glen's bathroom a few days later. The frog was still waiting to be rescued. Glen probably didn't even notice it. *He doesn't notice anything*. I moved Froggy to a dish filled with seashells and sand on top of the tank. We'd collected the shells years before on a shore vacation, back when we used to do things like walk on the beach.

The next afternoon, I went into my bathroom. There he sat on the edge of the toilet seat. Froggy. I burst out laughing. I ran to check Glen's bathroom. It positively sparkled! Toothpaste and shaving foam put away, the tub spotless. Victory! *Glen will be by to do his laundry tomorrow*, I thought. I had the perfect spot for Froggy: on top of the agitator in the washer. A sort of "thank you" gesture. Two days later I reached for some lotion in my medicine cabinet—and there it was, that silly green amphibian, staring me in the face. I giggled. *Right where he knew I'd notice it*, I thought. "Two can play at this game," I said. I went to Glen's bathroom and plopped Froggy on the bar of soap in Glen's shower.

This is sort of fun, I caught myself thinking. *Like the fun we used to have.* But I cut myself short. *Don't go there, Linda.* Our problems were too deep to be fixed by a little silliness. Besides, I had just rented an apartment for myself. I moved into the apartment a few days later and Glen moved back into the house. "I'll stop by when you're at work to pick up some clothes," I told him. That afternoon, when I opened up my lingerie drawer, there was Mikaila's frog, right where he didn't belong! My face turned beet red. Oh my! I marched into the bedroom and planted it on Glen's pillow under the bedspread. *That'll teach him.*

"How are things going?" the therapist asked us at our next session. Glen and I looked at each other.

Finally he said, his face perfectly serious, "Well, actually, we've been hiding this frog around . . . ." It was all I could do to keep from laughing. Glen told her how he found the frog on his pillow. I mentioned the lingerie drawer.

"It's not like us to be this playful," I said.

The therapist smiled. "Maybe that's the key for your marriage recovery, to learn how to have fun again. Laugh more and enjoy each other. You might be ready for the next step . . . to start dating each other again." I felt myself flush. Dating?

There, during our session, we made plans to go to a flea market and agreed we wouldn't discuss our relationship—just try to have fun. Nothing fancy, we both insisted. Our daughter Karen had other ideas. She called me that morning. "What are you planning to wear on your date?" she asked.

"Oh, just what I'm wearing to work," I answered, looking at my shirt and jeans and vaguely wondering how she knew about our date.

Karen sighed. "Mom, you can't wear the same thing you wear to work. You need something new and fun!"

That afternoon I stopped at Nordstrom's Last Chance. I couldn't help snorting at the name. Still, there was a stylish pair of black-and-white polka-dot Capri pants on sale. I matched them with a white V-neck T-shirt and shiny black sandals with cute straps. That night I put on makeup and dangling earrings. Standing in front of the mirror, I looked at myself. Not bad for someone going on a date for the first time in forty years.

There was a knock at the door. *Here we go. . . .* I took a deep breath and opened it. There stood Glen . . . but not the Glen I knew. Smartly dressed, hair combed, holding a bouquet of daisies. He even opened the car door for me! *Who is this guy?* We spent an hour browsing through the booths at the flea market.

"How about something a little more—" Glen started to say.

"Exciting?" I finished his sentence.

"Exactly," Glen said.

So we went to a barbecue place for dinner and some live country music. We talked about movies, work, even Glen's golf game—but nothing about our marriage. "I've got a confession to make," Glen said. "Karen called and told me I should bring you flowers and do all that other stuff."

"That little sneak! She told me what to do too!" I said. We chuckled at how we'd been tutored by our matchmaker daughter. I was beginning to remember what drew me to Glen in the first place. His good nature, his sense of humor, his honesty. *You know, if this were a real first date, I'd definitely see this guy again.* Glen dropped me at home.

"Should we do this again?" he asked, taking my hand.

How long had it been since we'd held hands? It wasn't all his fault. I'd let the distance build between us too. "Absolutely," I said. That night I prayed, *God, maybe Glen and I deserve another shot. I think You want us to be together. Help us rediscover our love.*

Now during our therapy sessions, we started talking about what we liked about each other, not what we didn't like. For the first time in years we began thinking of ourselves as a couple again. On days when I didn't see Glen, I found myself missing him. Missing us. Finally, the big test was a Fourth of July weekend camping trip in northern California. It was like a dream . . . a good one. By the time we got back, I knew I was ready to recommit to Glen. We finished our therapy and I moved back home.

We were back together again for a few weeks when I found a little surprise in my jewelry box—no, not a new diamond ring—the little rubber frog. Every now and then Froggy still appears in the most unexpected places. But that's the thing about love. It's the best surprise of all.

The Unopened Letter

by Bernard Lund

As a middle-school teacher for more than thirty years, I know a rambunctious classroom presents an interesting challenge for a teacher. Either you channel that overabundance of spirit and ability or you face a long, long school year. I'd been warned over the summer about what I'd be facing that fall. The performing-arts section was a collection of thirty-five of the school's most boisterous and talented kids. By fate or chance, I drew them for my homeroom. The year before, their teacher had gone so far as to tell our principal point-blank, "You put me back with those kids, and I'll quit!" Within a week, as my eighth graders jumped from their desks and burst into spontaneous song yet again, I felt flush up against the longest year of my career.

I taught a number of subjects in school, including twentieth-century history, to my homeroom kids. And that following Monday, I brought in my teaching aids—genuine rations books and war bonds, old newspapers, posters, letters—tricks of the trade that I'd found helped to make the lessons more real. To my surprise and relief, the performing-arts kids took to the artifacts even more than previous students had. At home that night I happened across a TV special on Bob Hope and his World War II USO troupes. As I watched those glamorous stars of stage and screen from the forties —Frances Langford, the Andrews Sisters, Kate Smith, Betty Hutton—bravely performing in Europe and the Pacific, I began picturing my students re-creating those acts for elderly servicemen in our corner of Nevada.

The next day in class I brought up my idea. It clicked immediately with the kids. We studied old USO films, watched World War II movies, read novels and magazines from the time and prepared a show to be performed in local nursing homes and senior centers. Our first booking was sure to be our toughest, just over two months away in the area VA hospital. During lunch periods, study halls and before school, the kids rehearsed. Their repertoire ranged from "Boogie Woogie Bugle Boy" and "Over the Rainbow" to "The White Cliffs of Dover" and "I Threw a Kiss in the Ocean."

Our research into the USO dovetailed with the rest of our World War II history lessons, my students studying troop movements and headlines of the day in old newspapers. On weekends I scoured the local antique shows, buying as many mementos from that era as I could afford, pieces the kids could pass to audiences to help set the mood before the shows.

In one dealer's stall, among the musty layers of newsprint and calendar pages and old highway maps, a rectangle of faded yellow caught my eye, a creased and careworn envelope. Printed boldly across its face was the banner Idle Gossip Sinks Ships and then the red smudge of a postmark, 1942. I studied the careful script letters—"To: Miss Lenore Pelka, 28 Henry Street, Staten Island, New York"—and ran my thumb over the return address—"Pvt. Bill Barnes, Co. F. 71st Infantry, APO 49, Ft. Lewis, Wash." I turned the envelope over. It had never been opened.

The hair on my arms went electric. The letter seemed instantly charged, almost alive in my hand. Miss Pelka had never unfolded the sheets inside or read the words from across the continent. What had Private Barnes told young Lenore? Was he about to see action? Were they words of love? Had he lived beyond the war to see her again? Or was it a Dear Jane letter? What had gone unread for so many years? I bought the letter for five dollars, and when I showed it to the class that next Monday, a hush fell over the room. It seemed the long-lost letter, unopened all those years, had grown more potent for its silence. One student burst out from the back of the room, "Let's open it up!"

"No," others yelled, "we can't do that!" Another said we should take a vote.

Carefully I laid the letter on my desk and opened the floor to debate. For the next two days we talked about the Army Post Office, about how difficult the war must have been for everyone, finding empathy for those torn from one another by distance and time. And most of all, we wrestled with an ethical dilemma—should we open the letter or should we respect the privacy of Private Barnes and Miss Pelka? "We have the legal right to open the letter," I reasoned, "but do we have the moral right? Are moral laws higher than legal? Are legal laws always moral?" The letter became a real presence in our classroom, one we couldn't seem to resolve. After some fifty-seven years, no veterans' groups or government agencies seemed able to help us deliver the envelope. But as the day of our big show at the VA hospital approached, our attention returned to our rehearsals, which took on a new urgency and vigor.

Before the show the kids mixed with the veterans, passing around the old newspapers and sheet music and asking the men about their war service. The children all bowed with attention to the voices of the men, some in wheelchairs, some with oxygen tanks. Only one vet sat removed from the rest, his wheelchair near a side door, and I watched fourteen-year-old Ainsley McPherson, who played Frances Langford, make her way over to him. She offered her hand to say hello, but the man jerked his chair away from her and shook his head. "I don't want to talk to you," he growled, "or anybody."

A cloud seemed to pass over Ainsley as she stood beside his chair. Then she said, "Okay," and joined the others in the center of the room. During the show, she sang her heart out on "On the Atchison, Topeka and the Santa Fe." And for the finale, she joined our Bob Hope in a duet of "Thanks for the Memory." That brought down the house. Everyone was yelling, cheering and clapping. After an encore, and after the room began to clear of those crowding the troupe, the same elderly vet near the side door wheeled over to Ainsley. "Forgive me, Angel," he said, "but the docs told me I don't have a month left." He took his glasses off to wipe his eyes. "Your singing was wonderful," he said, and Ainsley took his hand in both of hers.

A local newspaper mentioned the rousing success of the Sparks USO Touring Troupe the next morning, adding a note about the unopened letter we had found. On Memorial Day, a Dallas newsman called to say he'd seen the story posted on the Internet and had located Lenore Pelka! "She is now Mrs. William Barnes of Covina, California," said the man. The class and I decided the right thing to do was to rush the letter to Mrs. Barnes, unopened. She was overwhelmed.

She had indeed married the private a year after the letter had been written, in 1943, before he'd gone overseas. He had become a staff sergeant and received a Purple Heart during the war. She told us that he'd written to her several times a day. And this one lost letter was even more precious because he had died just three years earlier, after fifty-three years of marriage. "This is a piece of him," she told our class, "and I'll cherish it to the end of my days."

"What did it say?" we asked.

"Oh, it was just a postcard," she said, "from a USO." For our class, everything had come full circle.

Lunch Box Notes

by Catherine Madera

Finally, it was quiet. The kids were in bed, the dishwasher was running, a second load of wash was in the dryer. At last, a moment to myself. I get so few of these. Sinking down at the kitchen table, I noticed some sketches lying there. Sketches that my daughter, seven-year-old Haley, was always doing. I picked them up for a closer look. *Hmm.* There was a drawing of Mark, my husband, with Haley, crooked smiles on their squiggly faces. "Daddy loves me," it read. And there was one of Haley and her brother, twelve-year-old Nicholas, running through lime-green grass, a lemon-yellow sun beneath cotton-candy clouds. "Nicholas plays with me," she wrote. Then there was a sketch of a woman with short blonde hair and sharp blue eyes, staring at a box with her hands next to it. "Mommy loves to work on her computer," it read. I stared for a long time at that one.

Until a sad feeling made me turn away. Why hadn't Haley shown the two of us together doing something, as she had with her father and brother? Why was I by myself, working at the computer? Yes, I did a lot of work on the computer. I had a part-time job that kept me busy at home—in between taking the kids to school, church and their friends' houses. Not to mention keeping the house running, especially when Mark, a truck driver, was working long hours, often driving a truck to Seattle. But why was Haley so hard to reach? She was so different from her older brother. Nicholas was straightforward and logical. He was very easy to understand and talk to.

Haley always seemed to be lost in some imaginative world. She had long stories to tell me about made-up characters (whose names I could never seem to remember), and she was constantly arranging her stuffed animals into groups that made no sense to me until I would pick up one and she'd exclaim, "Mom, don't interrupt their tea party!" What hurt most was that Haley didn't picture me playing with her. I would try sometimes. I'd sit down at the tea party, but soon my mind would be running to all the things I had to get done: laundry, e-mails, dinner, work. I guess I just wasn't very imaginative. And no wonder. I lived in the real world 24/7. We read books together at night and I always admired her artwork, but as the latest batch showed, I wasn't in any of the pictures with her, as though I just did the chores, making the peanut-butter sandwiches and serving as chauffeur, yet never really connecting.

Twenty minutes later, my last chore of the night, I was making Haley's lunch for school when I noticed the napkin—as blank as all those pieces of paper before she started drawing on them. A thought came into my mind: *Haley needs to know how you see her.* Hesitantly, I picked up a colored marker. I didn't have a lot of artistic talent, but I started drawing anyway, as best I could, on the napkin. I made two stick figures holding hands, one taller than the other, and at the bottom I wrote, "Mommy loves Haley." I slipped the napkin into her lunch box. She didn't say anything about it when she came home from school the next afternoon. *Maybe she didn't even notice*, I thought. Or maybe my drawing was so bad she'd rather not say anything. Maybe she thought it was just some terrible mishap I'd had with a colored marker. But that night, as I was emptying out Haley's flowered lunch box, I noticed that instead of throwing her napkin away after lunch, she had left it carefully folded at the bottom.

I took out a new napkin and with a yellow marker drew a big sun with eyes and eyelashes and a smile on it. "You are my sunshine," I wrote. "Love, Mommy."

That day after school she started giggling as soon as she walked through the door. "I'm not your sunshine," she said.

"Yes, you are," I said. She came close for a hug and I started singing, "You are my sunshine, my only sunshine. You make me happy when skies are gray. . . ."

I put a note in Haley's lunch box every day after that. Pictures of our dog, our cat. Or I'd draw (badly) a flower or the tree in our backyard with the tire swing. But I'd always try to find something in it that reminded me of Haley—her stuffed bear, her pink bicycle, the ribbon in her hair. And I think, in a funny way, that the worse I drew, the more Haley loved the napkins, as if the effort meant so much more than the result. And clearly I struggled.

One night I went into the kitchen to turn off the lights before bedtime. The house was quiet. Haley and Nicholas were tucked into bed. Before I flicked off the light, I noticed something lying on the counter. A napkin. There were two hearts down at the bottom with squiggles connecting them and a message in pink: "Haley loves Mommy."

Call Me Coach

by Joyce Simonson

By the time I hit my late forties, life felt like it had reached a plateau. I'd married in my teens, and now my kids were grown and I was divorced, living alone in a small, quiet condo. I was still teaching history at Curtis High School on Staten Island, just a few miles from where I'd grown up. I'd been a teacher for seventeen years. I loved teaching, considered it my calling to impact my students' lives. Lately, though, it hadn't felt that way. Curtis had changed a lot. Staten Island had changed. Gone was the bucolic, semi-rural suburb with a view of teeming Manhattan. The island was packed and so was Curtis, with three thousand students in a school designed for sixteen hundred. Classes were big, the halls were crowded, days were hectic. I was running at full steam. Maybe beyond full steam.

It was at the start of that school year that I noticed the flyer posted in the school office: "Boys' soccer coach needed." I didn't pay much attention. I didn't know a thing about soccer. The closest I'd come to sports was working the food booth for my boys' Little League teams way back when.

The next day the note was still there. And the day after. A week went by. Finally I asked about it. The previous coach was busy with the girls' basketball team. No one seemed to want the job. The athletic director, Hank Butka, was planning to cancel the season.

I could have walked away. But for some mysterious reason—almost as if my feet had a mind of their own—I found myself heading to Hank's office.

"You're really going to cancel the season?" I asked him.

"If no one takes the job," he said. He didn't look too happy about it.

The words came out of my mouth before I knew what I was saying. "I'll do it."

Hank looked at me funny. "Joyce, you don't know a thing about soccer, do you?"

"No, but I know I can learn," I said.

"Have you ever played?" he asked.

"Um, no. But I know some other local coaches. I'll talk to them."

Hank wavered. "Your first game's in two weeks. The kids don't even have uniforms yet. You sure you're up for this?"

I nodded, trying to mean it.

A few days later, after a trip to a sporting goods store for uniforms and books on soccer, I called the team into my office. Luckily, there were nine returning seniors. Maybe they could help teach the younger kids. The boys slouched and milled around the office. They were from a medley of nations—Egypt, Pakistan, Bahamas, Honduras, Guatemala, Mexico, Poland, Costa Rica, Vietnam, Jamaica and one kid from Staten Island.

"Where's the coach?" Aldo Santos, from Honduras, asked.

"You're looking at her," I said.

Everyone froze. Twenty-three pairs of eyes locked on me.

"A woman?" burst out Aldo. He looked around, as if waiting for someone to tell him it was a joke. Silence. He snorted and stalked from the room. I let him go.

"We're practicing this afternoon," I said. "And every day this week. We have a game coming up."

"Um, Miss," someone mumbled. "We never practiced on school days before. Only before games."

"Well, maybe that's why this team has never had a winning season. Look, I'll be honest with you all. I don't know a lot about soccer. But I know about learning. And we're going to have to work—and learn—together this year. So let's stop talking and start playing."

There was some exasperated muttering, but everyone filed out onto the field. I began some passing drills and right away noticed something strange. The boys seemed very good—they all came from countries where kids start kicking soccer balls as soon as they can walk—but they never used each others' names. It was always, "Hey, red shirt!" "Yo, curly hair!" I called them together. "Doesn't anyone know anyone else's name?" They shook their heads. I ordered them to introduce themselves and assigned each boy a running partner.

That raised a new problem. "Miss, I can't be with him. He's Egyptian."

"What's wrong with that?"

"I'm from Honduras. We don't speak the same language. I'm not going to pass to him."

The other boys had similar objections.

I put my hands on my hips. "That is not acceptable. If I see anyone refusing to pass to someone from another country, I'm pulling you off the field. I don't care how good you are. Is that clear?"

They sulked through the rest of the practice. Aldo turned up and joined in, his attitude even worse. By the time I got home, I was exhausted. Crawling into bed, though, I realized I'd been so busy thinking about the day and planning the next practice, I hadn't noticed the quiet of my condo. It was like the kids were still with me.

Slowly, the team got better. As I'd warned, I pulled kids off the field for refusing to pass. That got their attention. Then we won a game and complaints tailed off. We won a second game and I stopped hearing comments about being a woman coach. One day, Aldo shyly asked if I could give him a ride home. How surprised was I to discover he lived in the same condo complex? I dropped him off and told him I was going to park my car. "It's okay, Miss, you don't have to come in with me."

"Aldo, I live here."

His eyes widened. A few minutes later he knocked on my door. "Um, Miss, my family's all out working. Would it be okay if I did some homework here?" Not a problem, I said, and soon my condo became Aldo's unofficial study hall.

A local newspaper, noticing we were winning, started covering our games. "Soccer Success Starts with Simonson." I posted the stories on a bulletin board and the boys pored over them, shouting excitedly when they saw their names. A film student from a nearby community college asked if she could make a documentary about the team. I said sure, as long as I could show footage to the boys. I bought pizza and popcorn and held film sessions in my office. The boys loved it, hooting at every pass and goal. They got along so well, I decided to try taking them bowling one weekend. They bowled about as well as I passed a soccer ball. We had a fantastic time.

One Saturday, three of the boys showed up at my place. By this point, I wasn't at all surprised by these visits. My condo, once so quiet, was now filled most afternoons and weekends with boister-ous soccer players. Steven, one of my forwards from Guatemala, and Jack and Michael, both Polish defenders, announced they wanted to take my Mercury Sable to be cleaned.

"We don't mean to be rude, Miss, but your car stinks," said Steven. "It smells like soccer balls and sweat." I couldn't argue with that, so I gave them the keys. A few hours later they returned, my car looking like new. "Don't worry about it," they said. "You think we could come in and watch a movie?"

We had made it to the playoffs. Then the semifinals. Then, to everyone's amazement, we were in the league championship, playing Lincoln High School in Brooklyn, a New York soccer power-house. More than two hundred people showed up at the Lincoln stadium, including a stunned Hank Butka. The boys played brilliantly, passing with confidence, working as a team. When the clock ran down, the score was tied 1-1 and the game went to overtime. Then to a second overtime. Finally, the winner was to be decided by a penalty shootout. The shots went back and forth, neither side scoring. Then Lincoln scored. We had to score or it was over. The ball was lined up, shot toward the goal—and missed. The crowd gasped. My heart fell. Then suddenly I saw my boys cheering. They were running around the field, hoisting their second-place trophy as if they'd won the championship. They surrounded me and swept me along, and it hit me: They had won. No Curtis team had ever come so far. Not anywhere near! Those boys had never made such good friends, never in their adopted country found such a home.

And neither, I suppose, had I. I often think back to that day I walked into Hank Butka's office and took on a job I knew nothing about. I felt compelled to do it, as if some mysterious force pushed me there, pushed me off my plateau and into a life I could never have imagined. Nineteen years later, I'm still grateful. That's how long I've been the soccer coach at Curtis High School. Or maybe I should say "Miss" Coach, like my kids call me.

I'm such a mom to them, I even became the legal guardian of one of my players, a West African immigrant named Tombo Berete, whose parents sent him to the United States to escape civil war in his native country. He's now grown up, married with kids—and working as my assistant coach.

These days my car still smells like soccer balls—and the sweaty soccer players I drive all over town. I actually retired from teaching in 2005. But not from coaching. My day doesn't really begin until I pull on my Reeboks, my white-and-maroon Curtis Warriors sweatshirt and the matching windbreaker that says "Coach Simonson" across the back. I pull out my keychain with the whistle attached and head to the soccer field, perched on a hill above New York harbor. The breeze blows fresh up there. Fresh like the game that gave this old teacher such new—and wonderful—life.

Adventures on the No. 5 Bus

by Mary Ann O'Roark

I was six years old when I took my first bus ride. It was on a visit to my grandmother in Steubenville, Ohio. We hurried up the hollyhock-lined alley to the stop and climbed aboard the rumbling city bus. Grandma Paisley greeted the driver by name. I watched out the window as we rode down past the Bond Bread sign (you could smell the bread baking), Woolworth's and the stately courthouse where Grandpa Paisley had been a judge. Then the bus chugged back up the hill. We got off at Mackey's confectioners for strawberry ice cream cones and then walked the rest of the way home. Even when I grew up and moved to new cities, I loved riding mass transit—to get a tour of the city, to feel like a local. I rode the yellow trolleys in Pittsburgh in college. A TWA stewardess based in San Francisco, I went blocks out of my way to hop on the clanging cable cars. It was fun being with all those other people, wondering what their lives were like and watching the world go by.

In 1964, I moved to New York City. For years I got around by walking or dashing underground to take the subway. But I sometimes felt small on the sidewalk amid the skyscrapers or a bit cut off in the underground tunnels. One drizzly day, as I lugged a shoulder bag full of manuscripts to work, I saw the bus coming. The bus! I climbed aboard. Instantly I felt at home again. And so began my mornings on the No. 5 bus. I'd leave my apartment and wait near a pretty park along the Hudson for the bus to come. I'd get a seat if I was lucky. Or I'd hold tight to the overhead bar as the bus swept down Broadway, passing Harriet's Heavenly Nail Salon, glorious Lincoln Center, the American Bible Society building and a place above a bodega where, according to the sign, you could "Learn to Scuba Dive" right in the middle of Manhattan. Finally we reached my stop on Thirty-third Street and Fifth Avenue, right next to the Empire State Building.

From the bus window, I've seen Amish women in sunbonnets, Hasidic men wearing broad-brimmed hats, a gaggle of girls whose earrings swung like wind chimes and a boy walking five dogs tugging him in different directions. There have been schoolkids breakdancing, truckloads of bagels being delivered and Mel Gibson making a movie. What a difference from Steubenville, Ohio! The passengers have been a cross section of ages, colors and nationalities. They read newspapers, novels, guidebooks and Bibles in half-a-dozen languages. Conversations rise and fall like music. Once a woman passed around a jar containing her latest kidney stone. On a winter morning the trip turned into a Seinfeld episode when a disgruntled passenger, a stubborn driver and an annoyed policeman exchanged words and the bus was declared "under arrest." I've even seen a Chihuahua jump out of a man's shirt.

One day the bus got stuck in traffic, and I glanced at my watch, a headache rising. *Dear God, I'm going to be late. Help me calm down.* That's when I looked out the window and saw a disheveled man pointing at our bus. "Look at all those normal people rushing to go to work!" he shouted. "They must be crazy!" I laughed out loud. Another time I wondered how I'd juggle a visit to a sick friend, a family wedding and a speech at a women's retreat. Then I saw a panel in the bus ceiling that said "Push up for ventilation." I took some deep breaths and settled down. A few weeks later, my anxieties kicked in again as I struggled to draft an article. On came a recorded warning about pickpockets: "Be alert for staged distractions." Aha! That's what my mind was doing, staging its own distractions of worry and doubt. I refocused and kept writing.

But the best help has come from other people on the bus. One morning last spring I was in a snit because—readers, you can choose a reason—I slept through the alarm/couldn't find a clean blouse/remembered that I forgot to clean the litter box. The bus pulled up and the door whooshed open to reveal a beaming driver. "Why are you lookin' so down?" he boomed. "Come aboard! Be happy! The world's a wonderful place!" His greeting changed my whole attitude.

Last July I sat by the window blinking back tears after having my twenty-year-old cat Lucy euthanized. *God, I could use some help here.* A few blocks later a woman who'd once lived in my apartment building boarded the bus.

"How are you?" Ann asked as she took the seat beside me.

"I had to have Lucy put to sleep yesterday. How's your dog, Toby?"

"Toby's in pretty bad shape," she said. "I think I'll have to do the same thing soon." We told stories about the animals we loved, patted each other's arms and wiped the tears from our eyes. "This is what Jewish people do when they sit shivah," Ann said. "After the death of a loved one, we tell stories and comfort each other. You and I are sitting shivah right here on the bus."

I thanked her. "Being with you today is an answer to prayer," I said. An answer to prayer. How many times a ride on the No. 5 bus had proven to be just that! All I had to do was pay attention to the answers all around me.

On September 11, 2001, on my way to work, traffic came to a complete standstill. Suddenly a woman wearing a headset gasped. "The radio says a plane crashed into the World Trade Center," she said. *Give strength and courage to those in danger*, I prayed. The next few days the bus was quiet, shock and sadness on everyone's face. A caretaker kissed the cheek of an elderly woman in a wheelchair. A father reassured his daughter, his big hand cradling her small fingers. The driver said, "We all have to watch out for each other." I thought of the words of Jesus: *I will not leave you comfortless.*

That comfort stayed with me in the following weeks as passengers started to chat and laugh again, pens came out for crossword puzzles, and a baby hurled a rubber alligator and a man in a business suit returned it to her again and again. These are the people who give me the heart to go on. They are the answers to my prayers. Answers that surround us every day when we become part of a community. For me, that community can be as close as a ride on the No. 5 bus.

The Mystery of Marshall

by Troylyn Ball

The nurse tucked my newborn baby into my arms and told me, "He's perfect." In that wonderful moment, everything else fell away—the eighteen-hour labor, the cesarean section, the anxious months anticipating my firstborn. My life became those ten tiny fingers reaching out to me, the sweet smell of his warm breath, the corn-silk hair on his head so soft it almost melted under my touch.

"He is perfect," I told the nurse. "And he has your lips, Charlie," I said, turning to my husband, who stood beside my bed rail. As he reached out and touched the bottom of the baby's foot with his fingertip, I felt my own feet curl, as if my son's reflex were my reflex and his feelings my feelings. Holding him to me, I thought, *I can't wait to show this boy the world and see it through his eyes.*

We named our son Marshall Stewart Ball, brought him home and began our life together as a family. We would walk our neighborhood in the early cool of evening with Marshall in the stroller. And down by Town Lake, on the paths where everyone goes to watch the bats fly at dusk, we would meet other couples out walking their babies. As the months passed and we got to be friends with these couples, we couldn't help but notice something odd: Marshall didn't seem to be developing as quickly as the other children.

In fact, at two months, Marshall remained at his birth weight and still didn't truly track us with his eyes the way babies are supposed to. *Does he see me at all?* I caught myself thinking. Our pediatrician became concerned too as our son continued to lag behind. At six months, while other babies were learning to sit, Marshall couldn't hold his head erect. Charlie and I vowed not to worry, telling each other that Marshall would eventually catch up to the other babies. It wasn't a race, it wasn't anything to lose sleep over, yet I prayed more and more with each passing day. *Lord, I want Marshall to look at me, to know that I am his mother and I love him.*

One night, as he approached his first birthday, I lay Marshall down on his stomach in the living room. He scrunched up with his knees drawn to his chest. "Charlie!" I called, sensing something was wrong. "Come quick!"

Charlie ran to the doorway. I glanced back at our baby. Marshall's body jerked out of control, twisting and convulsing on the floor. For an instant I was paralyzed with fear. Then I rushed to my baby and took him in my arms. "Don't worry, everything will be all right," I said, trying to reassure myself as well as him. We brought him to the hospital and learned about the grand mal seizures that we would soon be seeing as many as ten times a day. Each time, I felt that familiar fear and helplessness as I watched and tried to soothe him, praying all the while that the seizures would stop, as the doctors said, and that Marshall might simply enjoy getting to know the world around him, like other kids his age.

During our quiet moments alone in the mornings, I would sit and watch him. "What are you thinking, Marshall? What are you feeling inside there?" I'd ask him, his eyes drifting upward and away. "Marshall," I'd say, "I love you, your father loves you, and God loves you."

For the next two years, it seemed our lives were broken down into test after test, specialist after specialist, not one of them able to say what was wrong with Marshall. They would offer possible diagnoses—cerebral palsy or pervasive developmental delay—but not one spoke with any certainty or had a prognosis we could hang our hopes and prayers on. We worked at getting his seizures under control, but not one of the doctors could do anything but try to steel us to the idea that Marshall would, in all likelihood, never be able to speak, never be able to respond to us in a meaningful way.

Despite these dark predictions, a conviction grew in me: *Don't give up on Marshall. Don't give up, Troy. Don't give up on his abilities. Don't give up on Marshall.* I refused to believe the experts and refused to stop trying to reach my son, even as I looked at him and kept on wondering what was inside, what he was thinking.

By his third birthday, Marshall did not even have the muscle control to sit unsupported, never mind talk or crawl or play like other children. The less Marshall could do, though, the more I wanted to surround him with love. When we visited other children, their mothers would tell them not to run around Marshall, not to shout or yell or do anything a normal child does. The mothers would apologize, as if Marshall were sick, and I wanted to cry and say, "Let them play, let them run, let my son be a part of things."

But I would stay as silent as Marshall. I would scoop him up into my arms and head home. At night, Charlie and I would tuck him into bed and read him stories or poetry or pages of the Bible, and Marshall would listen quite rapt, it seemed, though silent, always silent.

How I longed to hear him babble—Dada or Mama, goo-goo—anything. How often I prayed for his words to come. I longed to know what he thought, how he felt, who he was. He was my son, my flesh and blood, yet at the same time he was a complete mystery to me. *Lord, does he even know us?* Anything is better than not knowing.

Then came that unforgettable morning. I like to think it was a cat that finally unlocked the door.

Marshall was three-and-a-half years old. I was holding him, doing the things mothers do with their children—counting games, word games, sing-alongs—showing him a new toy lying on the floor. "Marshall," I said, "this is the cat."

Holding the toy at his eye level, I pressed a button on it and out of the tiny speaker came the meow of a kitten.

I felt my son shift in my lap and tilt himself toward the button with the cat. Had he merely lost his balance? Was it just a fluke? My heart quickened. "Can you show me again, Marshall?" I asked. "Where's the cat?"

I held my breath and Marshall slowly, carefully bent and touched his forehead to the cat button. The tinny meow of that kitten seemed the most beautiful sound I had ever heard.

One by one, I called out each of the animals to Marshall. And one by one, he touched each of the right buttons.

Meow...

Moo...

Quack...

Woof...

"You understand!" I exclaimed, hugging him with one arm and wiping my eyes with the other. Finally, we had gotten through to him—or he to us—and I rocked him in my arms, saying, "I knew you were inside there, Marshall. I knew you were listening. I knew not to give up."

Charlie and I soon had every variation of that toy for Marshall, and our son would point out fog horns and fire sirens, chickens and elephants. It didn't take a specialist to tell us how much Marshall loved communicating with us. His face would go from slack and nonattentive to intense and engaged. With the help of family and tutors and therapists, Marshall soon graduated to blocks and dominoes, checkers and picture boards to help him interact. He still lacked the muscular strength to lift his arm, but with someone supporting his elbow, he could tap his hand on the button or picture he needed.

By the time Marshall turned five, we'd determined through tests that he could read and do basic math. We got an alphabet board for him. Each letter was a two-and-a-half-inch square, and the board soon became Marshall's lifeline to the world. Within weeks our son was not only tapping out letters but also words. His progress came haltingly, from yes-or-no answers to long strings of letters we could find no meaning in.

At five-and-a-half years old, still unable to pronounce the simplest word, Marshall sat in my lap one morning, his letter board before us, and slowly pointed out the letters to me. I jotted them down until Marshall stopped; then I held the tablet and began to decipher what he'd written. The hair on my arms went electric as I realized that the letters spelled words and the words flowed into lines of poetry:

> God is good and merciful,
> because he is also bright and intelligent.
> Seeing, feeling all that is true.
> Clearly he feels and listens to all our desires.
> Clearly he has everybody's
> dreams in mind.
> I see a God altogether lovely.

Charlie and I were dumbfounded. Within days of this revelation, we decided to contact a man we'd met at an art exhibition two years earlier, Dr. Laurence Becker. He was an educator specializing in the area of prodigies and savants. He told me he didn't work with the handicapped. Still, he agreed to see Marshall.

"Marshall," I said, "do you feel like writing for this nice man?"

The labor of writing began, me supporting Marshall's arm while Dr. Becker transcribed. "I really love writing," Marshall hammered out, at last.

"Good!" said Dr. Becker. "Write whatever you feel like, Marshall."

At that, Marshall began pointing out letters, which I called out to the doctor, who recorded them. The process took a long time, but when Marshall finished, he looked serene. "Oh my," the doctor said, his voice hardly more than a whisper.

"What's Marshall say?"

"Even though my individuality finds sweet knowing perfection," the doctor read aloud, "I listen for the answers to wishes from above."

"That's incredible," I said, "isn't it?"

"You have to nurture this boy's gift, Mrs. Ball—it's really something worth sharing with the world."

Three years ago, just before Christmas, Marshall indicated to me that he'd like to make a collection of his favorite poems as a gift for his father. We decided to print a hundred copies of that book, *Kiss of God*, to give to friends and family and, of course, Charlie. In the foreword, Marshall writes, "Questions nicely want good answers . . . I hope to gather thinkers, to give them my thoughts about love . . ."

We could never have imagined just how far Marshall's book has been able to reach since that first holiday. A local library invited him to be a guest author, and so many people wrote to us, asking for copies of the book, that we printed another five hundred. Then it found its way to a publisher and eventually into enough people's hearts that Marshall, a boy still unable to speak, found himself on some best-seller lists, with more than 195,000 copies of *Kiss of God* sold to date.

I am grateful to be a part of this journey with Marshall—this spiritual and intellectual odyssey of his—as we have worked almost every day at his writing. Each day is a blessing and an adventure for us with no destination in mind, only the journey. But that might be what we've learned best from Marshall, that every day is a wonderful gift to us.

Now, every time I touch his elbow, I feel more blessed than I ever thought possible, knowing that, as Marshall wrote, God feels and listens to our deepest desires, mother and son. There is, to me, no other explanation for how Marshall's words come together, one silent letter at a time, in marvelous poetry, giving me a glimpse into a world that is at once mysterious and altogether lovely.

The Cat Who Came Back

by Michael Sowders

I was foraging in the general store on my usual monthly run into town when a voice seemed to just barge into my thoughts: *Michael, why don't you pick up a few cans . . . just in case?* I was standing in front of a shelf full of cat food. *Just in case of what?* I wondered. *Just in case that darn stray cat comes sniffing around my place again?* If I was going to do anything with a can of cat food, I would probably throw it at him. I'd moved way out here in the middle of nowhere—a twelve-mile truck drive and then six more miles via snowmobile from town—so no one would bother me. But the urge to buy cat food kept at me. Finally I picked up a few cans and shoved them in with the rest of my groceries. I headed for the register.

I dreaded this part. I'd have to stand there while the girl rang me up. Sure, she was used to me, never asked questions. But it was uncomfortable standing there while she eyeballed each and every item, like I was being X-rayed or something. The cat food. That would get her attention. I stared at the wall above her head, down at the floor, at my hands.

"You got a cat?" she asked, her eyebrows arched as she rang up the cans.

"Nope," I said. Her face red, she went back to bagging my things without saying another word. Probably thought I was trying to stretch my food dollar. I paid for my stuff, piled into my pickup and hit the long, snowy road home. Home was a cabin I'd built myself, from scratch, using money from a small inheritance and some of my savings. My nearest neighbor—a real nice lady named Ina Rae—was two miles away. Close enough.

If I sound like a fellow who'd given up on life, well, that's not quite true. I'd given up on people. I suppose it started when I was small. My parents were kind of rough on me. I'd hide out in my room and stay below the radar. If this was the way people who were supposed to love you treated you, just imagine how the rest of the world must be, animals included.

I graduated high school by the skin of my teeth. College? Yeah, right. I hit the road and didn't look back. I hadn't talked to my folks since. In fact, I didn't even know where they lived anymore. I worked a whole bunch of jobs, eventually settling in as a janitor at a school. People left me alone unless something needed fixing. I made sure things stayed fixed. Sometimes I'd go down to the boiler room or into an empty classroom and read. One of my favorite books was *Walden* by Henry David Thoreau. Thoreau sought meaning by living alone in a cabin on a lake. That appealed to me. Self-discovery. No one to answer to. No one to talk to. Just me.

I traveled. Alaska, British Columbia, the Yukon, all over the Northwest. Eventually I got to Sandpoint, in northern Idaho, and decided to stick around for a while. Found myself a nice spot of land and built my own Walden. There was something in the air here, just a nice feeling. Peaceful. There was nothing better than sitting out on the deck and kicking back. I'd look at the mountains, the clouds and the pine trees until my mind got quiet and all I could hear was the babbling creek. Times like that, it was almost like I just dissolved into the air.

One cold day when the air froze your breath as soon as you exhaled, something under the picnic table caught my eye. A splash of gray against the winter white. I stooped over for a better look. A cat. "Shoo!" I yelled. The critter looked up at me. I stamped my foot and yelled again. The cat shot off the deck and disappeared. *How the heck did a little cat get out here in the middle of nowhere anyway?* I wondered. Well, it wasn't my problem, and I wasn't taking in boarders. All right, then. So how come I'd just bought cat food? I couldn't come up with an answer. I stopped the pickup and transferred everything to my snowmobile. Still had another six miles to go. Yep, I really was in the middle of nowhere. Once in a while I'd run into Ina Rae. She knew not to ask me too many questions. *Maybe you could get her to come take the cat,* I thought.

The snowmobile bounced along, jarring me back to my senses. *Get Ina Rae to take the cat? And then be caught up with her always telling you about how it's doing, asking if you want to visit?* No way. It was bad enough I had to deal with people in town once a month. I finally reached my cabin. No sign of the cat. I put away my provisions, shaking my head at myself for wasting good money on cat food.

Next morning, there he was, out on the deck. Just a ball of gray fur. He wasn't moving. I walked over. Was he dead? No. Still breathing. I couldn't just leave him out there. I cradled him close to my chest, carried him inside and sat down next to the stove. His fur was covered with ice. After a while he opened his eyes and stretched a bit. Then he reached a paw out toward me. "Hey," I said, shaking it. I set out the cat food in a bowl next to some water. He was wary at first, but when he finally dug in, he practically licked the dish clean.

I let him be while I did some chores. Frankly, I wondered how I'd ever get rid of him now. Then, just like that, he was gone. I felt panicky. "Here, cat!" I called from the deck. I went back in and searched all over. No cat.

Fine, I told myself. *Better that he doesn't start depending on you anyway.* He came back, though, scratching at the door. That night he jumped up onto the bed and settled down on my pillow. "Get out of here! It's bad enough I took you in. You are not sleeping with me!" I nudged the cat off the bed. He jumped right back on. The only way I got any sleep was to give in and let him stay.

The next morning I decided that maybe Ina Rae could give me some advice. "Michael, what a surprise!" she said when I showed up at her door.

"I found this cat," I told her, "and he's driving me nuts."

"Cats are all different," she told me. "But don't worry. He'll let you know what he needs. And he'll settle in eventually."

"He'd better not," I said. "Come spring, he's gone."

One morning I awoke to a quiet rumbling, like an outboard motor way off in the distance, as peaceful a sound as I'd ever heard. I lay back and just let it kind of vibrate through me, and for the first time in years I found myself thinking of my parents. Finally I turned my head. The cat was curled in a ball, eyes closed, purring contentedly. "What am I gonna call you?" I asked him. "Can't keep saying 'cat' all the time." I went through a bunch of possibilities, finally settling on Jake. Jake slept next to my head every night. He followed me on walks in the woods and nestled in my lap while I sat out on the deck. Ina Rae told me how happy I looked. Once, she wouldn't have dreamed of saying such a thing.

Time for my monthly supply run came. I loaded up on cat food. The poor checkout girl probably thought I'd developed a taste for it. Taking a big breath, I gave her the news. "I got a cat. His name's

Jake." It was the first time in a long time I'd told anyone a thing about myself. . . . Just a simple, insignificant fact, but for me it was a momentous occasion. You know something? It felt good. It felt like I'd opened a window and let some fresh air in. Now I was anxious to get home to my cat. Plowing through the backwoods of Idaho on my snowmobile, I couldn't help but think of how beautiful everything looked, almost as if I hadn't noticed it before. I really did live an isolated existence. Even Thoreau eventually rejoined society. Maybe other people weren't so bad after all, at least in small doses. I mean, look how wrong I'd been about cats.

And while I was at it, maybe I could track down my folks and give them a ring.

Humanities 101

by Marilyn Strube

I scanned the three-hundred-seat lecture hall on the first day of the fall 2000 semester at Madonna University. Things had definitely changed since I was last in school, twenty-nine years earlier. Guys didn't wear Harris Tweeds and girls didn't wear plaid skirts anymore. Ripped jeans and baggy sweatshirts outnumbered slacks and pressed shirts by far. Many of the kids had cell phones pressed to their ears. I picked a seat in a center row, hoping to blend in. But who was I kidding? Right before class, a student had asked me for directions. "I'm sorry," I'd said, "it's my first day too."

"Oh, I thought you were a professor," she said, walking away. Now, looking at the fresh, unlined faces around me, I felt ancient. It seemed like I was the only person in that room over twenty-five, let alone forty.

The lights dimmed and a professor who looked about my age took the stage and wrote "Humanities 101" on the blackboard with a flourish. "This course will be broken up into four disciplines: history, art, music and literature," she said. "After each segment we'll discuss what it means to be human." *Right now I'm feeling more like a fish out of water*, I thought.

The professor called roll. I slouched down in my seat to avoid the glances that I knew would come my way when she got down to my name. "Marilyn Strube?"

"Here," I said, trying to disappear into my seat. If only the kids around me knew how much I valued an opportunity they took for granted. After my husband Joe and I got married, I'd worked odd jobs to put him through college. The plan was for him to do the same for me when the time came. But then our first daughter was born. Four more followed and it was only now, with the two youngest in college themselves, that there was time and money enough for me to pursue my long-deferred dream of a degree. I wanted to be the best student I could possibly be.

Does anyone else? I saw some students sending e-mails on Palm Pilots while others played games on laptop computers. The professor launched into a lecture on the many ways in which American history has been recorded, from folk tales to databases. As other students typed, I struggled to take notes in my old-fashioned spiral notebook.

"Now I want you to break up into small groups and write down as many historically significant photographs as you can," said the professor. *As if I didn't feel awkward enough*, I thought. I reluctantly joined the other students in my row.

"There's the picture of the Challenger blowing up," one student said.

"How about the one of the man standing in front of the tank in Tiananmen Square?" said another.

"Or the one of Mrs. Kennedy in the limousine when President Kennedy got shot," I offered tentatively.

Afterward, we found we had thought of more photographs than any other group. One of the students, Mandi, leaned over and whispered to me, "It's great having someone older in our group." I knew she meant well, but her words only made me feel like more of an outsider. After all, what did I have in common with the other students? They were young, carefree, their whole lives ahead of them. For them, this humanities course was just a general education requirement to get out of the way, not the beginning of a lifelong dream.

Each time class met over the following weeks, I only felt more distant from my classmates. All they seemed to talk about were their weekend plans. When did they ever study? From the conversations I overheard between a couple of blonde girls down my row, it seemed they spent all their free time at a bar. Mandi was always sneaking food into the auditorium. Sometimes I even saw students dozing off. I felt bad for the professor when no one answered a question, so I often spoke up. Otherwise I kept to myself. Of course when a cluster of students would troop off together after class, I felt a twinge of envy. But I didn't see how I could possibly relate to any of them. What did these kids know about real life, real responsibilities? To them, college was probably just one long party bankrolled by Mom and Dad.

The morning of the Humanities midterm I got to campus early. I was sitting in my car with my notes on my lap when there was a tap at the window. "Hi, Mandi," I said, rolling it down.

"Hey, Marilyn, I thought that was you. A bunch of us are going to McDonald's for some last-minute cramming. Wanna come along?"

"No, thanks," I said, thinking I didn't want to waste precious study time making small talk. She was probably just being polite anyway.

"If it's a matter of money, I'll treat," she said. "I just got paid yesterday."

I looked up at her, surprised. "You work and take classes full-time?"

"Sure."

Maybe there was more to Mandi than met the eye. At McDonald's

I learned her parents had used all their savings to pay for her sister's recent wedding, so she worked afternoons as a nurse's aide. "That's why I'm always sneaking food into class. Gotta eat sometime!"

"How do you ever manage both work and school?" I asked, thinking about the hours I spent each evening studying.

"Oh, it's not that bad, actually. Lots of students do it. There's a guy in our class whose dad died last year. He has a soccer scholarship, but he still works two jobs so he can send money home to help out his mom."

Soon other students arrived and we started going over our class notes. We talked about jazz music, Impressionism, the Holocaust, Walt Whitman. *I never thought about that poem that way,* I thought, listening to a couple of the students. *These kids really are listening.* We went over virtually every area of the course. "Good luck," I said to them as we went into the exam. And I meant it. Maybe these kids hadn't had to wait thirty years to go to college, but that didn't mean it wasn't important to them.

A week later, Mandi and I compared exams. Mine was an A+! "I couldn't have done so well if I had to manage a job too," I told Mandi, who'd gotten a B.

"Well, then, if you really want to be impressed, look over there," she said, pointing down the row. I turned and saw the two blonde girls who seemed to live for the bar proudly exhibiting A+'s. "Both of them tend bar at O'Malley's," said Mandi. "They had to keep their books open under the counter and quiz each other between orders."

I had to laugh. How wrong I'd been about my classmates. Sometimes teaching comes from unexpected places. It turned out I had much more in common with my fellow students than I ever could have imagined. And that, I think, was the most valuable lesson of Humanities 101.

CHAPTER 10

What Really Matters

Our Daily Baguette

by Sandra Riendeau

I stared at the letter I was writing on my computer screen and bit into a chocolate croissant. The flaky, buttery pastry melted in my mouth. *C'était delicieux!* How could I put into words what these croissants—and the French bakery they came from—meant to our tiny New England town? And what good would my letter do anyway? I'd heard it that morning. The bakery was closing. *Fini.* I set the croissant on a plate and looked out the window. The sky was dark and gloomy, winter still not relinquishing its grip. April in Colebrook, New Hampshire. Not exactly a place songs are written about. Or anyone cares much about.

I resumed my typing. Senator Jeanne Shaheen: There are many of us in the Great North Woods who want to help bring Verlaine Daeron back home...

That morning, when I'd stopped by Le Rendez-Vous, the Main Street bakery run by Verlaine and her partner Marc Ounis had been abuzz. Marc told us the US embassy in Paris refused to renew Verlaine's visa as a business investor, saying the bakery's economic impact was "marginal." No visa, and Verlaine couldn't return from her trip to France. No Verlaine, no bakery.

Devastated, I'd come home and told my husband Jack. We've owned a timber-cutting operation here for years. "There must be something we can do," he said. "Why don't you write our senator?"

Easier said than done. Who'd believe that a town had been transformed by baguettes and some yellow paint?

I typed another sentence. *As you know, our town was awarded a NH Main Street grant, at the same time Verlaine and Marc Ounis came to our town to start their bakery.* I thought back to that day in 2000. Colebrook was practically a ghost town, buffeted by one economic downturn after another. The mood was as dark as our eight-month winters. Desperate for a boost, I'd helped the town win the grant. But business owners were wary of the program. It would take more than paint and new facades to revive Colebrook, they said. The truth was, we didn't believe in our town or ourselves.

Then, out of the blue, Verlaine and Marc arrived. Everyone was talking about the French couple. Who were they and what were they doing here? A few weeks later they bought an abandoned building at auction and covered the windows with paper. What were these foreigners up to? Then the coup de grâce: They painted the building bright yellow with maroon trim. Yellow and maroon!

By the time Le Rendez-Vous opened, the whole town was buzzing about the newcomers. The music, the décor, the food—everything seemed exotic, with names we couldn't pronounce. But Verlaine and Marc were so friendly, so upbeat, so unlike anything we'd ever experienced that it seemed rude to turn down a sample . . . or two . . . or three. Soon people were lined up out the door to buy madeleines and croissants. We were even learning French. *C'était magnifique!*

But that wasn't the amazing part. Within a month at least 70 percent of the buildings in our downtown were undergoing renovations worthy of the work done on Le Rendez-Vous, I typed in my letter to the senator. Yet that wasn't the biggest change. It seemed we'd all undergone a makeover. Everywhere you went people were smiling, quick to lend a hand, wanting to share an idea about a town project. Word spread about Le Rendez-Vous, and people from neighboring towns poured in. New businesses opened. The bakery became a place where town gatherings were held, where friends hung out, a comfy place to sit awhile and read.

I finished the letter, writing: Colebrook would be a very Plain Jane without Verlaine and Marc. We want them here where they belong. What can we do to help? I walked to the corner and dropped my letter in the mailbox. I said a short prayer, hoping God had a soft spot for French pastries. But it was hard to feel optimistic. In the past few months the Ethan Allen furniture factory had laid off a hundred workers. The Ford dealership had closed, along with our biggest restaurant. Now Le Rendez-Vous. Had our town really changed? Once again it seemed we were helpless against forces we couldn't control.

Every time I went to the bakery, Marc seemed more forlorn. It had been nearly a month since Verlaine's renewal was rejected, and still no word. Verlaine, he said, was calling him two or three times a day from Paris to see if he'd heard any news. I talked to friends who had written letters to our senators, to the state department officials. And I knew that some petitions were circulating around town. Would our efforts make a difference? Would anyone at the embassy read our letters?

One night at dinner, over spaghetti and toasted baguettes, I told Jack I dreaded going to the bakery. "It used to be the place I could count on to brighten my day," I said. "Now it feels like a death watch."

"I know," he said. "But I don't think people are giving up. They seem to think they can still make something happen."

"I worry it won't be enough," I said.

Two days later I went to Le Rendez-Vous, afraid the Closed sign might be in the window permanently. But Marc was behind the counter, beaming. "I have news!" he said. "Verlaine got called to go to the embassy tomorrow. They said they'll reconsider her case." For the rest of the day it felt as if the town was holding its breath. We were still sending out last-minute pleas—too late for letters but plenty of time to pray.

Early the next morning I went to Le Rendez-Vous. It seemed like the entire town had the same idea. Marc flung the door open. "They approved Verlaine's visa!" he cried. "Thanks to all of you. The embassy official's desk was covered in letters and petitions. Two pounds of letters! He said they must really like madeleines in that town."

I guess God does have a soft spot for French pastries! The crowd cheered. Then laughed. Then cheered some more. Our French friends had provided the yeast all those years ago, but we had risen to the occasion.

Saxophone Man

by Russell Martin Jr.

I'm a professional baseball player. That means I've heard the national anthem performed before games thousands of times, by solo singers, military choirs, marching bands, the occasional recording star. I place my cap over my heart, stand at attention at the top of the dugout steps and listen. We all do. But honestly, you don't always pay strict attention. It's hard to when your mind is on the game.

But this night was different. That was my dad out there, playing. He stood near home plate in Dodger Stadium last September, blowing into his old, tarnished saxophone ("Don't want a new one," he'd always say. "They don't make them like they used to."), playing to nearly 55,000 fans before our game that night against the Pittsburgh Pirates. I watched anxiously from the top step of the dugout and followed every note, praying for him to do his best.

A few bars into his performance, a funny thing happened. I realized our roles had reversed. All my life he'd rooted for me, prayed for me to do my best. Now I was rooting for him. For most of his days he'd been a street musician, but thanks to him, I was the Dodgers catcher.

Sports and music have been the mainstays in my life for as long as I can remember. Sports, because from early childhood that's what I loved—and did—best. Music, because that was as vital to my dad's life as, well, breathing. Our time together was important to me. He and Mom split when I was almost two, and during the school term I'd stay with Mom. She lived in Ottawa, Canada, two and a half hours from Dad's home in Montreal. Every other weekend I had with Dad, plus the entire summer.

Dad's place wasn't like Mom's. Mom worked as a government analyst and lived in a comfortable home in the suburbs. Dad moved around Montreal a lot, from apartment to apartment, according to what rent he could afford. He couldn't afford much. The biggest place he ever had was four and a half rooms. "Don't you want a place like Mom's?" I asked one day.

Dad sat me down. "Material things have never been important to me," he said. "What's important is happiness, fulfillment, chasing your dreams. My dream is music. Yours is baseball."

It's true. When I was just two, Dad tossed a ball in the living room. I caught it in two hops. "Did you see that?" he yelled, turning to his brother. "I think we've got a ballplayer here." Dad knew what he was talking about. He was more than a musician. He was also an athlete, an excellent baseball player, who was quick and strong and loved the game. When he was a kid, he'd talk his way into pickup games with older boys. "I'm Jackie Robinson's son," he'd say, and he was so good, they believed him.

From the time I was two, we spent every day we could at the local park, me with my little red bat and Montreal Expos cap, him with a bag of baseballs and two fielders' gloves. "Man!" he'd say when I got into one. "You really hit that ball!" At home we turned on the Expos game. Dad is a great storyteller, and all through the game he'd talk about Robinson—how he'd dance off third base, drive the pitcher crazy and then swipe home.

Most of all, I loved it when he went into his announcer's voice: "Now hitting for the Expos, Russell Martin," he'd say. "Bottom of the ninth. Here comes the pitch. There's a shot to deep right field. That ball is . . . out of here!" That's when I knew what I wanted most in life: to be a major-league ballplayer, to hear my name for real over a major-league stadium's booming PA.

Dad worked me hard, putting me through countless drills. Weird stuff, stuff he'd just make up. "I'm going to throw the ball over your head," he'd say. "I want you to dive for it, whether you reach it or not." Sometimes he'd hand me a broomstick and toss a badminton bird at me. "Let's see you hit it," he'd say. Or he'd put a towel over my bat and tell me to swing, to strengthen my hands.

Dad rose each morning before dawn and headed to the subway. There, he'd pick a spot on the platform and play his saxophone, the case open at his feet for donations. When rush hour was over, he returned home and we headed to the park to practice. We broke at lunch; then we returned to the field and practiced all afternoon. I'd be all tuckered out, but Dad went back to the subway station to play for the evening rush-hour crowd.

I never really thought much about how Dad earned his living. There was always food on the table—Dad would cook up a batch of stew or his fantastic chili, and we'd be set for the week. Each night we'd fill our bowls, turn on the tube and watch the Expos play. And we'd talk about life. Dad grew up in tough times. He had to make his own way. "You want to be a ballplayer, you're going to have to earn it," he'd say. "You're not a big guy. Nobody's going to hand you anything. You're going to have to work, work, work. And believe."

That I did. By the time I reached high school age, I was getting pretty good. That summer I asked Mom to let me live with Dad full-time. I didn't want to leave her, but there was a high school that had a great baseball program in Montreal where I could go to refine my game. Mom—who was always there for me and helped Dad out with my expenses—said okay. She even paid a bunch of the tuition for me. The school was across the city, an hour and a quarter subway-and-bus commute away. "You're going to have to make breakfast and get yourself to school," Dad said. "Before you get up, I'll be at work."

One day, passing through the station, I heard the mournful wail of a saxophone. I'd known for years Dad played in the subway, but I'd never seen him perform. The haunting notes poured out, as though the instrument itself were crying. Songs by Miles Davis, Thelonious Monk, Coltrane—my middle name. That must be Dad! I rushed to where he stood on the platform and watched and listened. The rush-hour crowd elbowed by. Some paused a minute to listen and drop coins into Dad's saxophone case. Most had their minds elsewhere and brushed past. Dad never batted an eye. He had an intent look on his face, like his whole soul was wrapped up in his music. *Wow,* I thought. *Dad is really good.*

"I saw you in the subway today on my way to school," I told him that night. "How come you just play during rush hours?" It occurred to me that he could have made a lot more money by playing there all day.

"I do it so that I can spend the day with you and help you practice," he said. "Like I told you, money isn't what's important in life." That's when it hit me how much my dad had done for me, how much he'd sacrificed for me, believed in me. I guess that when you have two people who believe in the same dream, it's twice as likely to come true. I could never pay my dad back. All I could do was be as passionate and devoted to my work as he was to his.

The day I made it to the Dodgers, I figured he'd be even happier than I was. But I couldn't get ahold of him. When Mom finally did, he was standing by the Saint Lawrence River, practicing his second instrument, the flute. He had a hard time talking. He was just too emotional. I flew him to Los Angeles as soon as I could. We were playing the Mets that night. Pitching for them was one of Dad's heroes, Pedro Martinez. I hit a double off of him. As I rounded first, I heard Dad screaming, "Yeah, that's my boy!"

The *Los Angeles Times* did a story about Dad and me. After that, it seemed everyone in the city knew Dad played the saxophone in the Montreal subway. One day he got a phone call from Frank McCourt, the Dodgers owner. "I want you to come back in September," he said, "to play the national anthem."

The night Dad performed, I was walking in from the bullpen, through the clubhouse, when he started playing. I raced to the dugout. There he was on the field, playing that sacred song. He played it slow and soulful, giving it a kind of deeper meaning. I watched him with awe and an indescribable pride.

My dad.

He got a standing ovation when he finished. Both dugouts too. The Pirates players came up to me, saying, "That was your dad? Man, he's amazing." Yeah, but not nearly as amazing as the two of us standing on the brilliant green grass of Dodger Stadium, sharing one dream together.

Doing (Too Much?) for Others

by Janet Holm McHenry

It was birthday number forty-two, but I'd sworn off celebrations. I saved them for my four children. My daughter Rebekah was already in her teens! That, plus the touches of gray in my hair, were reminders enough I was getting older. I didn't need cake and candles to mark the occasion. So my day had unfolded as usual. After teaching and working late in my elementary school classroom, I had sat through a college night course. Nobody could say I'd slowed down any, but I sure was beat when I pulled into the driveway.

The ringing phone greeted me. I answered it, dumping my books on top of the mess on the kitchen counter. It was Rebekah's science teacher. Rebekah had missed her second fund-raising meeting—and had been disqualified from the field trip. I felt queasy. This wasn't just any field trip. Only the top ten students from the entire school had been picked to go on a three-day excursion to the San Francisco area. To qualify, Rebekah had taken a difficult written and oral exam. She had gotten the best overall score. I'd never been more proud of her.

The field trip was the first academically related thing Rebekah had worked for. Because she was bright and learning came easily, she didn't put much effort into her studies. I worried about how she was going to get ahead. When Rebekah applied herself, she was a straight-A student. But friends had always come first for my big-hearted daughter. When someone needed her help, she dropped everything, studying included. That's why those A's appeared only occasionally. With my constant nagging, she seemed to be turning around, making straight A's two quarters in a row. I thought I was winning the battle when she earned a place on the trip.

Rebekah breezed by as I hung up the phone. I dove right in. "I thought this year was going to be about learning responsibility," I lectured. "Getting organized. Not forgetting things. Priorities. Why didn't you go to that meeting?"

"I had to . . . do something for someone," she mumbled.

"And what about you, young lady?" I shot back. "When are you going to do something for yourself, for your education, your future?" She looked at me like I was speaking another language. Frustrated, I stormed up to bed.

I lay there, staring at the ceiling. I had studied hard all my life, constantly trying to better myself, to improve my mind. I was still taking courses, for goodness' sake, and here was Rebekah, copping out in the eighth grade! Eighth grade seemed like a million years ago to me. *A million and one*, I thought wearily, remembering what day it was.

I was on the edge of sleep when my husband opened the door and peeked in. "Janet," he said quietly, "you need to come downstairs."

"I'm tired, Craig. Will you do something about dinner for the kids? It's been a long day. And did Rebekah tell you—"

"Yes, I know about Rebekah. And dinner's been taken care of. But please come down."

The urgency in his voice moved me from the bed down our winding staircase. What was going on? The bottom floor was pitch-black except for a glow from the kitchen. As I turned the last corner on the stairs, I saw the lit candles on a birthday cake. There was more: a clean kitchen, dinner on the table, presents around the cake. Moving closer, I saw that it was shaped like a T-shirt, with "The Best Mom on Earth" unevenly iced across its middle. Forty-two tiny flames vied for space around the message. Rebekah was standing behind the counter, tears dripping down her cheeks as fast as the wax from the skinny candles atop the cake.

"You missed your meeting because of me?" She nodded, wiping her eyes. I went over and hugged her close. "I'm sorry," I whispered.

After dinner, cake and presents, Rebekah and I had a long talk. I had never considered what it was like to be on the receiving end of her generosity. "Your friends are blessed, Rebekah. I see that now. But you worked so hard for that trip. . . ." I still could not quite fathom why she had given it up.

"You're worth it, Mom," she said with teenage nonchalance, but her big, warm eyes told me she meant it.

"I guess I should lighten up a bit, shouldn't I?" I asked her to forgive me for setting unreasonable standards. It was something I did to myself too.

Rebekah is now a young adult, making excellent grades in college, studying to be a teacher. In my opinion, she still overextends herself sometimes, but I am learning to let her be herself. For her own good and for all the people she touches with her good—and generous—heart.

The Dance Lesson

by Kathryn "Kitty" Slattery

When my widowed mother moved in to the in-law apartment attached to our house, I wasn't so sure it was going to work out. There had always been something unsettling about our relationship. I loved my mother, but we were different in so many ways, and I could never completely shake the feeling that she wanted me to be someone I wasn't or that I was somehow a disappointment.

Now Mom was eighty-eight, and it was hard to believe that she had been living in the apartment for ten years. Her macular degeneration had advanced to the point where she was legally blind, and she could no longer drive a car or recognize faces. You'd think I would admire the optimism and courage with which she faced this latest challenge. And I did, most of the time. But old habits die hard, and no matter how much I tried to change, too often I found myself irritated or impatient with her—and disappointed in myself.

One morning the two of us stood in the mudroom that separated our two back doors as my mother waited for a friend to pick her up to go shopping. She was talking about my husband Tom. She was very fond of Tom. But that day she repeated a phrase of hers that always bothered me. "You're so lucky to have found him, Kitty," she said, as though I had chased him down and snared him.

"Well, actually we found each other," I corrected her for what was certainly not the first time. "That's how I like to see it."

"You know, Kitty," she went on, "these are the best years of your lives. You two kids should do everything you can to make the most of them."

"Uh-huh," I replied, only half-listening. *Why does she insist on calling us "kids"?* And this wasn't the first time she had told me that these were "the best years of our lives." It was as though the previous twenty-five years of marriage barely counted.

Determined not to go there, I changed the subject. With our own two kids off at college, Tom had recently surprised me with ballroom dancing lessons. Tom and I could do a rudimentary slow dance, and we could more or less hold our own dancing to a wedding DJ. But we didn't know how to waltz or do the cha-cha or spin and swing to the jitterbug. "Guess what," I said. "Tom says he wants us to take dancing lessons."

"Dancing lessons!" my mother cried, her eyes lighting up behind her thick glasses. "What a wonderful idea! You two are going to love dancing." She and my father certainly had. As a little girl I remember peeking through the balustrade, watching the two of them dance to Benny Goodman or Peter Duchin on the record player in our living room. It used to embarrass me back then, the way Mom went into a girlish dip at the end of a song. She would look at my father with dreamy eyes and sigh, "Oh, John," and he would respond in his best Ralph Kramden voice, "Baby, you're the greatest!"

"I don't know," I said. "We're not like you and Dad." Seventh grade was the last time I had attempted ballroom dancing. Mom was the one who decided to sign me up for cotillion classes. I had never felt so out of place in all my life. I was about two heads taller than every boy. They stepped on my toes and their palms were sweaty. I couldn't wait to get home and tear off my little white gloves. "It's Tom's idea and I'm going along with it," I said.

"I can't wait to hear all about it!" A car horn honked. My mother's ride.

"Don't expect much," I muttered as she went out the door—my feeble attempt to diminish not only her expectations but my own.

The first dance lesson was mortifying. Just like seventh grade, I was self-conscious and awkward, even with my own husband. I placed my left hand on Tom's shoulder and extended my right arm. He rested his right hand on the small of my back and put his left hand in mine. So far, so good. But when we moved it was all wrong. "Left-two-three. Right-two-three . . . ," the instructor intoned. But whose left? Whose right? Tom's or mine? "Back-two-three. Forward-two-three. . . ." I felt like an idiot. Plus, I was getting hot. I stuck out my lower lip and blew a blast of cool air under my bangs. Ballroom dancing was not for me. There was nothing fun about it. My feet didn't do what they were supposed to do and my arms were as rigid as a toy soldier's. I couldn't wait to get out of the studio.

"What do you think?" I asked Tom in the car, massaging my aching toes.

"I think you need to get yourself a comfortable pair of shoes," he said.

We'd taken home a CD with a mix of music to practice with. Initially I resisted, but Tom insisted. The next night he pushed aside the coffee table and overstuffed chair in the sunroom to clear the hardwood floor.

"Do we have to?" I asked.

"We're supposed to," Tom said.

I thought again of my parents swirling and twirling in our living room and Mom with her coquettish dips. When it came to dancing, she was a natural. I was not.

Maybe it'll be better without the instructor staring at us, I thought. *Maybe I won't feel like a geeky seventh grader again.* I put my hand on Tom's shoulder and looked down at my feet as they shuffled in a clumsy box step. "Left, two, three . . . right, two, three." I thought of Mom with my father. They could dance, but things weren't always perfect for them.

I recalled the time just before Tom and I got married when I desperately needed to have a real heart-to-heart talk with my mother. I had been battling an eating disorder and I wanted her to know. I needed to tell her but was afraid of her reaction. Summoning up all my courage, I picked up the telephone and called her. I explained what I was going through. There was a long, long silence. Then she said, "You're not going to tell Tom about this, are you?" Now I looked up at my husband on our makeshift dance floor. Tom had never flinched when I told him about my bulimia. With his support and prayers I had managed to conquer it. Tom's love and faith were constant. I knew for certain he loved me. It wasn't a question of luck. It was something much deeper than that. I was blessed.

"Hey," Tom whispered to me on the dance floor, "you're good."

"No," I said, "it's you."

For a moment the two of us were lost together, without any awareness of time or space. We were really dancing. We could really do it. *Mom*, I thought, *I see why you loved to do this. It's so much fun . . . so romantic.* And there in our sunroom, in my husband's arms, with the music on the CD, I felt I could forgive her for all the things she said over the years that I had found hurtful. I could see how, in her own way, she wanted the best for me. A happy marriage, someone I could always depend on, someone to dance with. All the precious things that she had lost. I closed my eyes and prayed— a simple, silent prayer for my mother.

The next morning I bumped into Mom outside her back door, waiting for a friend to pick her up to go to a Ladies' Guild meeting at church. She wore a leopard-print silk scarf draped around her neck and a wide black belt cinched around her waist. "How are the dancing lessons?" she asked.

"Not bad," I said.

"Are you two practicing?" she asked me.

"You must have heard us in the sunroom," I said.

She smiled and her eyes got a faraway look. "Remember, Kitty," she said, "it may not always seem like it, but these are the best years of your lives. You two kids should do everything you can to make the most of them."

The old familiar words. This time, though, they didn't sting. Yes, maybe I was lucky—lucky to have these last years together with Mom. A chance to redo the past, a chance to heal from lingering hurts. The years wouldn't go on forever. She wasn't getting any younger and neither was I. "Yes," I said, "we're doing our best."

A car horn sounded. Her ride. "Bye, dear." As she descended the concrete steps, she gripped the white wooden handrail and her lips moved slightly as she counted each step, like me counting my dance steps. Before getting into her friend's car, she turned and waved to me. Even though I knew she couldn't see me, I waved back.

Mom's Grand Piano

by J. Fred Coots

In the parlor of our tenement flat in Brooklyn, standing at the place of honor next to our window, was an ancient, richly carved piano. Somehow, with the press of debts, Mother had managed to keep the piano. It was so out of place among our other furniture, people used to laugh at her. "Where'd Mrs. Coots ever get so fine a piano as that big one sitting by her window?" Then the story of Mother's marriage to a wealthy young man was told: how she had four children before her first husband died; how she had "made a mistake" when she remarried; how her new husband went through the family money and then passed on, leaving her penniless. But worst of all was when Mother's neighbors would accuse her of neglecting the children. "Imagine. There she is with her little ones hungry, and she won't sell that piano. . . ." Mother would just close her ears and play a hymn or a sonata. She played with the art of an angel.

As I grew older, I began to notice a pattern in Mother's playing. First thing in the evening, for instance, Mother would come in from her job—she peddled needles and pins—and instead of complaining, she would sit down to the piano and play. Or again on Saturday nights, I would come home from my own job down at Schwab's butcher shop with the eight or ten pounds of meat he would let me have in addition to my pay. Mom used to sit down then, too, and play. "You know, Son, a person's only hurt by life if he thinks he's hurt. There are ways to rise above being poor." Because of these patterns in my mother's playing, I misinterpreted what the piano meant to her. It seemed to me it was a symbol of her old wealth. I imagined her sitting down and dreaming of her beautiful home, as it used to be, and sort of sneering at poverty, as if it never existed.

Then one evening I came home complaining of pain in my legs. I had contracted inflammatory rheumatism and lay in bed for five years. During that illness, I began to understand the piano. The fever ballooned my joints till Mother had to suspend them from the ceiling with homemade pulleys to ease the pain. When I was in despair, Mother played. She came into my stuffy room with a prayer book and a hymn book, and she said: "Listen and learn." While she played the piano from the other room, I listened. I learned the hymns and I read the prayers. To the degree that I forgot myself, the pain vanished, the immediate dropped into perspective.

As I began to get better, Mother would help me into the parlor and get me to exercise my fingers at the piano. To my surprise, I discovered a real joy in music, and as spring came and I was again able to go about, Mother had to reverse her pleading, "Freddie, dear, why don't you run along outside now? The piano can wait."

The hundreds of hours spent at the old piano proved their worth. When I was well enough to start working again, I made my way to Tin Pan Alley and set siege. I was hired to play the new songs for dancers and entertainers. For a while, I forgot all about the fine piano in our home. When Mother passed on, I moved the old piano to my new quarters, more for sentimental reasons than anything else.

Then came the first real break. Eddie Dowling, the great old trouper, was to produce the annual "Friars Frolic" for the Friars Club. I asked Dowling if I could do the musical score for it. "Gee, yes, I'd be glad to let you try," Dowling said with a chuckle, "but I have commissioned Victor Herbert to do the score." Only a few days later, I learned that Herbert was suddenly involved in a new Broadway show. I went to Dowling and reminded him of his word. "All right, Freddie. You can have it."

This all happened around 1921—I've been on Broadway ever since. But in those early years, I began to learn the meaning of some old clichés: "In the scramble to the top, someone's bound to get hurt." "For every light on Broadway, there's a broken heart." I could somehow feel the trend toward a hard heart. I would come home in the evenings to my new, plushly furnished apartment, never whistling, never humming. Sometimes my stomach was tied in knots at the dog-eat-dog influences all around me in show business. I quickly picked up the common yardstick: "Money, old man. It's too bad, I know. It's artificial. But it's cash, J. Fred. How much've you got? That's the mark of success." But the success I was having left me empty.

I remember so well the night all this changed. I had come home busily discontented. As a rule, I managed to give myself so much work that I ignored the emptiness. It's an old trick, but it works— until for some reason you stop and think. That's what happened to me. I was at the piano, playing idly. Suddenly I found myself playing some of the old hymns. I remembered the tenement days, when we all had a lot less, and how we had managed to overcome adversity and misfortune. I sat up, alert, and began to play all the hymns I could recall. I recited the prayers I had learned while I was sick. Somehow the same drifting away from the immediate took place. I was not the all-successful J. Fred Coots, songwriter; I was just another man brought down to earth.

And there was the mystery of Mom's grand piano solved. It wasn't the symbol of her lost wealth. It was the opposite, the symbol of the spiritual in life. The spiritual that let her rise above the present. In adversity, it had proved helpful. But in success, as I have found in the years that have followed, it is simply essential.

Alone on the Farm

by Marsha Hedge

They were sleeping soundly, both of my girls. Too bad I couldn't say the same. I hadn't even changed out of my work boots. I slipped out of the house. Lately I'd been going for walks when I couldn't sleep. Tonight the summer moon cast a soft platinum glow on our rolling green fields, and I walked for a while, letting the stillness and the beauty ease the weariness in my bones.

My eyes fell to the spot by the end of our drive where my husband died. Had it been only a month? Dennis had been killed in a freak accident while using the four-wheeler to get around our farm. I felt a familiar stab in my heart and pulled my gaze away. Nothing could touch that ache. You love someone that much, one day without him seems like forever.

I went back inside. Time to get some rest. I had a long list of things to get done the next day. First, have breakfast with the girls— I wanted to keep their routine as normal as possible. Feed and water the cattle. In the afternoon, once the dew dried, I'd set to baling hay. My neighbors had offered to pitch in, but they had their own fields to worry about. Worrying. Farmers do a lot of that.

There was just so much to do on our 185 acres! Not that I wasn't used to country life. I grew up in Arkadelphia, Arkansas, population ten thousand. Living on a farm, where we could raise our girls to be self-sufficient, was our dream, Dennis's and mine. But being a full-time mom and part-time real-estate agent took most of my energy. Actually working the farm—Dennis had shouldered the bulk of that responsibility.

The place was a mess when we moved here. Dennis saw its potential, though. "We rebuild the fences, tend the pastures . . . it's going to make a nice little farm," he'd said. He pointed to a patch of grass out back, closer to the house. "We'll plant trees there, so our kids can play in the shade. Our grandbabies, too, someday."

Sure enough, eight years and a lot of sweat—mostly Dennis's (he was a workaholic)—had turned that mess into a farm. A home. The only home our girls—Rachel, ten, and Kelsey, six—had ever really known. I'd lost my dad at an early age, and I remembered how my mom held our home, my brothers and sister and me, together, managing her school secretary's salary so wisely that we never felt we wanted for anything. That's why I'd instinctively dug in my heels when people assumed I would sell the farm.

For the girls, I reminded myself as I sank into bed that night. So they can have a connection, through the land.

Yet the very next day I wondered. There I was, out in the middle of a field in the July heat, flat on my back under the hay baler, trying to untangle some twine that had wrapped around the machine's tines. How had my husband kept this farm running so smoothly—all the while working full-time as a veterinary medical officer for the Department of Agriculture?

Fences, cattle, hay . . . I didn't worry because Dennis took care of everything. His way. Capably. Meticulously. Perfectly.

A chunk of hay drifted into my eyes. I swatted it away. How could the Lord have taken Dennis from me? I was so angry at God, I couldn't even pray properly anymore. *Thanks, God,* I thought. *Now I do have to worry. About everything!*

"Marsha, you need a hand?" someone shouted.

I wriggled out from under the baler. It was my nearest neighbor, the one who had shown me how to replace the belts in the mower and attach it to the tractor when I'd cut the hay three days ago. I was embarrassed he'd taken time out to come over again. "Something's wrong with the twine motor," I told him. "That or the bale sensor." At least I'd gotten the terminology down.

"Hmm." He poked around the machine. "Yep, you're right on both counts. The computer chip on your bale sensor must be acting up. And the twine motor needs adjusting."

What next? I thought. *Is there anything else that can go wrong?*

"You look a little peaked, Marsha. You all right?"

"I'm okay," I said and turned the subject back to the baler. My neighbor agreed the baling would have to wait until I could get a repair tech to come out.

I made my way back to the house. I was so tired of depending on others. When would I learn to manage this place for myself? I collapsed in our living-room recliner. There, on the wall opposite, was my favorite picture of Dennis. My husband, wearing a ball cap studded with fishing lures, smiling at me.

I would have broken down completely if I hadn't heard a soft voice.

"Mama?" It was Kelsey. "I miss Daddy so much."

"Come here, Kelsey." I pulled her onto my lap. The next thing I knew, Rachel was there too, touching my shoulder. I covered her hand with mine, remembering how my mom had comforted me after my dad died. How strong she'd been for me and my siblings. If I could only do the same for my daughters!

I swallowed my pride and asked neighbors to help with the

baling. By the end of August there was enough hay cut, raked and baled to last our small forty-head herd through winter. Rachel and Kelsey were back in school, so I figured I'd return to real estate part-time.

Right. Except running the farm took so much time and energy that I couldn't add on showing properties and hope to have anything left for my daughters. There were fields to tend, cattle to feed and water, equipment and fences to maintain. Dawn to dusk, the chores were never-ending, even with the girls pitching in. Dennis and I had wanted to raise them to be self-sufficient, but it wasn't fair to ask them to take on more. Losing their dad was burden enough.

One Saturday they trooped along after me in the tangy fall air to fix fences. Rachel held the posts steady while I hammered. Kelsey was my gofer, fetching nails, tools and water. Tough way for two kids to spend a Saturday, but I didn't hear a single grumble. We finally finished. "We didn't do too bad, huh?" Rachel asked. Kelsey looked up at me proudly.

"Not bad at all," I said, throwing an arm around each of them as we walked slowly to the house. "We make a pretty good team."

I took a last glance back at the fence. To me, the section we'd repaired stood out, the cross-braces looking not quite so perfectly straight as the ones Dennis had put up. *I'm sorry*, I wanted to tell him. *No matter how hard we try, we can't do things right, the way you did.*

The months and the grief wore on. I got stuck in the mud driving around our rain-sodden fields to check on the cows. That winter I took over Dennis's job of keeping the stock pond from freezing over. The cattle had to drink, so I broke up the ice with an ax three times a day, leaving me wet and chilled to the bone. Sure, a less stubborn woman would have given up. But I had to keep going. For the girls.

I must have sounded as miserable as I felt because Mom took to calling every couple of days. She would claim she just wanted to say hi, chat with her granddaughters since the dreary weather was keeping them cooped up inside. But she was checking on me.

"Marsha, I've been meaning to tell you something," she said one day. "You've done a really good job keeping things going. I'm proud of you."

"I haven't done anything nearly as well as I should have," I said. "Not like you. How did you manage so well on your own?" She hadn't had much education or money, after all.

Mom was quiet for a moment. Then she said, "I wasn't on my own. I had help." She paused. "Marsha, only God could help me find the strength to do things my way. Without him, I don't know what I would have done. Accepting his help was the only real choice I had."

I considered that long after we hung up. I'd thought certain people, like my husband and my mother, were naturally more capable, with some inner resolve that went deeper than what the rest of us had. It hadn't occurred to me that strength might come from another source. The One whom I'd been so angry at for taking Dennis and leaving me to fend for myself.

God, you helped Mom. Help me. It was such a relief to ask that. I could almost hear Dennis chuckle somewhere up there in farmers' heaven and say, "Now you've got it, Marsha."

Once you turn to God, turning to others doesn't seem so hard. Come spring, I asked a neighbor to show me how to hook up the tractor equipment again. I snapped pictures of each step so I wouldn't forget.

And I haven't. I'm still working the farm. A local crew does the haying for a share of the bales. I had a freeze-proof drinking fountain installed for the cows. Rachel, Kelsey and I have become even more proficient at building fences. Good thing too, since we've added another 120 acres.

I used to think I was staying on here for the girls, the memory of their father, the legacy of the land. True. But I'm also staying for me. I look out back now, and I see the trees Dennis and I planted, growing, thriving. Just like our dream. One day I'll walk our grandkids under the shade of those trees and show them around the farm, show them why there's no place on God's green earth I'd rather be. And with a little help, this is where I'll stay.

Captain Southworth's Decision

by Scott Southworth

Christmas 2003. An orphanage in the middle of war-torn Baghdad. I was standing by a courtyard play area, talking to one of the nuns who cared for the children about a nine-year-old boy named Ala'a I'd gotten to know—okay, come to love—since my National Guard unit had started visiting the orphanage a few months before. Out of the blue, the nun said matter-of-factly, "A year from now we will have to move Ala'a to a government-run orphanage. He will be too big for us to care for him."

Immediately I pictured Ala'a, so tiny I could wrap my thumb and forefinger around his leg. My stomach felt like I was about to go into combat. This orphanage was run by nuns from Mother Teresa's Missionaries of Charity. It was an oasis of peace in a city of chaos. I knew about that government-run orphanage. It would be a death sentence for a boy like Ala'a, with cerebral palsy, no known relations and an American National Guard soldier for a best friend. I didn't even think. "Then I'll adopt him," I blurted out.

The nun looked at me, surprised. I was stunned too. What had I just said? Had I really offered to adopt a disabled child? From a war zone? I was a workaholic thirty-year-old bachelor with a career back home in Wisconsin. A career I might not even make it home to. Even if I did, what would I do with a nine-year-old? I didn't know how to raise kids. I'd only graduated law school a few years before. I lived with my parents, commuting seventy-five miles each way to Madison, the state capital, where I was chief of staff for my hometown state legislator.

I remembered my first day at the orphanage when Ala'a had pulled himself across the floor with his hands, planted himself right in front of me and smiled the most electric smile I'd ever seen. It didn't take him long to start calling me Baba, Arabic for father. We'd sit and talk—he'd learned crisply accented English from the Indian nuns—walk around and play games in his wheelchair. Sometimes he'd tell me about his prayers. His favorite place in the orphanage was the sisters' small, simple chapel. He prayed all the time, like he knew God was listening. Not like I prayed. Not like any grownup I knew prayed. How could I let him go? And yet—how could I possibly take him?

The nun drifted away, and soon it was time to leave. I said goodbye and, that night, lay in my bunk, mind racing. Outside, sounds of Baghdad's Green Zone—our military police unit was headquartered in a bombed-out former Baathist Party country club—hummed in the winter desert air. Had I just made a promise I couldn't keep? I didn't do that sort of thing. I'd been raised to honor my word. And yet—already I could hear my mom, worrying that combat stress was pushing me over the edge. Dad, who'd been in Vietnam, would understand. He sometimes talked of the kids he'd wanted to rescue from his own war zone long ago. But he was also committed to my public-service career. As committed as I was. I knew what he'd say: "Be very careful, son. You don't know what you're getting into." Praying for guidance, for an answer, for something, I finally fell asleep.

By the time I saw Ala'a again the next week, I'd sent e-mails, telling friends and family what I planned to do. The responses read as expected. Take a little time to think this through, Mom suggested. Dad and I didn't even discuss it.

A friend who was a single mom sent a long e-mail spelling out the difficulties of raising a child, the way it consumes all your time, the emotional commitment.

At the orphanage, Ala'a let me know he wanted to go to America. The nuns too said that all of the kids frequently talked about going there.

Every time I talked to my parents and my friends, I cautiously brought up Ala'a. They all knew if anyone would do something like this, it would be me. Still, they urged me to be careful.

Driving Baghdad's wary streets, talking to the Iraqi police officers it was our mission to train, thoughts kept revolving in my head like an endless slide show. One moment I saw Ala'a, so bright and funny, so faithful, so vulnerable. And then I saw myself, everything I owned packed in a few boxes in my parents' basement. My car, a Chrysler Concorde, not exactly wheelchair-ready. My salary as a state legislative aide, not nearly enough to support a family.

Back at the orphanage, I talked with an Iraqi doctor who helped supervise the children. "So, you're really serious," she said. I nodded. She looked at me more closely. "Captain Scott, do you realize how difficult it is to take care of a child with cerebral palsy?" I tried giving an optimistic answer. Quickly, she set me straight. "It is not like coming to an orphanage two times a week," she said. "Ala'a will be your responsibility every minute of every day. You will have to feed him, dress him, get him up and put him to bed. You will have to help him in the bathroom. Every day, Captain Scott. It is truly a heavy responsibility. Are you sure you're ready for it?"

I looked at her and swallowed, trying to nod.

That night I lay awake in my bunk, utterly dejected. I needed a straightforward answer from God. I needed a miracle to make this work. I was thankful for the doctor's words, but I had expected her to be as excited as I was. Instead, all she had pointed out were the challenges of taking care of a child like Ala'a. Trying to figure all of this out, I envisioned myself in heaven, explaining to Ala'a why I had decided not to adopt him. "Baba," he asked, "why didn't you take me home with you?" I stammered through a series of excuses.

"Well, Ala'a, you see, I had my career, and—" I sputtered out. The words sounded excruciatingly lame. I felt God's patient eyes on me. I tried another. "Ala'a, I don't know anything about taking care of a child with cerebral palsy. I have no experience with that. I'm sure someone else would do a better job. I don't make much money!" I cried. "I drive a Concorde! I have a seventy-five-mile commute!" The excuses became increasingly pathetic. I realized just how ashamed I'd feel if I really did leave him there in Baghdad. I would feel guilty for the rest of my life. I didn't need to think about my decision anymore.

It took seven months to get Ala'a out of Iraq. My tour of duty ended in July 2004, and I spent the next six months at home working with the Iraqi government and an immigration lawyer, bombarding the US embassy with my requests.

In the fall I was elected District Attorney in my county. In February 2005, I flew to Amman, Jordan, and then to Baghdad, where a translator from the orphanage had driven Ala'a through the city's violent streets. They hadn't told him I was coming to get him, in case insurgents found out. I walked through the airport—the same airport I had seen derelict right after the invasion—and there he was, in a wheelchair, surrounded by the orphanage Sisters. For a moment we were silent, too astonished by the journey the two of us were about to take. Then I went over and held him in my arms.

We flew to Chicago and then Wisconsin. I drove him to the apartment I had recently rented and showed him his bedroom, decorated by my mom. There were toys, books, an American flag, my old chest of drawers. He grinned his ecstatic grin. I grinned too. Laughed, in fact. I had spent months wondering whether I could really do this—me, a law-school graduate, American soldier, now prosecutor. All that, and it took an Iraqi orphan who couldn't walk to show me what real faith, real strength looks like.

I'm still not sure. Did I adopt Ala'a? Or did he adopt me?

Slow Down: America Ahead

by Fred Bauer

At summer's end last year, my family and I finished the most
unusual and most rewarding vacation we've ever taken: a cross-
country bicycle trip. That's right, the two-wheeled, two-pedaled kind
that is propelled by good old-fashioned pumping. "Why?" you may
ask, as my wife Shirley did when I first suggested that we take our
three children—ages thirteen, eleven and three—on such a trip. I
could answer: for the fun and adventure of it. But it was not just
that. More so, we were trying to break the dull-vacation habit.

Like many American families, we had often been guilty of over-
programming ourselves—stuffing too many caves, geysers, mountains, lakes, historical landmarks, canyons, birthplaces, rock
formations and Wild West extravaganzas into our two-week schedule. Inevitably, the highlight of these exhausting marathons came at
the moment we pulled up in front of our house and I turned off the
station-wagon ignition. The children invariably let out a war whoop
to express the joy of freedom, and Shirley and I would utter sighs of
relief that the vacation was over. And we discovered upon inquiring
around that many of our friends endure similar summer traumata
—complete with scoldings, shakings, spankings and cajoling

because their children won't quit fighting, be quiet, sit back and watch the scenery of the expensive trip that mother and father have planned for them.

Finally we decided to do something about our situation. The solution lay in finding a way to slow ourselves down. As avid campers, we knew the joys of the out-of-doors, so we wanted our vacation to be related to camping. But if we didn't travel by station wagon, how? We considered hiking and canoeing; then we hit on the idea of bicycling.

After we discovered the fun and good exercise in cycling that spring while we were conditioning ourselves, we laid plans for the adventure—a ten-week, New York-to-Los Angeles bicycling-camping trip. And on June 7 we left the Statue of Liberty loaded down with tent, sleeping bags, three changes of clothing, rain gear, bicycle-repair kit, spare parts, first-aid kit, emergency rations, a stove and Christopher, our three-year-old. Christopher rode on the back of my bicycle on a special seat, and his forty pounds proved to be a worthy handicap when we reached the mountains of Pennsylvania. Yet weight, mountains, heat, wind, storms or mechanical breakdowns could not quash our enthusiasm for cycling.

As we made our way across the country on the little-traveled back roads, our senses came alive to new sights, tastes, sounds and smells—ones that we had been too busy, too much in a hurry to appreciate before.

Included in the log we kept are such notes as:

Picked our own strawberries and made shortcake for a midmorning snack.

The meadows are alive with the song of bobwhites.

We saw a falling star as we set out at dawn this morning.

The aroma of honeysuckle is overpowering.

Also, we had time to visit with people who showed us unbelievable hospitality. For example, when we got caught short of a campground, we were often invited to pitch our tent in backyards or beside farm ponds. Outside Kansas City, one family fixed our breakfast. When rain caused us to seek shelter, invitations were never long in coming. On hot days, motorists stopped and shared ice or soft drinks from their coolers. One man sliced open a frosty watermelon.

The man who volunteered to drive us back over the Mississippi River to Alton told us about his and his wife's joy in life—serving as foster parents. They had helped raise about a dozen children other than their own.

But perhaps the most generous act came in Alton, Illinois, near St. Louis. Shirley forgot her purse at a laundromat, and we rode into Missouri without it. When she discovered the loss of several hundred dollars in traveler's checks, most of our cash, credit cards, house and car keys, we were seriously worried. However, a call back to the Alton police station revealed that a woman had already turned in the purse—intact.

All of these experiences formed a pattern that called attention to our interrelatedness as people—a bond I think Americans, with all our diversity, are prone to forget. At the same time, we were feeling such oneness with people that Shirley and I became poignantly aware of something else: The team spirit had permeated our family. Seldom had we been drawn so close.

Why? I'm not sure I can explain it, but I have some ideas. First, on the bicycle trip we were locked in a common goal, an unusual occurrence in the day-to-day living of most families. Too often we are scattered about as leaves in the wind, moving hither and yon on separate missions from sunup until long into the night.

Our conversations are staccato, laconic phrases uttered over the shoulder as one person comes and another leaves.

On our odyssey, we rode together, struggled against the elements together, ate together, slept together in the same tent. Our movements became interwoven. In the morning no one could leave until all were ready, until all had been fed, until all bikes were operating. We went hungry (for a little while) together, went thirsty (until we reached the next town and could fill our dry canteens) and we went without some sleep, all together. At night, before turning in, we often talked leisurely around a campfire. Strange, how stimulating some burning logs are to conversation, how different a fire is as a centerpiece than, say, a TV set, which stifles more than encourages family dialogue. And we appreciated one another. *Appreciation.* That's it in a word. We found time to appreciate the gifts of the outdoors, of people, of family, of life. And all of those gifts took on even more meaning because we experienced them together.

We didn't make it all the way to California on bikes. We were too slow to cover the distance in ten weeks, but somehow it didn't matter. The trip's success couldn't be measured in miles. Yet even in that respect, we did better than many figured we would, passing through twelve states and logging two thousand miles before we climbed aboard a train north of Albuquerque and traveled the rest of the way to the coast by more orthodox vehicles. We flew back East the middle of August and, as usual, we were glad to be home. But there were no lamentations about this vacation. Instead, we began making plans for another like it—maybe hiking the next time. Some people tell us a person misses too much of nature's beauty riding a bike.

What Is Given

by David Westerfield

Children raced up to the car, trying to sell us melons and bananas. Adults turned the street into a marketplace, lining the sidewalks with art and trinkets. I was in the African nation of Cameroon with three of my co-workers, and we were headed west, into a remote region of the country. The highway deteriorated into rutted dirt roads. The lush landscape, full of exotic birds, plants, trees and all kinds of animals, bounced by. Hours later, we came to a stop in a tiny village made of adobe bricks. There we were greeted by the chiefs of Batseng'la, Bawouwoua, Baletet, Baghonto and Fokamezo. These villages had been at war, but now the five chiefs wanted good relationships among their people. They had invited us to come to help them.

We'd heard about these five chiefs from Valentin Miafo-Donfack. He left Cameroon to study in the United States and ended up joining the staff of the Shreveport-Bossier Community Renewal program. We're a group of people who try to bring help and hope to all communities by connecting caring people who can improve education, housing and health care. Most important, we help build friendships. "Friendship," said our founder, Mack McCarter, "is the most powerful force of transformation in the universe." Valentin believed that the power of friendship could help change his homeland. Cameroon, he told us, was one of the most prosperous nations in all of Africa, thanks to large offshore oil deposits. But, because of corrupt businessmen and politicians, that wealth does not trickle down to the people, the vast majority of whom live in rural areas.

I experienced the shock of seeing abject poverty firsthand. None of these villages had running water; the women walked for miles every day to creeks or wells, carrying battered, leaky buckets. Electricity is a rare luxury. And a typical day's earnings are only about forty-five cents. We spent a week there, talking about how community renewal works. Before we left, we signed a compact with the chiefs, promising assistance in building a friendship house and a training center where they could learn how to work together.

That was in March 2005. Back in Shreveport, I often wondered about and prayed for the five chiefs. About their people and the incredible hardships they suffered daily. About how lucky we were to live in Louisiana. Then came Hurricane Katrina and the destruction and terrible suffering. We got an urgent message from Cameroon. Our friends had seen pictures of the hurricane damage. They feared for our lives, not knowing that Shreveport is five hours north of New Orleans. We got word back to them that we were all okay.

Not long after that, we heard from them again. The five chiefs had spread the news of what had happened. Some three thousand villagers scraped together whatever they could. One boy, nine-year-old Bernard Ngimfack, had spent two months working to make enough money for school supplies. "When the chief showed the pictures of Louisiana on the village television," he said, "I gave. Those people had come to my school, and they were very kind to us." Bernard donated twenty-five cents from his savings. Small gifts such as that added up—the villagers had raised eight hundred and sixty-five dollars. In rural Cameroon, that is truly a small fortune.

The five chiefs wanted to deliver it personally. Churches and other donors stepped forward to pay their airfare. "You came to see our community and help us," one chief said when we met them at the airport. "Now it is our turn to come and show you our friendship." He presented a hand-carved wooden box. Inside was their gift.

We took the chiefs down to New Orleans, where we were met by a group of National Guardsmen. It was surreal. The Lower Ninth Ward—what was left of it—was eerily quiet. Houses washed from their foundations, cars upside down, rubble everywhere. The neighborhood had been abandoned, forgotten. And walking through it all were soldiers in uniform and five Cameroonian chiefs in their colorful native clothes. The chiefs absorbed it in somber silence. At first I wondered what they were thinking. Then I remembered my visit to their country, the shock I'd felt at seeing how the people lived. And I knew that they understood more deeply than perhaps anyone.

We stopped a couple of blocks from where the Industrial Canal levee had breached. That's when we finally saw someone. A man came up to us and, out of curiosity, wanted to know what we all were doing there. We told him that the five chiefs had come all the way from Africa. "Wow! I'm from Biloxi, Mississippi, and I thought that was a long way to come," he said. He asked to talk to the chiefs. They told him why they had come. Immediately he shoved his hand into his pocket, fished around and pulled out a twenty-dollar bill. He dug some more. Another twenty. Then a ten. "Please," he said, handing the money to one of the chiefs, "take this to help your people. Let them know how much their gift means to us here." And then he walked away.

Later, the leader of the National Guardsmen asked us all to gather around. "That little boy, giving up part of his school money to help, well . . . that got to us," he said. "Me and the guys here want to give too. Take this to help your children get the supplies they need." He handed over several hundred dollars to one of the chiefs.

Just before the chiefs went back to Cameroon, we threw them a party. One of them asked if he could make an announcement. "We are here because of you and we now form one family," he said, receiving loud applause. "We are brothers and sisters. We believe in friendship. We believe in a world where life can be better for every human being." The chiefs and their people, he said, now call their five villages Doumbouo, which means "a meeting place; somewhere people can come together."

We had given to the five chiefs. And they had given back to us. A stranger from Biloxi—who knows what he had lost in the hurricane—gave out of his pocket. National Guardsmen, locals just back from Iraq, gave too. It didn't even matter how much. It wasn't about the money. It was about the bond, the irresistible human urge to help and to hope. It was also about friendship, the most powerful force of transformation in the whole universe.